TENNESSEE WILLIAMS: FOUR PLAYS

TENNESSEE WILLIAMS: FOUR PLAYS

Summer and Smoke
Orpheus Descending
Suddenly Last Summer
Period of Adjustment

A SIGNET CLASSIC

AMERICAN LIBRARY

PENGUIN BOOKS USA INC., NEW YORK
ED IN CANADA BY
NITED, MARKHAM, ONTARIO

℃

SIGNET CLASSIC TRADEMARK REG. U.S. PAT. OFF. AND FOREIGN COUNTRIES
REGISTERED TRADEMARK—MARCA REGISTRADA
HECHO EN DRESDEN, TN, U.S.A.

SIGNET, SIGNET CLASSIC, MENTOR, ONYX, PLUME, MERIDIAN
and NAL BOOKS are published *in the United States* by
New American Library, a division of Penguin Books USA Inc.,
1633 Broadway, New York, New York 10019,
in Canada by Penguin Books Canada Limited,
2801 John Street, Markham, Ontario L3R

First Signet Classic Printing, Novem

7 8 9 10 11 12 13

PRINTED IN THE UNITE

SUMMER
AND SMOKE

—◆—

Who, if I were to cry out,
would hear me among the angelic orders?
—Rilke

For Carson McCullers

characters

ALMA as a child
JOHN as a child
REV. WINEMILLER, her father
MRS. WINEMILLER, her mother
ALMA WINEMILLER
JOHN BUCHANAN, JR.
DR. BUCHANAN, his father
ROSA GONZALES
PAPA GONZALES, her father
NELLIE EWELL
MRS. BASSETT
ROGER DOREMUS
MR. KRAMER
ROSEMARY
VERNON
DUSTY

scenes

PART ONE

A SUMMER

PROLOGUE: The Fountain
SCENE 1 The same
SCENE 2 The Rectory Interior & Doctor's Office
SCENE 3 The Rectory Interior
SCENE 4 The Doctor's Office
SCENE 5 The Rectory Interior
SCENE 6 The Arbor

PART TWO

A WINTER

SCENE 7 The Rectory & Doctor's Office
SCENE 8 The Doctor's Office
SCENE 9 The Rectory & Doctor's Office
SCENE 10 The Fountain
SCENE 11 The Doctor's Office
SCENE 12 The Fountain

The entire action of the play takes place in Glorious Hill, Mississippi. The time is the turn of the Century through 1916.

author's production notes

As the concept of a design grows out of reading a play I will not do more than indicate what I think are the most essential points.

First of all—*The Sky*.

There must be a great expanse of sky so that the entire action of the play takes place against it. This is true of interior as well as exterior scenes. But in fact there are no really interior scenes, for the walls are omitted or just barely suggested by certain necessary fragments such as might be needed to hang a picture or to contain a doorframe.

During the day scenes the sky should be a pure and intense blue (like the sky of Italy as it is so faithfully represented in the religious paintings of the Renaissance) and costumes should be selected to form dramatic color contrasts to this intense blue which the figures stand against. (Color harmonies and other visual effects are tremendously important.)

In the night scenes, the more familiar constellations, such as Orion and the Great Bear and the Pleiades, are clearly projected on the night sky, and above them, splashed across the top of the cyclorama, is the nebulous radiance of the Milky Way. Fleecy cloud forms may also be projected on this cyclorama and made to drift across it.

So much for *The Sky*.

Now we descend to the so-called interior sets of the play. There are two of these "interior" sets, one being the parlor of an Episcopal Rectory and the other the home of a doctor next door to the Rectory. The architecture of these houses is barely suggested but is of an American Gothic design of the Victorian era. There are no actual doors or windows or walls. Doors and windows are represented by delicate frameworks of Gothic design. These frames have strings of ivy clinging to them, the leaves of emerald and amber. Sections of wall are used only where they are functionally required. There should be a fragment of wall in back of the Rectory sofa, supporting a romantic landscape in a gilt frame. In the doctor's house there should be a section of wall to support the chart of anatomy. Chirico has used fragmentary walls and interiors in a very evocative way in his painting called "Conversation among the Ruins." We will deal more specifically with these interiors as we come to them in the course of the play.

Now we come to the main exterior set which is a promontory in a park or public square in the town of Glorious Hill. Situated on this promontory is a fountain in the form of a stone angel, in a gracefully crouching position with wings lifted and her hands held together to form a cup from which water flows, a public drinking fountain. The stone angel of the fountain should probably be elevated so that it appears in the background of the interior scenes as a symbolic figure (Eternity) brooding over the course of the play. *This entire exterior set may be on an upper level, above that of the two fragmentary interiors.* I would like all three units to form an harmonious whole like one complete picture rather than three separate ones. An imaginative designer may solve these plastic problems in a variety of ways and should not feel bound by any of my specific suggestions.

There is one more set, a very small exterior representing an arbor, which we will describe when we reach it.
Everything possible should be done to give an unbroken fluid quality to the sequence of scenes.
There should be no curtain except for the intermission. The other divisions of the play should be accomplished by changes of lighting.
Finally, the matter of music. One basic theme should recur and the points of recurrence have been indicated here and there in the stage directions.

Rome, March, 1948.

Summer and Smoke was first produced by Margo Jones at her theater in Dallas, Texas. It was later produced and directed by Miss Jones in New York, opening at the Music Box Theater, October 6, 1948, with Margaret Phillips and Tod Andrews in the two leading roles; incidental music by Paul Bowles and setting by Jo Mielziner.

CAST OF THE NEW YORK PRODUCTION

ALMA as a child	ARLENE McQUADE
JOHN as a child	DONALD HASTINGS
REV. WINEMILLER	RAYMOND VAN SICKLE
MRS. WINEMILLER	MARGA ANN DEIGHTON
ALMA WINEMILLER	MARGARET PHILLIPS
JOHN BUCHANAN, Jr.	TOD ANDREWS
DR. BUCHANAN	RALPH THEADORE
ROSA GONZALES	MONICA BOYAR
PAPA GONZALES	SID CASSEL
NELLIE EWELL	ANNE JACKSON
MRS. BASSETT	BETTY GREENE LITTLE
ROGER DOREMUS	EARL MONTGOMERY
MR. KRAMER	RAY WALSTON
ROSEMARY	ELLEN JAMES
VERNON	SPENCER JAMES
DUSTY	WILLIAM LAYTON
A GIRL	HILDY PARKS

PART ONE

a summer

In the park near the angel of the fountain. At dusk of an evening in May, in the first few years of this Century.

Alma, as a child of ten, comes into the scene. She wears a middy blouse and has ribboned braids. She already has the dignity of an adult; there is a quality of extraordinary delicacy and tenderness or spirituality in her, which must set her distinctly apart from other children. She has a habit of holding her hands, one cupped under the other in a way similar to that of receiving the wafer at Holy Communion. This is a habit that will remain with her as an adult. She stands like that in front of the stone angel for a few moments; then bends to drink at the fountain.

While she is bent at the fountain, John, as a child, enters. He shoots a pea-shooter at Alma's bent-over back. She utters a startled cry and whirls about. He laughs.

JOHN:
Hi, Preacher's daughter. [_He advances toward her._] I been looking for you.

ALMA [_hopefully_]:
You have?

JOHN:
Was it you that put them handkerchiefs on my desk? [_Alma smiles uncertainly._] Answer up!

ALMA:
I put a box of handkerchiefs on your desk.

JOHN:
I figured it was you. What was the idea, Miss Priss?

ALMA:
You needed them.

JOHN:
Trying to make a fool of me?

ALMA:
Oh, no!

JOHN:
Then what was the idea?

ALMA:
You have a bad cold and your nose has been running all week. It spoils your appearance.

JOHN:
You don't have to look at me if you don't like my appearance.

ALMA:
I like your appearance.

JOHN [*coming closer*]:
Is that why you look at me all the time?

ALMA:
I—don't!

JOHN:
Oh, yeh, you do. You been keeping your eyes on me all the time. Every time I look around I see them cat eyes of yours looking at me. That was the trouble today when Miss Blanchard asked you where the river Amazon was. She asked you twice and you still didn't answer because you w' lookin' at me. What's the idea? What've'y' got on y' mind anyhow? Answer up!

ALMA:
I was only thinking how handsome you'd be if your face wasn't dirty. You know why your face is dirty? Because you don't use a handkerchief and you wipe your nose on the sleeve of that dirty old sweater.

JOHN [*indignantly*]:
Hah!

ALMA:
That's why I put the handkerchiefs on your desk and I wrapped them up so nobody would know what they were. It isn't my fault that you opened the box in front of everybody!

JOHN:
What did you think I'd do with a strange box on my desk? Just leave it there till it exploded or something? Sure I opened it up. I didn't expect to find no—*handkerchiefs!*—in it . . .

16

ALMA [*in a shy trembling voice*]:
I'm sorry that you were embarrassed. I honestly am awfully sorry that you were embarrassed. Because I wouldn't embarrass you for the world!

JOHN:
Don't flatter yourself that I was embarrassed. I don't embarrass that easy.

ALMA:
It was stupid and cruel of those girls to laugh.

JOHN:
Hah!

ALMA:
They should all realize that you don't have a mother to take care of such things for you. It was a pleasure to me to be able to do something for you, only I didn't want you to know it was me who did it.

JOHN:
Hee-haw! Ho-hum! Take 'em back! [*He snatches out the box and thrusts it toward her.*]

ALMA:
Please keep them.

JOHN:
What do I want with them?

[*She stares at him helplessly. He tosses the box to the ground and goes up to the fountain and drinks. Something in her face mollifies him and she sits down at the base of the fountain with a manner that does not preclude a more friendly relation. The dark gathers deeper.*]

ALMA:
Do you know the name of the angel?

JOHN:
Does she have a name?

ALMA:
Yes, I found out she does. It's carved in the base, but it's all worn away so you can't make it out with your eyes.

17

JOHN:
Then how do you know it?

ALMA:
You have to read it with your fingers. I did and it gave me cold shivers! *You* read it and see if it doesn't give *you* cold shivers! Go on! Read it with your fingers!

JOHN:
Why don't you tell me and save me the trouble?

ALMA:
I'm not going to tell you.

[*John grins indulgently and turns to the pediment, crouching before it and running fingers along the worn inscription.*]

JOHN:
E?

ALMA:
Yes, E is the first letter!

JOHN:
T?

ALMA:
Yes!

JOHN:
E?

ALMA:
E!

JOHN:
K?

ALMA:
No, no, not K!—*R!* [*He slowly straightens up.*]

JOHN:
Eternity?

ALMA:
Eternity!—Didn't it give you the cold shivers?

JOHN:
Nahh.
18

ALMA:
Well, it did me!

JOHN:
Because you're a preacher's daughter. Eternity. What is eternity?

ALMA [*in a hushed wondering voice*]:
It's something that goes on and on when life and death and time and everything else is all through with.

JOHN:
There's no such thing.

ALMA:
There is. It's what people's souls live in when they have left their bodies. My name is Alma and Alma is Spanish for soul. Did you know that?

JOHN:
Hee-haw! Ho-hum! Have you ever seen a dead person?

ALMA:
No.

JOHN:
I have. They made me go in the room when my mother was dying and she caught hold of my hand and wouldn't let me go—and so I screamed and hit her.

ALMA:
Oh, you didn't do that.

JOHN [*somberly*]:
Uh-huh. She didn't look like my mother. Her face was all ugly and yellow and—terrible—bad-smelling! And so I hit her to make her let go of my hand. They told me that I was a devil!

ALMA:
You didn't know what you were doing.

JOHN:
My dad is a doctor.

ALMA:
I know.

JOHN:
He wants to send me to college to study to be a doctor but I wouldn't be a doctor for the world. And have to go in a room and watch people dying! . . . Jesus!

ALMA:
You'll change your mind about that.

JOHN:
Oh, no, I won't. I'd rather *be* a devil, like they called me and go to South America on a boat! . . . Give me one of them handkerchiefs. [*She brings them eagerly and humbly to the fountain. He takes one out and wets it at the fountain and scrubs his face with it.*] Is my face clean enough to suit you now?

ALMA:
Yes!—Beautiful!

JOHN:
What!

ALMA:
I said "Beautiful"!

JOHN:
Well—let's—kiss each other.

[*Alma turns away.*]

JOHN:
Come on, let's just try it!

[*He seizes her shoulders and gives her a quick rough kiss. She stands amazed with one hand cupping the other.*

[*The voice of a child in the distance calls "Johnny! Johnny!"*

[*He suddenly snatches at her hair-ribbon, jerks it loose and then runs off with a mocking laugh.*

[*Hurt and bewildered, Alma turns back to the stone angel, for comfort. She crouches at the pediment and touches the inscription with her fingers. The scene dims out with music.*]

Before the curtain rises a band is heard playing a patriotic anthem, punctuated with the crackle or fireworks.

The scene is the same as for the Prologue. It is the evening of July 4th in a year shortly before the first World War. There is a band concert and a display of fireworks in the park. During the scene the light changes from faded sunlight to dusk. Sections of roof, steeples, weather-vanes, should have a metallic surface that catches the mellow light on the backdrop; when dusk has fallen the stars should be visible.

As the curtain rises, the Rev. and Mrs. Winemiller come in and sit on the bench near the fountain. Mrs. Winemiller was a spoiled and selfish girl who evaded the responsibilities of later life by slipping into a state of perverse childishness. She is known as Mr. Winemiller's "Cross."

MR. WINEMILLER [*suddenly rising*]:
There is Alma, getting on the bandstand! [*Mrs. Winemiller is dreamily munching popcorn.*]

AN ANNOUNCER'S VOICE [*at a distance*]:
The Glorious Hill Orchestra brings you Miss Alma Winemiller, The Nightingale of the Delta, singing . . . "La Golondrina."

MR. WINEMILLER [*sitting back down again*]:
This is going to provoke a lot of criticism.

[*The song commences. The voice is not particularly strong, but it has great purity and emotion. John Buchanan comes along. He is now a Promethean figure, brilliantly and restlessly alive in a stagnant society. The excess of his power has not yet found a channel. If it remains without one, it will burn him up. At present he is unmarked by the dissipations in which he relieves his demoniac unrest; he has the fresh and shining look of an epic hero. He walks leisurely before the Winemillers' bench, negligently touching the crown of his hat but not glancing at them; climbs the steps to the base of the fountain, then turns and looks*]

21

in the direction of the singer. A look of interest touched with irony appears on his face. A couple, strolling in the park, pass behind the fountain.]

THE GIRL:
Look who's by the fountain!

THE MAN:
Bright as a new silver dollar!

JOHN:
Hi, Dusty! Hi, Pearl!

THE MAN:
How'd you make out in that floating crap game?

JOHN:
I floated with it as far as Vicksburg, then sank.

THE GIRL:
Everybody's been calling: "Johnny, Johnny—where's Johnny?"

[*John's father, Dr. Buchanan, comes on from the right, as Rev. and Mrs. Winemiller move off the scene to the left, toward the band music. Dr. Buchanan is an elderly man whose age shows in his slow and stiff movements. He walks with a cane. John sees him coming, but pretends not to and starts to walk off.*]

DR. BUCHANAN:
John!

JOHN [*slowly turning around, as the couple move off*]:
Oh! Hi, Dad. . . . [*They exchange a long look.*] I—uh—meant to wire you but I must've forgot. I got tied up in Vicksburg Friday night and just now got back to town. Haven't been to the house yet. Is everything . . . going okay? [*He takes a drink of water at the fountain.*]

DR. BUCHANAN [*slowly, in a voice hoarse with emotion*]:
There isn't any room in the medical profession for wasters, drunkards and lechers. And there isn't any room in my house for wasters—drunkards—lechers! [*A child is heard calling "I sp-yyyyy!" in the distance.*] I married late in life. I brought over five hundred children into this world before I had one of my own. And by God it looks like I've
22

given myself the rottenest one of the lot. . . . [*John laughs uncertainly.*] You will find your things at the Alhambra Hotel.

JOHN:
Okay. If that's how you want it.

[*There is a pause. The singing comes through on the music. John tips his hat diffidently and starts away from the fountain. He goes a few feet and his father suddenly calls after him.*]

DR. BUCHANAN:
John! [*John pauses and looks back.*] Come here.

JOHN:
Yes, Sir? [*He walks back to his father and stands before him.*]

DR. BUCHANAN [*hoarsely*]:
Go to the Alhambra Hotel and pick up your things and— bring them back to the house.

JOHN [*gently*]:
Yes, Sir. If that's how you want it. [*He diffidently extends a hand to touch his father's shoulder.*]

DR. BUCHANAN [*brushing the hand roughly off*]:
You! . . . You infernal *whelp*, you!

[*Dr. Buchanan turns and goes hurriedly away. John looks after him with a faint, affectionate smile, then sits down on the steps with an air of relief, handkerchief to forehead, and a whistle of relief. Just then the singing at the bandstand ends and there is the sound of applause. Mrs. Winemiller comes in from the left, followed by her husband.*]

MRS. WINEMILLER:
Where is the ice cream man?

MR. WINEMILLER:
Mother, hush! [*He sees his daughter approaching.*] Here we are, Alma!

[*The song ends. There is applause. Then the band strikes up the Santiago Waltz.*]

[*Alma Winemiller enters. Alma had an adult quality as a child and now, in her middle twenties, there is something prematurely spinsterish about her. An excessive propriety and self-consciousness is apparent in her nervous laughter; her voice and gestures belong to years of church entertainments, to the position of hostess in a rectory. People her own age regard her as rather quaintly and humorously affected. She has grown up mostly in the company of her elders. Her true nature is still hidden even from herself. She is dressed in pale yellow and carries a yellow silk parasol.*]

[*As Alma passes in front of the fountain, John slaps his hands resoundingly together a few times. She catches her breath in a slight laughing sound, makes as if to retreat, with a startled "Oh!", but then goes quickly to her parents. The applause from the crowd continues.*]

MR. WINEMILLER:
They seem to want to hear you sing again, Alma.

[*She turns nervously about, touching her throat and her chest. John grins, applauding by the fountain. When the applause dies out, Alma sinks faintly on the bench.*]

ALMA:
Open my bag, Father. My fingers have frozen stiff! [*She draws a deep labored breath.*] I don't know what came over me—absolute panic! Never, never again, it isn't worth it— the tortures that I go through!

MR. WINEMILLER [*anxiously*]:
You're having one of your nervous attacks?

ALMA:
My heart's beating so! It seemed to be in my *throat* the whole time I was singing! [*John laughs audibly from the fountain.*] Was it noticeable, Father?

MR. WINEMILLER:
You sang extremely well, Alma. But you know how I feel about this, it was contrary to my wishes and I cannot imagine why you wanted to do it, especially since it seemed to upset you so.

ALMA:
I don't see how anyone could object to my singing at a

24

patriotic occasion. If I had just sung well! But I barely got through it. At one point I thought that I wouldn't. The words flew out of my mind. Did you notice the pause? Blind panic! They really never came back, but I went on singing —I think I must have been improvising the lyric! Whew! Is there a handkerchief in it?

MRS. WINEMILLER [*suddenly*]:
Where is the ice cream man?

ALMA [*rubbing her fingers together*]:
Circulation is slowly coming back . . .

MR. WINEMILLER:
Sit back quietly and take a deep breath, Alma.

ALMA:
Yes, my handkerchief—now . . .

MRS. WINEMILLER:
Where is the ice cream man?

MR. WINEMILLER:
Mother, there isn't any ice cream man.

ALMA:
No, there isn't any ice cream man, Mother. But on the way home Mr. Doremus and I will stop by the drug store and pick up a pint of ice cream.

MR. WINEMILLER:
Are you intending to stay here?

ALMA:
Until the concert is over. I promised Roger I'd wait for him.

MR. WINEMILLER:
I suppose you have noticed who is by the fountain?

ALMA:
Shhh!

MR. WINEMILLER:
Hadn't you better wait on a different bench?

ALMA:
This is where Roger will meet me.

25

MR. WINEMILLER:
Well, Mother, we'll run along now. [*Mrs. Winemiller has started vaguely toward the fountain, Mr. Winemiller firmly restraining her.*] This way, this way, Mother! [*He takes her arm and leads her off.*]

MRS. WINEMILLER [*calling back, in a high, childish voice*]:
Strawberry, Alma. Chocolate, chocolate and strawberry mixed! Not vanilla!

ALMA [*faintly*]:
Yes, yes, Mother—vanilla . . .

MRS. WINEMILLER [*furiously*]:
I said *not* vanilla. [*shouting*] Strawberry!

MR. WINEMILLER [*fiercely*]:
Mother! We're attracting attention. [*He propels her forcibly away.*]

[*John laughs by the fountain. Alma moves her parasol so that it shields her face from him. She leans back closing her eyes. John notices a firecracker by the fountain. He leans over negligently to pick it up. He grins and lights it and tosses it toward Alma's bench. When it goes off she springs up with a shocked cry, letting the parasol drop.*]

JOHN [*jumping up as if outraged*]:
Hey! Hey, you! [*He looks off to the right. Alma sinks back weakly on the bench. John solicitously advances.*] Are you all right?

ALMA:
I can't seem to—catch my breath! Who threw it?

JOHN:
Some little rascal.

ALMA:
Where?

JOHN:
He ran away quick when I hollered!

ALMA:
There ought to be an ordinance passed in this town forbidding firecrackers.

26

JOHN:
Dad and I treated fifteen kids for burns the last couple of days. I think you need a little restorative, don't you? [*He takes out a flask.*] Here!

ALMA:
What is it?

JOHN:
Apple-jack brandy.

ALMA:
No thank you.

JOHN:
Liquid dynamite.

ALMA:
I'm sure.

[*John laughs and returns it to his pocket. He remains looking down at her with one foot on the end of her bench. His steady, smiling look into her face is disconcerting her.*

[*In Alma's voice and manner there is a delicacy and elegance, a kind of "airiness," which is really natural to her as it is, in a less marked degree, to many Southern girls. Her gestures and mannerisms are a bit exaggerated but in a graceful way. It is understandable that she might be accused of "putting on airs" and of being "affected" by the other young people of the town. She seems to belong to a more elegant age, such as the Eighteenth Century in France. Out of nervousness and self-consciousness she has a habit of prefacing and concluding her remarks with a little breathless laugh. This will be indicated at points, but should be used more freely than indicated; however, the characterization must never be stressed to the point of making her at all ludicrous in a less than sympathetic way.*]

ALMA:
You're—home for the summer? [*John gives an affirmative grunt.*] Summer is not the pleasantest time of year to renew an acquaintance with Glorious Hill—is it? [*John gives an indefinite grunt. Alma laughs airily.*] The Gulf wind has failed us this year, disappointed us dreadfully this summer.

We used to be able to rely on the Gulf wind to cool the nights off for us, but this summer has been an exceptional season. [*He continues to grin disconcertingly down at her; she shows her discomfiture in flurried gestures.*]

JOHN [*slowly*]:
Are you—disturbed about something?

ALMA:
That firecracker was a shock.

JOHN:
You should be over that shock by now.

ALMA:
I don't get over shocks quickly.

JOHN:
I see you don't.

ALMA:
You're planning to stay here and take over some of your father's medical practice?

JOHN:
I haven't made up my mind about anything yet.

ALMA:
I hope so, we all hope so. Your father was telling me that you have succeeded in isolating the germ of that fever epidemic that's broken out at Lyon.

JOHN:
Finding something to kill it is more of a trick.

ALMA:
You'll do that! He's so positive that you will. He says that you made a special study of bacter—bacter . . .

JOHN:
Bacteriology!

ALMA:
Yes! At Johns Hopkins! That's in Boston, isn't it?

JOHN:
No. Baltimore.

ALMA:
Oh, Baltimore. Baltimore, Maryland. Such a beautiful combination of names. And bacteriology—isn't that something you do with a microscope?

JOHN:
Well—partly. . . .

ALMA:
I've looked through a telescope, but never a microscope. What . . . what do you—see?

JOHN:
A—universe, Miss Alma.

ALMA:
What kind of a universe?

JOHN:
Pretty much the same kind that you saw through the lens of a telescope—a mysterious one. . . .

ALMA:
Oh, yes. . . .

JOHN:
Part anarchy—and part order!

ALMA:
The footprints of God!

JOHN:
But not God.

ALMA [*ecstatically*]:
To be a doctor! And deal with these mysteries under the microscope lens . . . I think it is more religious than being a priest! There is so much suffering in the world it actually makes one sick to think about it, and most of us are so helpless to relieve it. . . . But a physician! Oh, my! With his magnificent gifts and training what a joy it must be to know that he is equipped and appointed to bring relief to all of this fearful suffering—and fear! And it's an expanding profession, it's a profession that is continually widening its horizons. So many diseases have already come under scientific control but the commencement is just—beginning! I mean there is so much more that is yet to be done, such as

29

mental afflictions to be brought under control. . . . And with your father's example to inspire you! Oh, my!

JOHN:
I didn't know you had so many ideas about the medical profession.

ALMA:
Well, I am a great admirer of your father, as well as a patient. It's such a comfort knowing that he's right next door, within arm's reach as it were!

JOHN:
Why? Do you have fits?

ALMA:
Fits? [*She throws back her head with a peal of gay laughter.*] Why no, but I do have attacks!—of nervous heart trouble. Which can be so alarming that I run straight to your father!

JOHN:
At two or three in the morning?

ALMA:
Yes, as late as that, even . . . occasionally. He's very patient with me.

JOHN:
But does you no good?

ALMA:
He always reassures me.

JOHN:
Temporarily?

ALMA:
Yes . . .

JOHN:
Don't you want more than that?

ALMA:
What?

JOHN:
It's none of my business.

ALMA:
What were you going to say?

JOHN:
You're Dad's patient. But I have an idea . . .

ALMA:
Please go on! [*John laughs a little.*] Now you have to go on!
You can't leave me up in the air! What were you going
to tell me?

JOHN:
Only that I suspect you need something more than a little
temporary reassurance.

ALMA:
Why? Why? You think it's more serious than . . . ?

JOHN:
You're swallowing air.

ALMA:
I'm what?

JOHN:
You're swallowing air, Miss Alma.

ALMA:
I'm swallowing air?

JOHN:
Yes, you swallow air when you laugh or talk. It's a little
trick that hysterical women get into.

ALMA [*uncertainly*]:
Ha-ha . . . !

JOHN:
You swallow air and it presses on your heart and gives you
palpitations. That isn't serious in itself but it's a symptom
of something that is. Shall I tell you frankly?

ALMA:
Yes!

JOHN:
Well, what I think you have is a *doppelganger!* You have a
doppelganger and the *doppelganger* is badly irritated.

31

ALMA:
Oh, my goodness! I have an irritated *doppelganger!* [*She tries to laugh, but is definitely uneasy.*] How awful that sounds! What exactly *is* it?

JOHN:
It's none of *my* business. You are not *my* patient.

ALMA:
But that's downright wicked of you! To tell me I have some-thing awful-sounding as that, and then refuse to let me know what it is! [*She tries to laugh again, unsuccessfully.*]

JOHN:
I shouldn't have said anything! I'm not your doctor. . . .

ALMA:
Just how did you arrive at this—diagnosis of my case? [*She laughs.*] But of course you're teasing me. Aren't you? . . . There, the Gulf wind is stirring! He's actually moving the leaves of the palmetto! And listen to them complaining. . . .

[*As if brought in by this courier from the tropics, Rosa Gonzales enters and crosses to the fountain. Her indolent walk produces a sound and an atmosphere like the Gulf wind on the palmettos, a whispering of silk and a slight rattle of metallic ornaments. She is dressed in an almost outrageous finery, with lustrous feathers on her hat, green-ish blue, a cascade of them, also diamond and emerald earrings.*]

JOHN [*sharply*]:
Who is that?

ALMA:
I'm surprised that you don't know.

JOHN:
I've been away quite a while.

ALMA:
That's the Gonzales girl. . . . Her father's the owner of the gambling casino on Moon Lake. [*Rosa drinks at the foun-tain and wanders leisurely off.*] She smiled at you, didn't she?

JOHN:
I thought she did.
32

ALMA:
I hope that you have a strong character. [*He places a foot on the end of the bench.*]

JOHN:
Solid rock.

ALMA [*nervously*]:
The pyrotechnical display is going to be brilliant.

JOHN:
The what?

ALMA:
The fireworks.

JOHN:
Aw!

ALMA:
I suppose you've lost touch with most of your *old* friends here.

JOHN [*laconically*]:
Yeah.

ALMA:
You must make some *new* ones! I belong to a little group that meets every ten days. I think you'd enjoy them, too. They're young people with—intellectual and artistic interests. . . .

JOHN [*sadly*]:
Aw, I see . . . intellectual. . . .

ALMA:
You must come!—sometime—I'm going to remind you of it. . . .

JOHN:
Thanks. Do you mind if I sit down?

ALMA:
Why, certainly not, there's room enough for two! Neither of us are—terribly large in diameter! [*She laughs shrilly.*]

[*A girl's voice is heard calling: "Goodbye, Nellie!" and another answers: "Goodbye!" Nellie Ewell enters—a girl of sixteen with a radiantly fresh healthy quality.*]

33

ALMA:
Here comes someone much nicer! One of my adorable little vocal pupils, the youngest and prettiest one with the least gift for music.

JOHN:
I know that one.

ALMA:
Hello, there, Nellie dear!

NELLIE:
Oh, Miss Alma, your singing was so beautiful it made me cry.

ALMA:
It's sweet of you to fib so. I sang terribly.

NELLIE:
You're just being modest, Miss Alma. Hello, Dr. John! Dr. John?

JOHN:
Yeah?

NELLIE:
That book you gave me is too full of long words.

JOHN:
Look 'em up in the dictionary, Nellie.

NELLIE:
I did, but you know how dictionaries are. You look up one long word and it gives you another and you look up that one and it gives you the long word you looked up in the first place. [*John laughs.*] I'm coming over tomorrow for you to explain it all to me. [*She laughs and goes off.*]

ALMA:
What book is she talking about?

JOHN:
A book I gave her about the facts of nature. She came over to the office and told me her mother wouldn't tell her anything and she had to know because she'd fallen in love.

ALMA:
Why the precocious little—imp! [*She laughs.*]

34

JOHN:
What sort of a mother has she?

ALMA:
Mrs. Ewell's the merry widow of Glorious Hill. They say that she goes to the depot to meet every train in order to make the acquaintance of traveling salesmen. Of course she is ostracized by all but a few of her own type of women in town, which is terribly hard for Nellie. It isn't fair to the child. Father didn't want me to take her as a pupil because of her mother's reputation, but I feel that one has a duty to perform toward children in such—circumstances. . . . And I always say that life is such a mysteriously complicated thing that no one should really presume to judge and condemn the behavior of anyone else!

[There is a faraway "puff" and a burst of golden light over their heads. Both look up. There is a long-drawn "Ahhh . . ." from the invisible crowd. This is an effect that will be repeated at intervals during the scene.]

There goes the first sky-rocket! Oh, look at it burst into a million stars!

[John leans way back to look up and allows his knees to spread wide apart so that one of them is in contact with Alma's. The effect upon her is curiously disturbing.]

JOHN [after a moment]:
Do you have a chill?

ALMA:
Why, no!—no. Why?

JOHN:
You're shaking.

ALMA:
Am I?

JOHN:
Don't you feel it?

ALMA:
I have a touch of malaria lingering on.

JOHN:
You have malaria?

35

ALMA:
Never severely, never really severely. I just have touches of it that come and go. [*She laughs airily.*]

JOHN [*with a gentle grin*]:
Why do you laugh that way?

ALMA:
What way?

[*John imitates her laugh. Alma laughs again in embarrassment.*]

JOHN:
Yeah. That way.

ALMA:
I do declare, you haven't changed in the slightest. It used to delight you to embarrass me and it still does!

JOHN:
I guess I shouldn't tell you this, but I heard an imitation of you at a party.

ALMA:
Imitation? Of what?

JOHN:
You.

ALMA:
I?—I? Why, *what* did they imitate?

JOHN:
You singing at a wedding.

ALMA:
My voice?

JOHN:
Your gestures and facial expression!

ALMA:
How mystifying!

JOHN:
No, I shouldn't have told you. You're upset about it.

36

ALMA:

I'm not in the least upset, I am just mystified.

JOHN:

Don't you know that you have a reputation for putting on airs a little—for gilding the lily a bit?

ALMA:

I have no idea what you are talking about.

JOHN:

Well, some people seem to have gotten the idea that you are just a little bit—affected!

ALMA:

Well, well, well, well. [*She tries to conceal her hurt.*] That may be so, it may seem so to some people. But since I am innocent of any such attempt at affectation, I really don't know what I can do about it.

JOHN:

You have a rather fancy way of talking.

ALMA:

Have I?

JOHN:

Pyrotechnical display instead of fireworks, and that sort of thing.

ALMA:

So?

JOHN:

And how about that accent?

ALMA:

Accent? This leaves me quite speechless! I have sometimes been accused of having a put-on accent by people who disapprove of good diction. My father was a Rhodes scholar at Oxford, and while over there he fell into the natural habit of using the long A where it is correct to use it. I suppose I must have picked it up from him, but it's entirely unconscious. Who gave this imitation at this party you spoke of?

JOHN [*grinning*]:

I don't think she'd want that told.

ALMA:
Oh, it was a *she* then?

JOHN:
You don't think a man could do it?

ALMA:
No, and I don't think a lady would do it either!

JOHN:
I didn't think it would have made you so mad, or I wouldn't have brought it up.

ALMA:
Oh, I'm not mad. I'm just mystified and amazed as I always am by unprovoked malice in people. I don't understand it when it's directed at me and I don't understand it when it is directed at anybody else. I just don't understand it, and perhaps it is better not to understand it. These people who call me affected and give these unkind imitations of me— I wonder if they stop to think that I have had certain difficulties and disadvantages to cope with—which may be partly the cause of these peculiarities of mine—which they find so offensive!

JOHN:
Now, Miss Alma, you're making a mountain out of a mole-hill!

ALMA:
I wonder if they stop to think that my circumstances are somewhat different from theirs? My father and I have a certain—cross—to bear!

JOHN:
What cross?

ALMA:
Living next door to us, you should know what cross.

JOHN:
Mrs. Winemiller?

ALMA:
She had her breakdown while I was still in high school. And from that time on I have had to manage the Rectory and take over the social and household duties that would

ordinarily belong to a minister's wife, not his daughter. And that may have made me seem strange to some of my more critical contemporaries. In a way it may have—deprived me of—my youth. . . .

[*Another rocket goes up. Another "Ahhh . . ." from the crowd.*]

JOHN:
You ought to go out with young people.

ALMA:
I am not a recluse. I don't fly around here and there giving imitations of other people at parties. But I am not a recluse by any manner of means. Being a minister's daughter I have to be more selective than most girls about the—society I keep. But I do go out now and then. . . .

JOHN:
I have seen you in the public library and the park, but only two or three times have I seen you out with a boy and it was always someone like this Roger Doremus.

ALMA:
I'm afraid that you and I move in different circles. If I wished to be as outspoken as you are, which is sometimes just an excuse for being rude—I might say that I've yet to see you in the company of a—well, a—reputable young woman. You've heard unfavorable talk about me in your circle of acquaintances and I've heard equally unpleasant things about you in mine. And the pity of it is that you are preparing to be a doctor. You're intending to practice your father's profession here in Glorious Hill. [*She catches her breath in a sob.*] Most of us have no choice but to lead useless lives! But you have a gift for scientific research! You have a chance to serve humanity. Not just to go on enduring for the sake of endurance, but to serve a noble, humanitarian cause, to relieve human suffering. And what do you do about it? Everything that you can to alienate the confidence of nice people who love and respect your father. While he is devoting himself to the fever at Lyon you drive your automobile at a reckless pace from one disorderly roadhouse to another! You say you have seen two things through the microscope, anarchy and order? Well, obviously *order* is not the thing that impressed you . . . conducting yourself like some overgrown schoolboy who wants to be known as the wildest fellow in town! And you—a gifted young doctor—

Magna cum Laude! [*She turns aside, touching her eyelids with a handkerchief.*] You know what I call it? I call it a *desecration!* [*She sobs uncontrollably. Then she springs up from the bench. John catches her hand.*]

JOHN:
You're not going to run off, are you?

ALMA:
Singing in public always—always upsets me!—Let go of my hand. [*He holds on to it, grinning up at her in the deepening dusk. The stars are coming out in the cyclorama with its leisurely floating cloud-forms. In the distance the band is playing "La Golondrina."*] Please let go of my hand.

JOHN:
Don't run off mad.

ALMA:
Let's not make a spectacle of ourselves.

JOHN:
Then sit back down.

[*A skyrocket goes up. The crowd "Ahhh . . . s."*]

ALMA:
You threw that firecracker and started a conversation just in order to tease me as you did as a child. You came to this bench in order to embarrass me and to hurt my feelings with the report of that vicious—imitation! No, let go of my hand so I can leave, now. You've succeeded in your purpose. I *was* hurt, I *did* make a fool of myself as you intended! So let me go now!

JOHN:
You're attracting attention! Don't you know that I really *like* you, Miss Alma?

ALMA:
No, you don't.

[*Another skyrocket.*]

JOHN:
Sure I do. A lot. Sometimes when I come home late at night I look over at the Rectory. I see something white at the

window. Could that be you, Miss Alma? Or, is it your *doppelganger*, looking out of the window that faces my way?

ALMA:
Enough about *doppelganger*—whatever that is!

JOHN:
There goes a nice one, Roman candle they call it!

[*This time the explosion is in back of them. A Roman candle shoots up puffs of rainbow-colored light in back of the stone angel of the fountain. They turn in profile to watch it.*]

JOHN [*counting the puffs of light*]:
Four—five—six—that's all? No—seven! [*There is a pause. Alma sits down slowly.*]

ALMA [*vaguely*]:
Dear me . . . [*She fans herself.*]

JOHN:
How about going riding?

ALMA [*too eagerly*]:
When . . . now?

[*Rosa Gonzales has wandered up to the fountain again. John's attention drifts steadily toward her and away from Alma.*]

JOHN [*too carelessly*]:
Oh . . . some afternoon.

ALMA:
Would you observe the speed limit?

JOHN:
Strictly with you, Miss Alma.

ALMA:
Why then, I'd be glad to—John.

[*John has risen from the bench and crosses to the fountain.*]

JOHN:
And wear a hat with a plume!

41

ALMA:
I don't have a hat with a plume!

JOHN:
Get one!

[*Another skyrocket goes up, and there is another long
"Ahhh . . ." from the crowd. John saunters up to the
fountain. Rosa has lingered beside it. As he passes her
he whispers something. She laughs and moves leisurely
off. John takes a quick drink at the fountain, then follows
Rosa, calling back "Good night" to Alma. There is a
sound of laughter in the distance. Alma sits motionless
for a moment, then touches a small white handkerchief to
her lips and nostrils. Mr. Doremus comes in, carrying a
French horn case. He is a small man, somewhat like a
sparrow.*]

ROGER:
Whew! Golly! Moses! —Well, how did it go, Miss Alma?

ALMA:
How did—what—go?

ROGER [*annoyed*]:
My solo on the French horn.

ALMA [*slowly, without thinking*]:
I paid no attention to it. [*She rises slowly and takes his arm.*]
I'll have to hang on your arm—I'm feeling so dizzy!

[*The scene dims out. There is a final skyrocket and a last
"Ahhh . . ." from the crowd in the distance. Music is
heard, and there is light on the angel.*]

scene two

Inside the Rectory, which is lighted, Mrs. Winemiller comes
in and makes her way stealthily to the love seat, where she
seats herself. Opening her parasol, she takes out a fancy
white-plumed hat which she had concealed there. Rising, she
turns to the mirror on the wall over the love seat and tries
on the hat. She draws a long, ecstatic breath as she places it

squarely on her head. At that moment the telephone rings. Startled, she snatches off the hat, hides it behind the center table and quickly resumes her seat. The telephone goes on ringing. Alma comes in to answer it.

ALMA:
Hello. . . . Yes, Mr. Gillam. . . . She did?. . . . Are you sure? . . . How shocking! . . . [*Mrs. Winemiller now retrieves the hat, seats herself in front of Alma and puts the hat on.*] Thank you, Mr. Gillam . . . the hat is here.

[*Mr. Winemiller comes in. He is distracted.*]

MR. WINEMILLER:
Alma! Alma, your mother . . . !

ALMA [*coming in*]:
I know, Father, Mr. Gillam just phoned. He told me she picked up a white plumed hat and he pretended not to notice in order to save you the embarrassment, so I—I told him to just charge it to us.

MR. WINEMILLER:
That hat looks much too expensive.

ALMA:
It's fourteen dollars. You pay six of it, Father, and I'll pay eight. [*She gives him the parasol.*]

MR. WINEMILLER:
What an insufferable cross we have to bear. [*He retires despairingly from the room.*]

[*Alma goes over to her mother and seats her in a chair at the table.*]

ALMA:
I have a thousand and one things to do before my club meeting tonight, so you work quietly on your picture puzzle or I shall take the hat back, plume and all.

MRS. WINEMILLER [*throwing a piece of the puzzle on the floor*]:
The pieces don't fit! [*Alma picks up the piece and puts it on the table.*] The pieces don't fit!

43

[*Alma stands for a moment in indecision. She reaches for the phone, then puts it down. Then she takes it up again, and gives a number. The telephone across the way in the doctor's office rings and that part of the scene lights up. John comes in.*]

JOHN [*answering the phone*]:
Hello?

ALMA:
John! [*She fans herself rapidly with a palm leaf clutched in her free hand and puts on a brilliant, strained smile as if she were actually in his presence.*]

JOHN:
Miss Alma?

ALMA:
You recognized my voice?

JOHN:
I recognized your laugh.

ALMA:
Ha-ha! How are you, you stranger you?

JOHN:
I'm pretty well, Miss Alma. How're you doing?

ALMA:
Surviving, just surviving! Isn't it fearful?

JOHN:
Uh-huh.

ALMA:
You seem unusually laconic. Or perhaps I should say more than usually laconic.

JOHN:
I had a big night and I'm just recovering from it.

ALMA:
Well, sir, I have a bone to pick with you!

JOHN:
What's that, Miss Alma? [*He drains a glass of bromo.*]
44

ALMA:
The time of our last conversation on the Fourth of July, you said you were going to take me riding in your automobile.

JOHN:
Aw. Did I say that?

ALMA:
Yes indeed you did, sir! And all these hot afternoons I've been breathlessly waiting and hoping that you would remember that promise. But now I know how insincere you are. Ha-ha! Time and again the four-wheeled phenomenon flashes by the Rectory and I have yet to put my—my quaking foot in it!

[*Mrs. Winemiller begins to mock Alma's speech and laughter.*]

JOHN:
What was that, Miss Alma? I didn't understand you.

ALMA:
I was just reprimanding you, sir! Castigating you verbally! Ha-ha!

MRS. WINEMILLER [*grimacing*]:
Ha-ha.

JOHN:
What about, Miss Alma? [*He leans back and puts his feet on table.*]

ALMA:
Never mind. I know how busy you are! [*She whispers.*] Mother, *hush!*

JOHN:
I'm afraid we have a bad connection.

ALMA:
I hate telephones. I don't know why but they always make me laugh as if someone were poking me in the ribs! I swear to goodness they do!

JOHN:
Why don't you just go to your window and I'll go to mine and we can holler across?

ALMA:
The yard's so wide I'm afraid it would crack my voice! And I've got to sing at somebody's wedding tomorrow.

JOHN:
You're going to sing at a wedding?

ALMA:
Yes. "The Voice That Breathed O'er Eden!" And I'm as hoarse as a frog! [*Another gale of laughter almost shakes her off her feet.*]

JOHN:
Better come over and let me give you a gargle.

ALMA:
Nasty gargles—I hate them!

MRS. WINEMILLER [*mockingly*]:
Nasty gargles—I hate them!

ALMA:
Mother, shhh!—please! As you no doubt have gathered, there is some interference at this end of the line! What I wanted to say is—you remember my mentioning that little club I belong to?

JOHN:
Aw! Aw, yes! Those intellectual meetings!

ALMA:
Oh, now, don't call it that. It's just a little informal gathering every Wednesday and we talk about the new books and read things out loud to each other!

JOHN:
Serve any refreshments?

ALMA:
Yes, we serve refreshments!

JOHN:
Any liquid refreshments?

ALMA:
Both liquid and solid refreshments.

JOHN:
Is this an invitation?

ALMA:
Didn't I promise I'd ask you? It's going to be tonight!—at eight at my house, at the Rectory, so all you'll have to do is cross the yard!

JOHN:
I'll try to make it, Miss Alma.

ALMA:
Don't say try as if it required some Herculean effort! All you have to do is . . .

JOHN:
Cross the yard! Uh-huh—reserve me a seat by the punch bowl.

ALMA:
That gives me an idea! We *will* have punch, fruit punch, with claret in it. Do you like claret?

JOHN:
I just dote on claret.

ALMA:
Now you're being sarcastic! Ha-ha-ha!

JOHN:
Excuse me, Miss Alma, but Dad's got to use this phone.

ALMA:
I won't hang up till you've said you'll come without fail!

JOHN:
I'll be there, Miss Alma. You can count on it.

ALMA:
Au revoir, then! Until eight.

JOHN:
G'bye, Miss Alma.

[*John hangs up with an incredulous grin. Alma remains holding the phone with a dazed smile until the office interior has dimmed slowly out.*]

MRS. WINEMILLER:
Alma's in love—in love. [*She waltzes mockingly.*]

ALMA [*sharply*]:
Mother, you are wearing out my patience! Now I am expecting another music pupil and I have to make preparations for the club meeting so I suggest that you . . . [*Nellie rings the bell.*] Will you go up to your room? [*Then she calls sweetly.*] Yes, Nellie, coming, Nellie. All right, stay down here then. But keep your attention on your picture puzzle or there will be no ice cream for you after supper!

[*She admits Nellie, who is wildly excited over something. This scene should be played lightly and quickly.*]

NELLIE:
Oh, Miss Alma!
[*She rushes past Alma in a distracted manner, throws herself on the sofa and hugs herself with excited glee.*]

ALMA:
What is it, Nellie? Has something happened at home? [*Nellie continues her exhilaration.*] Oh, now, Nellie, stop that! Whatever it is, it can't be *that* important!

NELLIE [*blurting out suddenly*]:
Miss Alma, haven't you ever had—*crushes?*

ALMA:
What?

NELLIE:
Crushes?

ALMA:
Yes—I suppose I have. [*She sits down.*]

NELLIE:
Did you know that I used to have a crush on *you*, Miss Alma?

ALMA:
No, Nellie.

NELLIE:
Why do you think that I took singing lessons?
48

ALMA:
I supposed it was because you wished to develop your voice.

NELLIE [cutting in]:
Oh, you know, and I know, I never had any voice. I had a crush on you though. Those were the days when I had crushes on girls. Those days are all over, and now I have crushes on boys. Oh, Miss Alma, you know about Mother, how I was brought up so nobody nice except you would have anything to do with us—Mother meeting the trains to pick up the traveling salesmen and bringing them home to drink and play poker—all of them acting like pigs, pigs, pigs!

MRS. WINEMILLER [mimicking]:
Pigs, pigs, pigs!

NELLIE:
Well, I thought I'd always hate men. Loathe and despise them. But last night— Oh!

ALMA:
Hadn't we better run over some scales until you are feeling calmer?

NELLIE [cutting in]:
I'd heard them downstairs for hours but didn't know who it was—I'd fallen asleep—when all of a sudden my door banged open. He'd thought it was the bathroom!

ALMA [nervously]:
Nellie, I'm not sure I want to hear any more of this story.

NELLIE [interrupting]:
Guess who it was?

ALMA:
I couldn't possibly guess.

NELLIE:
Someone you know. Someone I've seen you with.

ALMA:
Who?

NELLIE:
The wonderfullest person in all the big wide world! When

49

he saw it was me he came and sat down on the bed and held my hand and we talked and talked until Mother came up to see what had happened to him. You should have heard him bawl her out. Oh, he laid the law down! He said she ought to send me off to a girl's school because she wasn't fit to bring up a daughter! Then she started to bawl him out. You're a fine one to talk, she said, you're not fit to call yourself a doctor. [*Alma rises abruptly*.]

ALMA:
John Buchanan?

NELLIE:
Yes, of course, Dr. Johnny.

ALMA:
Was—with—your—mother?

NELLIE:
Oh, he wasn't her beau! He had a girl with him, and Mother had somebody else!

ALMA:
Who—did—he—have?

NELLIE:
Oh, some loud tacky thing with a Z in her name!

ALMA:
Gonzales? Rosa Gonzales?

NELLIE:
Yes, that was it! [*Alma sits slowly back down*.] But him! Oh, Miss Alma! He's the *wonderfullest* person that I . . .

ALMA [*interrupting*]:
Your mother was right! He isn't fit to call himself a doctor! I hate to disillusion you, but this wonderfullest person is pitiably weak.

[*Someone calls "Johnny" outside*.]

NELLIE [*in hushed excitement*]:
Someone is calling him now!

ALMA:
Yes, these people who shout his name in front of his house
50

are of such a character that the old doctor cannot permit them to come inside the door. And when they have brought him home at night, left him sprawling on the front steps, sometimes at daybreak—it takes two people, his father and the old cook, one pushing and one pulling, to get him upstairs. [*She sits down.*] All the gifts of the gods were showered on him. . . . [*The call of "Johnny" is repeated.*] But all he cares about is indulging his senses! [*Another call of "Johnny."*]

NELLIE:
Here he comes down the steps! [*Alma crosses toward the window.*] Look at him jump!

ALMA:
Oh.

NELLIE:
Over the banisters. Ha-ha!

ALMA:
Nellie, don't lean out the window and have us caught spying.

MRS. WINEMILLER [*suddenly*]:
Show Nellie how *you* spy on him! Oh, she's a good one at spying. She stands behind the curtain and *peeks* around it, and . . .

ALMA [*frantically*]:
Mother!

MRS. WINEMILLER:
She spies on him. Whenever he comes in at night she rushes downstairs to watch him out of this window!

ALMA [*interrupting her*]:
Be still!

MRS. WINEMILLER [*going right on*]:
She called him just now and had a fit on the telephone! [*The old lady cackles derisively. Alma snatches her cigarette from her and crushes it under her foot.*] Alma's in love! Alma's in love!

ALMA [*interrupting*]:
Nellie, Nellie, please go.

51

NELLIE [*with a startled giggle*]:
All right, Miss Alma, I'm going. [*She crosses quickly to the door, looking back once with a grin.*] Good night, Mrs. Winemiller!

[*Nellie goes out gaily, leaving the door slightly open. Alma rushes to it and slams it shut. She returns swiftly to Mrs. Winemiller, her hands clenched with anger.*]

ALMA:
If ever I hear you say such a thing again, if ever you dare to repeat such a thing in my presence or anybody else's—then it will be the last straw! You understand me? Yes, you understand me! You act like a child, but you have the devil in you. And God will punish you—yes! I'll punish you too. I'll take your cigarettes from you and give you no more. I'll give you no ice cream either. Because I'm tired of your malice. Yes, I'm tired of your malice and your self-indulgence. People wonder why I'm tied down here! They pity me—think of me as an old maid already! In spite of I'm young. Still young! It's you—it's you, you've taken my youth away from me! I wouldn't say that—I'd try not even to think it—if you were just kind, just simple! But I could spread my life out like a rug for you to step on and you'd step on it, and not even say "Thank you, Alma!" Which is what you've done always—and now you dare to tell a disgusting lie about me—in front of that girl!

MRS. WINEMILLER:
Don't you think I hear you go to the window at night to watch him come in and . . .

ALMA:
Give me that plumed hat, Mother! It goes back now, it goes back!

MRS. WINEMILLER:
Fight! Fight!

[*Alma snatches at the plumed hat. Mrs. Winemiller snatches too. The hat is torn between them. Mrs. Winemiller retains the hat. The plume comes loose in Alma's hand. She stares at it a moment with a shocked expression.*]

ALMA [*sincerely*]:
Heaven have mercy upon us!

52

Inside the Rectory.

The meeting is in progress, having just opened with the reading of the minutes by Alma. She stands before the green plush sofa and the others. This group includes Mr. Doremus, Vernon, a willowy younger man with an open collar and Byronic locks, the widow Bassett, and a wistful older girl with a long neck and thick-lensed glasses.

ALMA [*reading*]:
Our last meeting which fell on July fourteenth . . .

MRS. BASSETT:
Bastille Day!

ALMA:
Pardon me?

MRS. BASSETT:
It fell on Bastille Day! But, honey, that was the meeting before last.

ALMA:
You're perfectly right. I seem to be on the wrong page. . . .
[*She drops the papers.*]

MRS. BASSETT:
Butterfingers!

ALMA:
Here we are! July twenty-fifth! Correct?

MRS. BASSETT:
Correct! [*A little ripple of laughter goes about the circle.*]

ALMA [*continuing*]:
It was debated whether or not we ought to suspend operations for the remainder of the summer as the departure of several members engaged in the teaching profession for their summer vacations . . .

MRS. BASSETT:
Lucky people!

ALMA:
. . . had substantially contracted our little circle.

MRS. BASSETT:
Decimated our ranks! [*There is another ripple of laughter.*]

[*John appears outside the door-frame and rings the bell.*]

ALMA [*with agitation*]:
Is that—is that—the doorbell?

MRS. BASSETT:
It sure did sound like it to me.

ALMA:
Excuse me a moment. I think it may be . . .

[*She crosses to the door-frame and makes the gesture of
opening the door. John steps in, immaculately groomed
and shining, his white linen coat over his arm and a white
Panama hat in his hand. He is a startling contrast to the
other male company, who seem to be outcasts of a state
in which he is a prominent citizen.*]

ALMA [*shrilly*]:
Yes, it is—our guest of honor! Everybody, this is Dr. John
Buchanan, Jr.

JOHN [*easily glancing about the assemblage*]:
Hello, everybody.

MRS. BASSETT:
I never thought he'd show up. Congratulations, Miss Alma.

JOHN:
Did I miss much?

ALMA:
Not a thing! Just the minutes—I'll put you on the sofa.
Next to me. [*She laughs breathlessly and makes an uncertain
gesture. He settles gingerly on the sofa. They all stare at
him with a curious sort of greediness.*] Well, now! we are
completely assembled!

MRS. BASSETT [*eagerly*]:
Vernon has his verse play with him tonight!
54

ALMA [*uneasily*]:
Is that right, Vernon? [*Obviously, it is. Vernon has a pile of papers eight inches thick on his knees. He raises them timidly with downcast eyes.*]

ROGER [*quickly*]:
We decided to put that off till cooler weather. Miss Rosemary is supposed to read us a paper tonight on William Blake.

MRS. BASSETT:
Those dead poets can keep!

[*John laughs.*]

ALMA [*excitedly jumping up*]:
Mrs. Bassett, everybody! This is the way I feel about the verse play. It's too important a thing to read under any but ideal circumstances. Not only atmospheric—on some cool evening with music planned to go with it!—but everyone present so that nobody will miss it! Why don't we . . .

ROGER:
Why don't we take a standing vote on the matter?

ALMA:
Good, good, perfect!

ROGER:
All in favor of putting the verse play off till cooler weather, stand up!

[*Everybody rises but Rosemary and Mrs. Bassett. Rosemary starts vaguely to rise, but Mrs. Bassett jerks her arm.*]

ROSEMARY:
Was this a vote?

ROGER:
Now, Mrs. Bassett, no rough tactics, please!

ALMA:
Has everybody got fans? John, you haven't got one!

[*She looks about for a fan for him. Not seeing one, she*

takes Roger's out of his hand and gives it to John. Roger is non-plussed. Rosemary gets up with her paper.]

ROSEMARY:
The poet—William Blake.

MRS. BASSETT:
Insane, insane, that man was a mad fanatic! [*She squints her eyes tight shut and thrusts her thumbs into her ears. The reactions range from indignant to conciliatory.*]

ROGER:
Now, Mrs. Bassett!

MRS. BASSETT:
This is a free country. I can speak my opinion. And I have read up on him. Go on, Rosemary. I wasn't criticizing your paper. [*But Rosemary sits down, hurt.*]

ALMA:
Mrs. Bassett is only joking, Rosemary.

ROSEMARY:
No, I don't want to read it if she feels that strongly about it.

MRS. BASSETT:
Not a bit, don't be silly! I just don't see why we should encourage the writings of people like that who have already gone into a drunkard's grave!

VARIOUS VOICES [*exclaiming*]:
Did he? I never heard that about him. Is that true?

ALMA:
Mrs. Bassett is mistaken about that. Mrs. Bassett, you have confused Blake with someone else.

MRS. BASSETT [*positively*]:
Oh, no, don't tell me. I've read up on him and know what I'm talking about. He traveled around with that Frenchman who took a shot at him and landed them both in jail! Brussels, Brussels!

ROGER [*gaily*]:
Brussels sprouts!

MRS. BASSETT:
That's where it happened, fired a gun at him in a drunken
56

stupor, and later one of them died of T.B. in the gutter! All right. I'm finished. I won't say anything more. Go on with your paper, Rosemary. There's nothing like contact with culture!

[*Alma gets up.*]

ALMA:
Before Rosemary reads her paper on Blake, I think it would be a good idea, since some of us aren't acquainted with his work, to preface the critical and biographical comments with a reading of one of his loveliest lyric poems.

ROSEMARY:
I'm not going to read anything at all! Not I!

ALMA:
Then let me read it then. [*She takes a paper from Rosemary.*] . . . This is called "Love's Secret."

[*She clears her throat and waits for a hush to settle. Rosemary looks stonily at the carpet. Mrs. Bassett looks at the ceiling. John coughs.*]

> Never seek to tell thy love,
> Love that never told can be,
> For the gentle wind doth move
> Silently, invisibly.
> I told my love, I told my love,
> I told him all my heart.
> Trembling, cold in ghastly fear
> Did my love depart.
>
> No sooner had he gone from me
> Than a stranger passing by,
> Silently, invisibly,
> Took him with a sigh!

[*There are various effusions and enthusiastic applause.*]

MRS. BASSETT:
Honey, you're right. That isn't the man I meant. I was thinking about the one who wrote about "the bought red lips." Who was it that wrote about the "bought red lips"?

[*John has risen abruptly. He signals to Alma and points to his watch. He starts to leave.*]

ALMA [*springing up*]:
John!

JOHN [*calling back*]:
I have to call on a patient!

ALMA:
Oh, John!

[*She calls after him so sharply that the group is startled into silence.*]

ROSEMARY [*interpreting this as a cue to read her paper*]:
"The poet, William Blake, was born in 1757 . . ."

[*Alma suddenly rushes to the door and goes out after John.*]

ROGER:
Of poor but honest parents.

MRS. BASSETT:
No supercilious comments out of you, sir. Go on Rosemary. [*She speaks loudly*.] She has such a beautiful *voice!*

[*Alma returns inside, looking stunned.*]

ALMA:
Please excuse the interruption, Rosemary. Dr. Buchanan had to call on a patient.

MRS. BASSETT [*archly*]:
I bet I know who the patient was. Ha-ha! That Gonzales girl whose father owns Moon Lake Casino and goes everywhere with two pistols strapped on his belt. Johnny Buchanan will get himself shot in that crowd!

ALMA:
Why, Mrs. Bassett, what gave you such an idea? I don't think that John even knows that Gonzales girl!

MRS. BASSETT:
He knows her, all right. In the Biblical sense of the word, if you'll excuse me!

ALMA:
No, I will not excuse you! A thing like that is inexcusable!
58

MRS. BASSETT:
Have you fallen for him, Miss Alma? Miss Alma has fallen for the young doctor! They tell me he has lots of new lady patients!

ALMA:
Stop it! [*She stamps her foot furiously and crushes the palm leaf fan between her clenched hands.*] I won't have malicious talk here! You drove him away from the meeting after I'd bragged so much about how bright and interesting you all were! You put your worst foot forward and simpered and chattered and carried on like idiots, idiots! What am I saying? I—I—please excuse me!

[*She rushes out the inner door.*]

ROGER:
I move that the meeting adjourn.

MRS. BASSETT:
I second the motion.

ROSEMARY:
I don't understand. What happened?

MRS. BASSETT:
Poor Miss Alma!

ROGER:
She hasn't been herself lately. . . .

[*They all go out. After a moment Alma reenters with a tray of refreshments, looks about the deserted interior and bursts into hysterical laughter. The light dims out.*]

scene four

In the doctor's office.

John has a wound on his arm which he is bandaging with Rosa's assistance.

JOHN:
Hold that end. Wrap it around. Pull it tight.

[*There is a knock at the door. They look up silently. The knock is repeated.*]

I better answer before they wake up the old man.

[*He goes out. A few moments later he returns followed by Alma. He is rolling down his sleeve to conceal the bandage. Alma stops short at the sight of Rosa.*]

Wait outside, Rosa. In the hall. But be quiet!

[*Rosa gives Alma a challenging look as she withdraws from the lighted area. John explains about Rosa.*]

A little emergency case.

ALMA:
The patient you had to call on. [*John grins.*] I want to see your father.

JOHN:
He's asleep. Anything I can do?

ALMA:
No, I think not. I have to see your father.

JOHN:
It's 2 A.M., Miss Alma.

ALMA:
I know, I'm afraid I'll have to see him.

JOHN:
What's the trouble?

[*The voice of John's father is heard, calling from above.*]

DR. BUCHANAN:
John! What's going on down there?

JOHN [*at the door*]:
Nothing much, Dad. Somebody got cut in a fight.

DR. BUCHANAN:
I'm coming down.

JOHN:
No. Don't! Stay in bed! [*He rolls up his sleeve to show*

Alma the bandaged wound. She gasps and touches her lips.]
I've patched him up, Dad. You sleep!

[JOHN *executes the gesture of closing a door quietly on the hall.*]

ALMA:
You've been in a brawl with that—woman! [*John nods and rolls the sleeve back down. Alma sinks faintly into a chair.*]

JOHN:
Is your *doppelganger* cutting up again?

ALMA:
It's your father I want to talk to.

JOHN:
Be reasonable, Miss Alma. You're not that sick.

ALMA:
Do you suppose I would come here at two o'clock in the morning if I were not seriously ill?

JOHN:
It's no telling what you would do in a state of hysteria. [*He puts some powders in a glass of water.*] Toss that down, Miss Alma.

ALMA:
What is it?

JOHN:
A couple of little white tablets dissolved in water.

ALMA:
What kind of tablets?

JOHN:
You don't trust me?

ALMA:
You are not in any condition to inspire much confidence. [*John laughs softly. She looks at him helplessly for a moment, then bursts into tears. He draws up a chair beside hers and puts his arm gently about her shoulders.*] I seem to be all to pieces.

JOHN:
The intellectual meeting wore you out.

ALMA:
You made a quick escape from it.

JOHN:
I don't like meetings. The only meetings I like are between two people.

ALMA:
Such as between yourself and the lady outside?

JOHN:
Or between you and me.

ALMA [*nervously*]:
Where is the . . . ?

JOHN:
Oh. You've decided to take it?

ALMA:
Yes, if you . . .

[*She sips and chokes. He gives her his handkerchief. She touches her lips with it.*]

JOHN:
Bitter?

ALMA:
Awfully bitter.

JOHN:
It'll make you sleepy.

ALMA:
I do hope so. I wasn't able to sleep.

JOHN:
And you felt panicky?

ALMA:
Yes. I felt walled in.

JOHN:
You started hearing your heart?

ALMA:
Yes, like a drum!

JOHN:
It scared you?

ALMA:
It always does.

JOHN:
Sure. I know.

ALMA:
I don't think I will be able to get through the summer.

JOHN:
You'll get through, Miss Alma.

ALMA:
How?

JOHN:
One day will come after another and one night will come after another till sooner or later the summer will be all through with and then it will be fall, and you will be saying, I don't see how I'm going to get through the fall.

ALMA:
Oh . . .

JOHN:
That's right. Draw a deep breath!

ALMA:
Ah . . .

JOHN:
Good. Now draw another!

ALMA:
Ah . . .

JOHN:
Better? Better?

ALMA:
A little.

JOHN:
Soon you'll be much better. [*He takes out a big silver watch and holds her wrist.*] Did y' know that time is one side of the four-dimensional continuum we're caught in?

ALMA:
What?

JOHN:
Did you know space is curved, that it turns back onto itself like a soap-bubble, adrift in something that's even less than space. [*He laughs a little as he replaces the watch.*]

ROSA [*faintly from outside*]:
Johnny!

JOHN [*looking up as if the cry came from there*]:
Did you know that the Magellanic clouds are a hundred thousand light years away from the earth? No? [*Alma shakes her head slightly.*] That's something to think about when you worry over your heart, that little red fist that's got to keep knocking, knocking against the big black door.

ROSA [*more distinctly*]:
Johnny!

[*She opens the door a crack.*]

JOHN:
Calla de la boca! [*The door closes and he speaks to Alma.*] There's nothing wrong with your heart but a little functional disturbance, like I told you before. You want me to check it? [*Alma nods mutely. John picks up his stethoscope.*]

ALMA:
The lady outside, I hate to keep her waiting.

JOHN:
Rosa doesn't mind waiting. Unbutton your blouse.

ALMA:
Unbutton . . . ?

JOHN:
The blouse.

ALMA:
Hadn't I better—better come back in the morning, when your father will be able to . . . ?

JOHN:
Just as you please, Miss Alma. [*She hesitates. Then begins to unbutton her blouse. Her fingers fumble.*] Fingers won't work?

ALMA [*breathlessly*]:
They are just as if frozen!

JOHN [*smiling*]:
Let me. [*He leans over her.*] Little pearl buttons . . .

ALMA:
If your father discovered that woman in the house . . .

JOHN:
He won't discover it.

ALMA:
It would distress him terribly.

JOHN:
Are you going to tell him?

ALMA:
Certainly not! [*He laughs and applies the stethoscope to her chest.*]

JOHN:
Breathe! . . . Out! . . . Breathe! . . . Out!

ALMA:
Ah . . .

JOHN:
Um-hmmm . . .

ALMA:
What do you hear?

JOHN:
Just a little voice saying—"Miss Alma is lonesome!" [*She rises and turns her back to him.*]

ALMA:

If your idea of helping a patient is to ridicule and insult . . .

JOHN:

My idea of helping you is to tell you the truth. [*Alma looks up at him. He lifts her hand from the chair arm.*] What is this stone?

ALMA:

A topaz.

JOHN:

Beautiful stone. . . . Fingers still frozen?

ALMA:

A little. [*He lifts her hand to his mouth and blows his breath on her fingers.*]

JOHN:

I'm a poor excuse for a doctor, I'm much too selfish. But let's try to think about you.

ALMA:

Why should you bother about me? [*She sits down.*]

JOHN:

You know I like you and I think you're worth a lot of consideration.

ALMA:

Why?

JOHN:

Because you have a lot of feeling in your heart, and that's a rare thing. It makes you too easily hurt. Did I hurt you tonight?

ALMA:

You hurt me when you sprang up from the sofa and rushed from the Rectory in such—in such mad haste that you left your coat behind you!

JOHN:

I'll pick up the coat sometime.

ALMA:

The time of our last conversation you said you would take me riding in your automobile sometime, but you forgot to.

JOHN:
I didn't forget. Many's the time I've looked across at the Rectory and wondered if it would be worth trying, you and me. . . .

ALMA:
You decided it wasn't?

JOHN:
I went there tonight, but it wasn't you and me. . . . Fingers warm now?

ALMA:
Those tablets work quickly. I'm already feeling drowsy. [*She leans back with her eyes nearly shut.*] I'm beginning to feel almost like a water lily. A water lily on a Chinese lagoon.

[*A heavy iron bell strikes three.*]

ROSA:
Johnny?

[*Alma starts to rise.*]

ALMA:
I *must* go.

JOHN:
I will call for you Saturday night at eight o'clock.

ALMA:
What?

JOHN:
I'll give you this box of tablets but watch how you take them. Never more than one or two at a time.

ALMA:
Didn't you say something else a moment ago?

JOHN:
I said I would call for you at the Rectory Saturday night.

ALMA:
Oh . . .

JOHN:
Is that all right? [*Alma nods speechlessly. She remains with the box resting in the palm of her hand as if not knowing it was there. John gently closes her fingers on the box.*]

ALMA:
Oh! [*She laughs faintly.*]

ROSA [*outside*]:
Johnny!

JOHN:
Do you think you can find your way home, Miss Alma?

[*Rosa steps back into the office with a challenging look. Alma catches her breath sharply and goes out the side door.*

[*John reaches above him and turns out the light. He crosses to Rosa by the anatomy chart and takes her roughly in his arms. The light lingers on the chart as the interior dims out.*]

scene five

In the Rectory.

Before the light comes up a soprano voice is heard singing "From the Land of the Sky Blue Waters."

As the curtain rises, Alma gets up from the piano. Mr. and Mrs. Winemiller, also, are in the lighted room.

ALMA:
What time is it, Father? [*He goes on writing. She raises her voice.*] What time is it, Father?

MR. WINEMILLER:
Five of eight. I'm working on my sermon.

ALMA:
Why don't you work in the study?

MR. WINEMILLER:
The study is suffocating. So don't disturb me.

ALMA:
Would there be any chance of getting Mother upstairs if someone should call?

MR. WINEMILLER:
Are you expecting a caller?

ALMA:
Not expecting. There is just a chance of it.

MR. WINEMILLER:
Whom are you expecting?

ALMA:
I said I wasn't expecting anyone, that there was just a possibility . . .

MR. WINEMILLER:
Mr. Doremus? I thought that this was his evening with his mother?

ALMA:
Yes, it is his evening with his mother.

MR. WINEMILLER:
Then who is coming here, Alma?

ALMA:
Probably no one. Probably no one at all.

MR. WINEMILLER:
This is all very mysterious.

MRS. WINEMILLER:
That tall boy next door is coming to see her, that's who's coming to see her.

ALMA:
If you will go upstairs, Mother, I'll call the drug store and ask them to deliver a pint of fresh peach ice cream.

MRS. WINEMILLER:
I'll go upstairs when I'm ready—good and ready, and you can put that in your pipe and smoke it, Miss Winemiller!

[*She lights a cigarette. Mr. Winemiller turns slowly away with a profound sigh.*]

ALMA:
I may as well tell you who might call, so that if he calls there will not be any unpleasantness about it. Young Dr. John Buchanan said he might call.

MRS. WINEMILLER:
See!

MR. WINEMILLER:
You can't be serious.

MRS. WINEMILLER:
Didn't I tell you?

ALMA:
Well, I am.

MR. WINEMILLER:
That young man might come here?

ALMA:
He asked me if he might and I said, yes, if he wished to. But it is now after eight so it doesn't look like he's coming.

MR. WINEMILLER:
If he does come you will go upstairs to your room and I will receive him.

ALMA:
If he does come I'll do no such thing, Father.

MR. WINEMILLER:
You must be out of your mind.

ALMA:
I'll receive him myself. You may retire to your study and Mother upstairs. But if he comes I'll receive him. I don't judge people by the tongues of gossips. I happen to know that he has been grossly misjudged and misrepresented by old busybodies who're envious of his youth and brilliance and charm!

MR. WINEMILLER:
If you're not out of your senses, then I'm out of mine.

ALMA:
I daresay we're all a bit peculiar, Father. . . .

MR. WINEMILLER:
Well, I have had one almost insufferable cross to bear and perhaps I can bear another. But if you think I'm retiring into my study when this young man comes, probably with a whiskey bottle in one hand and a pair of dice in the other, you have another think coming. I'll sit right here and look at him until he leaves. [*He turns back to his sermon.*]

[*A whistle is heard outside the open door.*]

ALMA [*speaking quickly*]:
As a matter of fact I think I'll walk down to the drug store and call for the ice cream myself. [*She crosses to the door, snatching up her hat, gloves and veil.*]

MRS. WINEMILLER:
There she goes to him! Ha-ha! [*Alma rushes out.*]

MR. WINEMILLER [*looking up*]:
Alma! Alma!

MRS. WINEMILLER:
Ha-ha-haaaaa!

MR. WINEMILLER:
Where is Alma?—Alma! [*He rushes through the door.*] Alma!

MRS. WINEMILLER:
Ha-ha! Who got fooled? Who got fooled! Ha-haaaa! Insufferable cross yourself, you old—windbag. . . .

[*The curtain comes down.*]

A delicately suggested arbor, enclosing a table and two chairs. Over the table is suspended a torn paper lantern. This tiny set may be placed way downstage in front of the two interiors, which should be darkened out, as in the fountain scenes. In the background, as it is throughout the play, the angel of the fountain is dimly visible.

Music from the nearby pavilion of the Casino can be used when suitable for background.

John's voice is audible before he and Alma enter.

JOHN [*from the darkness*]:
I don't understand why we can't go in the casino.

ALMA:
You do understand. You're just pretending not to.

JOHN:
Give me one reason.

ALMA [*coming into the arbor*]:
I am a minister's daughter.

JOHN:
That's no reason. [*He follows her in. He wears a white linen suit, carrying the coat over his arm.*]

ALMA:
You're a doctor. That's a better reason. You can't any more afford to be seen in such places than I can—less!

JOHN [*bellowing*]:
Dusty!

DUSTY [*from the darkness*]:
Coming!

JOHN:
What are you fishing in that pocketbook for?

72

ALMA:
Nothing.

JOHN:
What have you got there?

ALMA:
Let go!

JOHN:
Those sleeping tablets I gave you?

ALMA:
Yes.

JOHN:
What for?

ALMA:
I need one.

JOHN:
Now?

ALMA:
Yes.

JOHN:
Why?

ALMA:
Why? Because I nearly died of heart failure in your automobile. What possessed you to drive like that? A demon?

[*Dusty enters.*]

JOHN:
A bottle of vino rosso.

DUSTY:
Sure. [*He withdraws.*]

JOHN:
Hey! Tell Shorty I want to hear the "Yellow Dog Blues."

ALMA:
Please give me back my tablets.

JOHN:
You want to turn into a dope-fiend taking this stuff? I said take one when you need one.

ALMA:
I need one now.

JOHN:
Sit down and stop swallowing air. [*Dusty returns with a tall wine bottle and two thin-stemmed glasses.*] When does the cockfight start?

DUSTY:
'Bout ten o'clock, Dr. Johnny.

ALMA:
When does *what start?*

JOHN:
They have a cock-fight here every Saturday night. Ever seen one?

ALMA:
Perhaps in some earlier incarnation of mine.

JOHN:
When you wore a brass ring in your nose?

ALMA:
Then maybe I went to exhibitions like that.

JOHN:
You're going to see one tonight.

ALMA:
Oh, no, I'm not.

JOHN:
That's what we came here for.

ALMA:
I didn't think such exhibitions were legal.

JOHN:
This is Moon Lake Casino where anything goes.

ALMA:
And you're a frequent patron?

JOHN:
I'd say constant.

ALMA:
Then I'm afraid you must be serious about giving up your medical career.

JOHN:
You bet I am! A doctor's life is walled in by sickness and misery and death.

ALMA:
May I be so presumptuous as to inquire what you'll do when you quit?

JOHN:
You may be so presumptious as to inquire.

ALMA:
But you won't tell me?

JOHN:
I haven't made up my mind, but I've been thinking of South America lately.

ALMA [*sadly*]:
Oh . . .

JOHN:
I've heard that cantinas are lots more fun than saloons, and senoritas are caviar among females.

ALMA:
Dorothy Sykes' brother went to South America and was never heard of again. It takes a strong character to survive in the tropics. Otherwise it's a quagmire.

JOHN:
You think my character's weak?

ALMA:
I think you're confused, just awfully, awfully confused, as confused as I am—but in a different way. . . .

JOHN [*stretching out his legs*]:
Hee-haw, ho-hum.

ALMA:
You used to say that as a child—to signify your disgust!

JOHN [*grinning*]:
Did I?

ALMA [*sharply*]:
Don't sit like that!

JOHN:
Why not?

ALMA:
You look so indolent and worthless.

JOHN:
Maybe I am.

ALMA:
If you must go somewhere, why don't you choose a place with a bracing climate?

JOHN:
Parts of South America are as cool as a cucumber.

ALMA:
I never knew that.

JOHN:
Well, now you do.

ALMA:
Those Latins all dream in the sun—and indulge their senses.

JOHN:
Well, it's yet to be proven that anyone on this earth is crowned with so much glory as the one that uses his senses to get all he can in the way of—satisfaction.

ALMA:
Self-satisfaction?

JOHN:
What other kind is there?

76

ALMA:
I will answer that question by asking you one. Have you ever seen, or looked at a picture, of a Gothic cathedral?

JOHN:
Gothic cathedrals? What about them?

ALMA:
How everything reaches up, how everything seems to be straining for something out of the reach of stone—or human —fingers? . . . The immense stained windows, the great arched doors that are five or six times the height of the tallest man—the vaulted ceiling and all the delicate spires— all reaching up to something beyond attainment! To me— well, that is the secret, the principle back of existence—the everlasting struggle and aspiration for more than our human limits have placed in our reach. . . . Who was that said that—oh, so beautiful thing!—"All of us are in the gutter, but some of us are looking at the stars!"

JOHN:
Mr. Oscar Wilde.

ALMA [*somewhat taken aback*]:
Well, regardless of who said it, it's still true. Some of us are looking at the stars! [*She looks up raptly and places her hand over his.*]

JOHN:
It's no fun, holding hands with gloves on, Miss Alma.

ALMA:
That's easily remedied. I'll just take the gloves off. [*Music is heard.*]

JOHN:
Christ! [*He rises abruptly and lights a cigarette.*] Rosa Gonzales is dancing in the Casino.

ALMA:
You *are* unhappy. You hate me for depriving you of the company inside. Well, you'll escape by and by. You'll drive me home and come back out by yourself. . . . I've only gone out with three young men at all seriously, and with each one there was a desert between us.

JOHN:
What do you mean by a desert?

ALMA:
Oh—wide, wide stretches of uninhabitable ground.

JOHN:
Maybe you made it that way by being stand-offish.

ALMA:
I made quite an effort with one or two of them.

JOHN:
What kind of an effort?

ALMA:
Oh, I—tried to entertain them the first few times. I would play and sing for them in the Rectory parlor.

JOHN:
With your father in the next room and the door half open?

ALMA:
I don't think that was the trouble.

JOHN:
What was the trouble?

ALMA:
I—I didn't have my heart in it. [*She laughs uncertainly.*] A silence would fall between us. You know, a silence?

JOHN:
Yes. I know a silence.

ALMA:
I'd try to talk and he'd try to talk and neither would make a go of it.

JOHN:
The silence would fall?

ALMA:
Yes, the enormous silence.

JOHN:
Then you'd go back to the piano?
78

ALMA:
I'd twist my ring. Sometimes I twisted it so hard that the band cut my finger! He'd glance at his watch and we'd both know that the useless undertaking had come to a close. . . .

JOHN:
You'd call it quits?

ALMA:
Quits is—what we'd call it. . . . One or two times I was rather sorry about it.

JOHN:
But you didn't have your heart in it?

ALMA:
None of them really engaged my serious feelings.

JOHN:
You do have serious feelings—of that kind?

ALMA:
Doesn't everyone—sometimes?

JOHN:
Some women are cold. Some women are what is called frigid.

ALMA:
Do I give that impression?

JOHN:
Under the surface you have a lot of excitement, a great deal more than any other woman I have met. So much that you have to carry these sleeping pills with you. The question is why? [*He leans over and lifts her veil.*]

ALMA:
What are you doing that for?

JOHN:
So that I won't get your veil in my mouth when I kiss you.

ALMA [*faintly*]:
Do you want to do that?

79

JOHN [*gently*]:
Miss Alma. [*He takes her arms and draws her to her feet.*] Oh, Miss Alma, Miss Alma! [*He kisses her.*]

ALMA [*in a low, shaken voice*]:
Not "Miss" any more. Just Alma.

JOHN [*grinning gently*]:
"Miss" suits you better, Miss Alma. [*He kisses her again. She hesitantly touches his shoulders, but not quite to push him away. John speaks softly to her.*] Is it so hard to forget you're a preacher's daughter?

ALMA:
There is no reason for me to forget that I am a minister's daughter. A minister's daughter's no different from any other young lady who tries to remember that she *is* a lady.

JOHN:
This lady stuff, is that so important?

ALMA:
Not to the sort of girls that you may be used to bringing to Moon Lake Casino. But suppose that some day . . . [*She crosses out of the arbor and faces away from him.*] suppose that some day you—*married*. . . . The woman that you selected to be your wife, and not only your wife but—the mother of your children! [*She catches her breath at the thought.*] Wouldn't you want that woman to be a lady? Wouldn't you want her to be somebody that you, as her husband, and they as her precious children—could look up to with very deep respect? [*There is a pause.*]

JOHN:
There's other things between a man and a woman besides respect. Did you know that, Miss Alma?

ALMA:
Yes. . . .

JOHN:
There's such a thing as intimate relations.

ALMA:
Thank you for telling me that. So plainly.
80

JOHN:

It may strike you as unpleasant. But it does have a good deal to do with—connubial felicity, as you'd call it. There are some women that just give in to a man as a sort of obligation imposed on them by the—cruelty of nature! [*He finishes his glass and pours another.*] And there you are.

ALMA:

There *I* am?

JOHN:

I'm speaking generally.

ALMA:

Oh.

[*Hoarse shouts go up from the Casino.*]

JOHN:

The cock-fight has started!

ALMA:

Since you have spoken so plainly, I'll speak plainly, too. There are some women who turn a possibly beautiful thing into something no better than the coupling of beasts!—but love is what you bring to it.

JOHN:

You're right about that.

ALMA:

Some people bring just their bodies. But there are some people, there are some women, John—who can bring their hearts to it, also—who can bring their souls to it!

JOHN [*derisively*]:

Souls again, huh?—those Gothic cathedrals you dream of!

[*There is another hoarse prolonged shout from the Casino.*]

Your name is Alma and Alma is Spanish for soul. Some time I'd like to show you a chart of the human anatomy that I have in the office. It shows what our insides are like, and maybe you can show me where the beautiful soul is located on the chart. [*He drains the wine bottle.*] Let's go watch the cock-fight.

ALMA:
No! [*There is a pause.*]

JOHN:
I know something else we could do. There are rooms above the Casino. . . .

ALMA [*her back stiffening*]:
I'd heard that you made suggestions like that to girls that you go out with, but I refused to believe such stories were true. What made you think I might be amenable to such a suggestion?

JOHN:
I counted your pulse in the office the night you ran out because you weren't able to sleep.

ALMA:
The night I was ill and went to your father for help.

JOHN:
It was me you went to.

ALMA:
It was your father, and you wouldn't call your father.

JOHN:
Fingers frozen stiff when I . . .

ALMA [*rising*]:
Oh! I want to go home. But I won't go with you. I will go in a taxi! [*She wheels about hysterically.*] Boy! Boy! Call a taxi!

JOHN:
I'll call one for you, Miss Alma.—Taxi! [*He goes out of the arbor.*]

ALMA [*wildly*]:
You're not a gentleman!

JOHN [*from the darkness*]:
Taxi!

ALMA:
You're not a gentleman!

[*As he disappears she makes a sound in her throat like a hurt animal. The light fades out of the arbor and comes up more distinctly on the stone angel of the fountain.*]

PART TWO

a winter

scene seven

*The sky and the southern constellations, almost impercep-
tibly moving with the earth's motion, appear on the great
cyclorama.*

*The Rectory interior is lighted first, disclosing Alma and
Roger Doremus seated on the green plush sofa under the
romantic landscape in its heavy gilt frame. On a tiny table
beside them is a cut glass pitcher of lemonade with cherries
and orange slices in it, like a little aquarium of tropical fish.
Roger is entertaining Alma with a collection of photographs
and postcards, mementoes of his mother's trip to the Orient.
He is enthusiastic about them and describes them in phrases
his mother must have assimilated from a sedulous study of
literature provided by Cook's Tours. Alma is less enthusiastic; she is preoccupied with the sounds of a wild party
going on next door at the doctor's home. At present there is
Mexican music with shouts and stamping.*

*Only the immediate area of the sofa is clearly lighted; the
fountain is faintly etched in light and the night sky walls
the interior.*

ROGER:
And this is Ceylon, The Pearl of the Orient!

ALMA:
And who is this fat young lady?

ROGER:
That is Mother in a hunting costume.

ALMA:
The hunting costume makes her figure seem bulky. What
was your mother hunting?

ROGER [*gaily*]:
Heaven knows what she was hunting! But she found Papa.

ALMA:
Oh, she met your father on this Oriental tour?

ROGER:
Ha-ha!—yes. . . . He was returning from India with dysentery and they met on the boat.

ALMA [*distastefully*]:
Oh . . .

ROGER:
And here she is on top of a ruined temple!

ALMA:
How did she get up there?

ROGER:
Climbed up, I suppose.

ALMA:
What an active woman.

ROGER:
Oh, yes, active—is no word for it! Here she is on an elephant's back in Burma.

ALMA:
Ah!

ROGER:
You're looking at it upside down, Miss Alma!

ALMA:
Deliberately—to tease you. [*The doorbell rings.*] Perhaps that's your mother coming to fetch you home.

ROGER:
It's only ten-fifteen. I never leave till ten-thirty.

[*Mrs. Bassett comes in.*]

ALMA:
Mrs. Bassett!

MRS. BASSETT:
I was just wondering who I could turn to when I saw the Rectory light and I thought to myself, Grace Bassett, you trot yourself right over there and talk to Mr. Winemiller!

ALMA:
Father has retired.

MRS. BASSETT:
Oh, what a pity. [*She sees Roger.*] Hello, Roger! . . . I saw that fall your mother took this morning. I saw her come skipping out of the Delta Planters' Bank and I thought to myself, now isn't that remarkable, a woman of her age and weight so light on her feet? And just at that very moment— *down she went!* I swear to goodness I thought she had broken her hip! Was she bruised much?

ROGER:
Just shaken up, Mrs. Bassett.

MRS. BASSETT:
Oh, how lucky! She certainly must be made out of India rubber! [*She turns to Alma.*] Alma—Alma, if it is not too late for human intervention, your father's the one right person to call up old Dr. Buchanan at the fever clinic at Lyon and let him know!

ALMA:
About—what?

MRS. BASSETT:
You must be stone-deaf if you haven't noticed what's been going on next door since the old doctor left to fight the epidemic. One continual orgy! Well, not five minutes ago a friend of mine who works at the County Courthouse called to inform me that young Dr. John and Rosa Gonzales have taken a license out and are going to be married tomorrow!

ALMA:
Are you—quite certain?

MRS. BASSETT:
Certain? I'm always certain before I speak!

ALMA:
Why would he—do such a thing?

MRS. BASSETT:
August madness! They say it has something to do with the falling stars. Of course it might also have something to do with the fact that he lost two or three thousand dollars at the Casino which he can't pay except by giving himself to Gonzales' daughter. [*She turns to Alma.*] Alma, what are you doing with that picture puzzle?

ALMA [*with a faint, hysterical laugh*]:
The pieces don't fit.

MRS. BASSETT [*to Roger*]:
I shouldn't have opened my mouth.

ALMA:
Will both of you please go!

[*Roger goes out.*]

MRS. BASSETT:
I knew this was going to upset you. Good night, Alma. [*She leaves. Alma suddenly springs up and seizes the telephone.*]

ALMA:
Long distance. . . . Please get me the fever clinic at Lyon. . . . I want to speak to Dr. Buchanan.

[*The light in the Rectory dims out and light comes on in the doctor's office. Rosa's voice is heard calling.*]

ROSA:
Johnny!

[*The offstage calling of John's name is used throughout the play as a cue for theme music.*

[*John enters the office interior. He is dressed, as always, in a white linen suit. His face has a look of satiety and confusion. He throws himself down in a swivel chair at the desk.*

[*Rosa Gonzales comes in. She is dressed in a Flamenco costume and has been dancing. She crosses and stands before the anatomy chart and clicks her castanets to catch his attention, but he remains looking up at the roofless dark. She approaches him.*]

ROSA:
You have blood on your face!

JOHN:
You bit my ear.

ROSA:
Ohhh . . . [*She approaches him with exaggerated concern.*]

JOHN:
You never make love without scratching or biting or something. Whenever I leave you I have a little blood on me. Why is that?

ROSA:
Because I know I can't hold you.

JOHN:
I think you're doing a pretty good job of it. Better than anyone else. Tomorrow we leave here together and Father or somebody else can tell old Mrs. Arbuckle her eighty-five years are enough and she's got to go now on the wings of carcinoma. Dance, Rosa! [*Accordion music is heard. She performs a slow and joyless dance around his chair. John continues while she dances.*] Tomorrow we leave here together. We sail out of Galveston, don't we?

ROSA:
You say it but I don't believe it.

JOHN:
I have the tickets.

ROSA:
Two pieces of paper that you can tear in two.

JOHN:
We'll go all right, and live on fat remittances from your Papa! Ha-ha!

ROSA:
Ha-ha-ha!

JOHN:
Not long ago the idea would have disgusted me, but not now. [*He catches her by the wrist.*] Rosa! Rosa Gonzales! Did anyone ever slide downhill as fast as I have this summer? Ha-ha! Like a greased pig. And yet every evening I put on a clean white suit. I have a dozen. Six in the closet and six in the wash. And there isn't a sign of depravity in my face. And yet all summer I've sat around here like *this*, remembering last night, anticipating the next one! The trouble with me is, I should have been *castrated!* [*He flings his wine glass at the anatomy chart. She stops dancing.*] Dance, Rosa! Why don't you dance? [*Rosa shakes her head dumbly.*] What is the matter, Rosa? Why don't you go on

dancing? [*The accordion continues; he thrusts her arm savagely over her head in the Flamenco position.*]

ROSA [*suddenly weeping*]:
I can't dance any more! [*She throws herself to the floor, pressing her weeping face to his knees. The voice of her father is heard, bellowing, in the next room.*]

GONZALES:
The sky is the limit!

[*John is sobered.*]

JOHN:
Why does your father want me for a son-in-law?

ROSA [*sobbing*]:
I want you—I, I want you!

JOHN [*raising her from the floor*]:
Why do you?

ROSA [*clinging to him*]:
Maybe because—I was born in Piedras Negras, and grew up in a one room house with a dirt floor, and all of us had to sleep in that one room, five Mexicans and three geese and a little game-cock named Pepe! Ha-ha! [*She laughs hysterically.*] Pepe was a good fighter! That's how Papa began to make money, winning bets on Pepe! Ha-ha! We all slept in the one room. And in the night, I would hear the love-making. Papa would grunt like a pig to show his passion. I thought to myself, how dirty it was, love-making, and how dirty it was to be Mexicans and all have to sleep in one room with a dirt floor and not smell good because there was not any bathtub! [*The accordion continues.*]

JOHN:
What has that got to do with . . . ?

ROSA:
Me wanting you? You're tall! You smell good! And, oh, I'm so glad that you never grunt like a pig to show your passion! [*She embraces him convulsively.*] Ah, but *quien sabe!* Something might happen tonight, and I'll wind up with some dark little friend of Papa's.

GONZALES [*imperiously*]:
Rosa! Rosa!
92

ROSA:
Si, si, Papa, aqui estoy!

GONZALES [*entering unsteadily*]:
The gold beads . . . [*He fingers a necklace of gold beads that Rosa is wearing.*] Johnny . . . [*He staggers up to John and catches him in a drunken embrace.*] Listen! When my girl Rosa was little she see a string a gold bead and she want those gold bead so bad that she cry all night for it. I don' have money to buy a string a gold bead so next day I go for a ride up to Eagle Pass and I walk in a dry good store and I say to the man: "Please give me a string a gold bead." He say: "Show me the money," and I say: "Here is the money!" And I reach down to my belt and I pull out—not the money—but this! [*He pulls out a revolver.*] Now—now I have money, but I still have this! [*laughing*] She got the gold bead. Anything that she want I get for her with this [*He pulls out a roll of bills.*] or this! [*He waves the revolver.*]

JOHN [*pushing Gonzales away*]:
Keep your stinking breath out of my face, Gonzales!

ROSA:
Dejalo, dejalo, Papa!

GONZALES [*moving unsteadily to the couch, with Rosa supporting him*]:
Le doy la tierra y si tierra no basta—le doy el cielo! [*He collapses onto the couch.*] The sky is the limit!

ROSA [*to John*]:
Let him stay there. Come on back to the party.

[*Rosa leaves the room. John goes over to the window facing the Rectory and looks across. The light comes up in the Rectory living room as Alma enters, dressed in a robe. She goes to the window and looks across at the doctor's house. As Alma and John stand at the windows looking toward each other through the darkness music is heard. Slowly, as if drawn by the music, John walks out of his house and crosses over to the Rectory. Alma remains motionless at the window until John enters the room, behind her. The music dies away and there is a murmur of wind. She slowly turns to face John.*]

93

JOHN:

I took the open door for an invitation. The Gulf wind is blowing tonight . . . cools things off a little. But my head's on fire. . . . [*Alma says nothing. John moves a few steps toward her.*] The silence? [*Alma sinks onto the love seat, closing her eyes.*] Yes, the enormous silence. [*He goes over to her.*] I will go in a minute, but first I want you to put your hands on my face. . . . [*He crouches beside her.*] Eternity and Miss Alma have such cool hands. [*He buries his face in her lap. The attitude suggests a stone Pieta. Alma's eyes remain closed.*]

[*On the other side of the stage Dr. Buchanan enters his house and the light builds a little as he looks around in the door of his office. The love theme music fades out and the Mexican music comes up strongly, with a definitely ominous quality, as Rosa enters the office from the other side.*]

ROSA:

Johnny! [*She catches sight of Dr. Buchanan and checks herself in surprise.*] Oh! I thought you were Johnny! . . . But you are Johnny's father. . . . I'm Rosa Gonzales!

DR. BUCHANAN:

I know who you are. What's going on in my house?

ROSA [*nervously*]:

John's giving a party because we're leaving tomorrow. [*defiantly*] Yes! Together! I hope you like the idea, but if you don't, it don't matter, because *we* like the idea and my father likes the idea.

GONZALES [*drunkenly, sitting up on the couch*]:

The sky is the limit!

[*Dr. Buchanan slowly raises his silver-headed cane in a threatening gesture.*]

DR. BUCHANAN:

Get your—swine out of—my house! [*He strikes Gonzales with his cane.*]

GONZALES [*staggering up from the couch in pain and surprise*]:

Aieeeee!

ROSA [*breathlessly, backing against the chart of anatomy*]:
No! No, Papa!

DR. BUCHANAN [*striking at the chest of the bull-like man with his cane*]:
Get your swine out, I said! Get them out of my house!

[*He repeats the blow. The drunken Mexican roars with pain and surprise. He backs up and reaches under his coat.*]

ROSA [*wildly and despairingly*]:
No, no, no, no, no, no!

[*She covers her face against the chart of anatomy. A revolver is fired. There is a burst of light. The cane drops. The music stops short. Everything dims out but a spot of light on Rosa standing against the chart of anatomy with closed eyes and her face twisted like that of a tragic mask.*]

ROSA [*senselessly*]:
Aaaaaahhhhhh . . . Aaaaaahhhhhh . . .

[*The theme music is started faintly and light disappears from everything but the wings of the stone angel.*]

scene eight

The doctor's office.

The stone angel is dimly visible above.

John is seated in a hunched position at the table. Alma enters with a coffee tray. The sounds of a prayer come through the inner door.

JOHN:
What is that mumbo-jumbo your father is spouting in there?

ALMA:
A prayer.

JOHN:
Tell him to quit. We don't want that worn-out magic.

ALMA:
You may not want it, but it's not a question of what you want any more. I've made you some coffee.

JOHN:
I don't want any.

ALMA:
Lean back and let me wash your face off, John. [*She presses a towel to the red marks on his face.*] It's such a fine face, a fine and sensitive face, a face that has power in it that shouldn't be wasted.

JOHN:
Never mind that. [*He pushes her hand away.*]

ALMA:
You have to go in to see him.

JOHN:
I couldn't. He wouldn't want me.

ALMA:
This happened because of his devotion to you.

JOHN:
It happened because some meddlesome Mattie called him back here tonight. Who was it did that?

ALMA:
I did.

JOHN:
It *was* you then!

ALMA:
I phoned him at the fever clinic in Lyon as soon as I learned what you were planning to do. I wired him to come here and stop it.

JOHN:
You brought him here to be shot.

ALMA:
You can't put the blame on anything but your weakness.

JOHN:
You call me weak?

ALMA:
Sometimes it takes a tragedy like this to make a weak person strong.

JOHN:
You—white-blooded spinster! You so right people, pious pompous mumblers, preachers and preacher's daughter, all muffled up in a lot of worn-out magic! And I was supposed to minister to your neurosis, give you tablets for sleeping and tonics to give you the strength to go on mumbling your worn-out mumbo-jumbo!

ALMA:
Call me whatever you want, but don't let your father hear your drunken shouting. [*She tries to break away from him.*]

JOHN:
Stay here! I want you to look at something. [*He turns her about.*] This chart of anatomy, look!

ALMA:
I've seen it before. [*She turns away.*]

JOHN:
You've never dared to look at it.

ALMA:
Why should I?

JOHN:
You're scared to.

ALMA:
You must be out of your senses.

JOHN:
You talk about weakness but can't even look at a picture of human insides.

ALMA:
They're not important.

JOHN:
That's your mistake. You think you're stuffed with rose-

leaves. Turn around and look at it, it may do you good!

ALMA:
How can you behave like this with your father dying and you so . . .

JOHN:
Hold still!

ALMA:
. . . so much to blame for it!

JOHN:
No more than you are!

ALMA:
At least for this little while . . .

JOHN:
Look here!

ALMA:
. . . you could feel some shame!

JOHN [*with crazy, grinning intensity*]:
Now listen here to the anatomy lecture! This upper story's the brain which is hungry for something called truth and doesn't get much but keeps on feeling hungry! This middle's the belly which is hungry for food. This part down here is the sex which is hungry for love because it is sometimes lonesome. I've fed all three, as much of all three as I could or as much as I wanted— You've fed none—nothing. Well—maybe your belly a little—watery subsistance— But love or truth, nothing but—nothing but hand-me-down notions!—attitudes!—poses [*He releases her.*] Now you can go. The anatomy lecture is over.

ALMA:
So that is your high conception of human desires. What you have here is not the anatomy of a beast, but a man. And I —I reject your opinion of where love is, and the kind of truth you believe the brain to be seeking!—There is something not shown on the chart.

JOHN:
You mean the part that Alma is Spanish for, do you?
98

ALMA:
Yes, that's not shown on the anatomy chart! But it's there, just the same, yes, there! Somewhere, not seen, but there. And it's *that* that I loved you with—that! Not what you mention!—Yes, did love you with, John, did nearly *die* of when you hurt me! [*He turns slowly to her and speaks gently.*]

JOHN:
I wouldn't have made love to you.

ALMA [*uncomprehendingly*]:
What?

JOHN:
The night at the Casino—I wouldn't have made love to you. Even if you had consented to go upstairs. I couldn't have made love to you. [*She stares at him as if anticipating some unbearable hurt.*] Yes, yes! Isn't that funny? I'm more afraid of your soul than you're afraid of my body. You'd have been as safe as the angel of the fountain—because I wouldn't feel *decent* enough to touch you. . . .

[*Mr. Winemiller comes in.*]

MR. WINEMILLER:
He's resting more easily now.

ALMA:
Oh . . . [*She nods her head. John reaches for his coffee cup.*] It's cold. I'll heat it.

JOHN:
It's all right.

MR. WINEMILLER:
Alma, Dr. John wants you.

ALMA:
I . . .

MR. WINEMILLER:
He asked if you would sing for him.

ALMA:
I—couldn't—now.

JOHN:
Go in and sing to him, Miss Alma!

[*Mr. Winemiller withdraws through the outer door. Alma looks back at John hunched over the coffee cup. He doesn't return her look. She passes into the blurred orange space beyond the inner door, leaving it slightly open. After a few minutes her voice rises softly within, singing. John suddenly rises. He crosses to the door, shoves it slowly open and enters.*]

JOHN [*softly and with deep tenderness*]:
Father?

[*The light dims out in the house, but lingers on the stone angel.*]

scene nine

The cyclorama is the faint blue of a late afternoon in autumn. There is band-music—a Sousa march, in the distance. As it grows somewhat louder, Alma enters the Rectory interior in a dressing gown and with her hair hanging loose. She looks as if she had been through a long illness, the intensity drained, her pale face listless. She crosses to the window frame but the parade is not in sight so she returns weakly to the sofa and sits down closing her eyes with exhaustion.

The Rev. and Mrs. Winemiller enter the outer door frame of the Rectory, a grotesque-looking couple. Mrs. Winemiller has on her plumed hat, at a rakish angle, and a brilliant scarf about her throat. Her face wears a roguish smile that suggests a musical comedy pirate. One hand holds the minister's arm and with the other she is holding an ice cream cone.

MR. WINEMILLER:
Now you may let go of my arm, if you please! She was on her worst behavior. Stopped in front of the White Star Pharmacy on Front Street and stood there like a mule;

wouldn't budge till I bought her an ice cream cone. I had it wrapped in tissue paper because she had promised me that she wouldn't eat it until we got home. The moment I gave it to her she tore off the paper and walked home licking it every step of the way!—just—just to humiliate me! [*Mrs. Winemiller offers him the half-eaten cone, saying "Lick?"*]

MR. WINEMILLER:
No, thank you!

ALMA:
Now, now, children.

[*Mr. Winemiller's irritation shifts to Alma.*]

MR. WINEMILLER:
Alma! Why don't you get dressed? It hurts me to see you sitting around like this, day in, day out, like an invalid when there is nothing particularly wrong with you. I can't read your mind. You may have had some kind of disappointment, but you must not make it an excuse for acting as if the world had come to an end.

ALMA:
I have made the beds and washed the breakfast dishes and phoned the market and sent the laundry out and peeled the potatoes and shelled the peas and set the table for lunch. What more do you want?

MR. WINEMILLER [*sharply*]:
I want you to either get dressed or stay in your room. [*Alma rises indifferently, then her father speaks suddenly.*] At night you get dressed. Don't you? Yes, I heard you slipping out of the house at two in the morning. And that was not the first time.

ALMA:
I don't sleep well. Sometimes I have to get up and walk for a while before I am able to sleep.

MR. WINEMILLER:
What am I going to tell people who ask about you?

ALMA:
Tell them I've changed and you're waiting to see in what way.

[*The band music becomes a little louder.*]

MR. WINEMILLER:
Are you going to stay like this indefinitely?

ALMA:
Not indefinitely, but you may wish that I had.

MR. WINEMILLER:
Stop twisting that ring! Whenever I look at you you're twisting that ring. Give me that ring! I'm going to take that ring off your finger! [*He catches her wrist. She breaks roughly away from him.*]

MRS. WINEMILLER [*joyfully*]:
Fight! Fight!

MR. WINEMILLER:
Oh, I give up!

ALMA:
That's better. [*She suddenly crosses to the window as the band music gets louder.*] Is there a parade in town?

MRS. WINEMILLER:
Ha-ha—yes! They met him at the station with a great big silver loving-cup!

ALMA:
Who? Who did they . . . ?

MRS. WINEMILLER:
That boy next door, the one you watched all the time!

ALMA:
Is that true, Father?

MR. WINEMILLER [*unfolding his newspaper*]:
Haven't you looked at the papers?

ALMA:
No, not lately.

MR. WINEMILLER [*wiping his eyeglasses*]:
These people are grasshoppers, just as likely to jump one way as another. He's finished the work his father started, stamped out the fever and gotten all the glory. Well, that's

how it is in this world. Years of devotion and sacrifice are overlooked an' forgotten while someone young an' lucky walks off with the honors!

[*Alma has crossed slowly to the window. The sun brightens and falls in a shaft through the frame.*]

ALMA [*suddenly crying out*]:
There he is! [*She staggers away from the window. There is a roll of drums and then silence. Alma now speaks faintly.*] What . . . happened? Something . . . struck me! [*Mr. Winemiller catches her arm to support her.*]

MR. WINEMILLER:
Alma . . . I'll call a doctor.

ALMA:
No, no, don't. Don't call anybody to help me. I want to die!

[*She collapses on the sofa.*]

[*The band strikes up again and recedes down the street. The Rectory interior dims out. Then the light is brought up in the doctor's office. John enters, with his loving-cup. He is sprucely dressed and his whole manner suggests a new-found responsibility. While he is setting the award on the table, removing his coat and starched collar, Nellie Ewell appears in the door behind him. She stands by the anatomy chart and watches him until he discovers her presence. Nellie has abruptly grown up, and wears very adult clothes, but has lost none of her childish impudence and brightness. John gives a startled whistle as he sees her. Nellie giggles.*]

JOHN:
High heels, feathers . . . and paint!

NELLIE:
Not paint!

JOHN:
Natural color?

NELLIE:
Excitement.

JOHN:
Over what?

NELLIE:
Everything! You! You here! Didn't you see me at the depot? I shouted and waved my arm off! I'm home for Thanksgiving.

JOHN:
From where?

NELLIE:
Sophie Newcombe's. [*He remains staring at her, unbelieving. At last she draws a book from under her arm.*] Here is that nasty book you gave me last summer when I was pretending such ignorance of things!

JOHN:
Only pretending?

NELLIE:
Yes. [*He ignores the book. She tosses it on the table.*] . . . Well? [*John laughs uneasily and sits on the table.*] Shall I go now, or will you look at my tongue? [*She crosses to him, sticking out her tongue.*]

JOHN:
Red as a berry!

NELLIE:
Peppermint drops! Will you have one? [*She holds out a sack.*]

JOHN:
Thanks [*Nellie giggles as he takes one.*] What's the joke, Nellie?

NELLIE:
They make your mouth so sweet!

JOHN:
So?

NELLIE:
I always take one when I hope to be kissed.

JOHN [*after a pause*]:
Suppose I took you up on that?

NELLIE:
I'm not scared. Are you?
104

[*He gives her a quick kiss. She clings to him, raising her hand to press his head against her own. He breaks free after a moment and turns the light back on.*]

JOHN [*considerably impressed*]:
Where did you learn such tricks?

NELLIE:
I've been away to school. But they didn't teach me to love.

JOHN:
Who are you to be using that long word?

NELLIE:
That isn't a long word!

JOHN:
No? [*He turns away from her.*] Run along Nellie before we get into trouble.

NELLIE:
Who's afraid of trouble, you or me?

JOHN:
I am. Run along! Hear me?

NELLIE:
Oh, I'll go. But I'll be back for Christmas!

[*She laughs and runs out. He whistles and wipes his forehead with a handkerchief.*]

An afternoon in December. At the fountain in the park. It is very windy.

Alma enters. She seems to move with an effort against the wind. She sinks down on the bench.

A widow with a flowing black veil passes across the stage and pauses by Alma's bench. It is Mrs. Bassett.

MRS. BASSETT:
Hello Alma.

ALMA:
Good afternoon, Mrs. Bassett.

MRS. BASSETT:
Such wind, such wind!

ALMA:
Yes, it nearly swept me off my feet. I had to sit down to catch my breath for a moment.

MRS. BASSETT:
I wouldn't sit too long if I were you.

ALMA:
No, not long.

MRS. BASSETT:
It's good to see you out again after your illness.

ALMA:
Thank you.

MRS. BASSETT:
Our poor little group broke up after you dropped out.

ALMA [*insincerely*]:
What a pity.

MRS. BASSETT:
You should have come to the last meeting.

ALMA:
Why, what happened?

MRS. BASSETT:
Vernon read his verse play!

ALMA:
Ah, how was it received?

MRS. BASSETT:
Maliciously, spitefully and vindictively torn to pieces, the way children tear the wings of butterflies. I think next Spring we might reorganize. [*She throws up her black-gloved hands in a deploring gesture.*]

[*Nellie Ewell appears. She is dressed very fashionably and carrying a fancy basket of Christmas packages.*]

NELLIE:
Miss Alma!

MRS. BASSETT [*rushing off*]:
Goodbye!

NELLIE:
Oh, there you are!

ALMA:
Why Nellie . . . Nellie Ewell!

NELLIE:
I was by the Rectory. Just popped in for a second; the holidays are so short that every minute is precious. They told me you'd gone to the park.

ALMA:
This is the first walk I've taken in quite a while.

NELLIE:
You've been ill!

ALMA:
Not ill, just not very well. How you've grown up, Nellie.

NELLIE:
It's just my clothes. Since I went off to Sophie Newcombe I've picked out my own clothes, Miss Alma. When Mother

107

had jurisdiction over my wardrobe, she tried to keep me looking like a child!

ALMA:
Your voice is grown-up, too.

NELLIE:
They're teaching me diction, Miss Alma. I'm learning to talk like you, long A's and everything, such as "cahn't" and "bahth" and "lahf" instead of "laugh." Yesterday I slipped. I said I "lahfed and lahfed till I nearly died laughing." Johnny was so amused at me!

ALMA:
Johnny?

NELLIE:
Your nextdoor neighbor!

ALMA:
Oh! I'm sure it must be a very fashionable school.

NELLIE:
Oh yes, they're preparing us to be young ladies in society. What a pity there's no society here to be a young lady in ... at least not for me, with Mother's reputation!

ALMA:
You'll find other fields to conquer.

NELLIE:
What's this I hear about *you?*

ALMA:
I have no idea, Nellie.

NELLIE:
That you've quit teaching singing and gone into retirement.

ALMA:
Naturally I had to stop teaching while I was ill and as for retiring from the world ... it's more a case of the world retiring from me.

NELLIE:
I know somebody whose feelings you've hurt badly.
108

ALMA:
Why, who could that be, Nellie?

NELLIE:
Somebody who regards you as an angel!

ALMA:
I can't think who might hold me in such esteem.

NELLIE:
Somebody who says that you refused to see him.

ALMA:
I saw nobody. For several months. The long summer wore me out so.

NELLIE:
Well, anyhow, I'm going to give you your present. [*She hands her a small package from the basket.*]

ALMA:
Nellie, you shouldn't have given me anything.

NELLIE:
I'd like to know why not!

ALMA:
I didn't expect it.

NELLIE:
After the trouble you took with my horrible voice?

ALMA:
It's very sweet of you, Nellie.

NELLIE:
Open it!

ALMA:
Now?

NELLIE:
Why, sure.

ALMA:
It's so prettily wrapped I hate to undo it.

NELLIE:
I love to wrap presents and since it was for you, I did a specially dainty job of it.

ALMA [*winding the ribbon about her fingers*]:
I'm going to save this ribbon. I'm going to keep this lovely paper too, with the silver stars on it. And the sprig of holly . . .

NELLIE:
Let me pin it on your jacket, Alma.

ALMA:
Yes, do. I hardly realized that Christmas was coming. . . . [*She unfolds the paper, revealing a lace handkerchief and a card.*] What an exquisite handkerchief.

NELLIE:
I hate to give people handkerchiefs, it's so unimaginative.

ALMA:
I love to get them.

NELLIE:
It comes from Maison Blanche.

ALMA:
Oh, does it really?

NELLIE:
Smell it!

ALMA:
Sachet *Roses!* Well, I'm just more touched and pleased than I can possibly tell you!

NELLIE:
The card!

ALMA:
Card?

NELLIE:
You dropped it. [*She snatches up the card and hands it to Alma.*]

ALMA:
Oh, how clumsy of me! Thank you, Nellie. "Joyeux Noel
. . . to Alma . . . from Nellie and . . . [*She looks up slowly.*] *John?*"

NELLIE:
He helped me wrap presents last night and when we came to yours we started talking about you. Your ears must have burned!

[*The wind blows loudly. Alma bends stiffly forward.*]

ALMA:
You mean you—spoke well of me?

NELLIE:
"Well of"! We raved, simply raved! Oh, he told me the influence you'd had on him!

ALMA:
Influence?

NELLIE:
He told me about the wonderful talks he'd had with you last summer when he was so mixed up and how you in-spired him and you more than anyone else was responsible for his pulling himself together, after his father was killed, and he told me about . . . [*Alma rises stiffly from the bench.*] Where are you going, Miss Alma?

ALMA:
To drink at the fountain.

NELLIE:
He told me about how you came in the house that night like an angel of mercy!

ALMA [*laughing harshly by the fountain*]:
This is the only angel in Glorious Hill. [*She bends to drink.*] Her body is stone and her blood is mineral water.

[*The wind is louder.*]

NELLIE:
How penetrating the wind is!

ALMA:
I'm going home, Nellie. You run along and deliver your presents now.... [*She starts away.*]

NELLIE:
But wait till I've told you the wonderfullest thing I . . .

ALMA:
I'm going home now. Goodbye.

NELLIE:
Oh— Goodbye, Miss Alma.

[*She snatches up her festive basket and rushes in the other direction with a shrill giggle as the wind pulls at her skirts. The lights dim out.*]

scene eleven

An hour later. In John's office.

The interior is framed by the traceries of Victorian architecture and there is one irregular section of wall supporting the anatomy chart. Otherwise the stage is open to the cyclorama.

In the background mellow golden light touches the vane of a steeple (a gilded weathercock). Also the wings of the stone angel. A singing wind rises and falls throughout scene.

John is seated at a white enameled table examining a slide through a microscope.

[*A bell tolls the hour of five as Alma comes hesitantly in. She wears a russet suit and a matching hat with a plume. The light changes, the sun disappearing behind a cloud, fading from the steeple and the stone angel till the bell stops tolling. Then it brightens again.*]

ALMA:
No greetings? No greetings at all?

JOHN:
Hello, Miss Alma.

ALMA [*speaking with animation to control her panic*]:
How white it is here, such glacial brilliance! [*She covers her eyes, laughing.*]

JOHN:
New equipment.

ALMA:
Everything new but the chart.

JOHN:
The human anatomy's always the same old thing.

ALMA:
And such a tiresome one! I've been plagued with sore throats.

JOHN:
Everyone has here lately. These Southern homes are all improperly heated. Open grates aren't enough.

ALMA:
They burn the front of you while your back is freezing!

JOHN:
Then you go into another room and get chilled off.

ALMA:
Yes, yes, chilled to the bone.

JOHN:
But it never gets quite cold enough to convince the damn fools that a furnace is necessary so they go on building without them.

[*There is the sound of wind.*]

ALMA:
Such a strange afternoon.

JOHN:
Is it? I haven't been out.

ALMA:
The Gulf wind is blowing big, white—what do they call

them? cumulus?—clouds over! Ha-ha! It seemed determined to take the plume off my hat, like that fox terrier we
had once named Jacob, snatched the plume off a hat and
dashed around and around the back yard with it like a
trophy!

JOHN:
I remember Jacob. What happened to him?

ALMA:
Oh, Jacob. Jacob was such a mischievous thief. We had to
send him out to some friends in the country. Yes, he ended
his days as—a country squire! The tales of his exploits . . .

JOHN:
Sit down, Miss Alma.

ALMA:
If I'm disturbing you . . . ?

JOHN:
No—I called the Rectory when I heard you were sick. Your
father told me you wouldn't see a doctor.

ALMA:
I needed a rest, that was all. . . . You were out of town
mostly. . . .

JOHN:
I was mostly in Lyon, finishing up Dad's work in the fever
clinic.

ALMA:
Covering yourself with sudden glory!

JOHN:
Redeeming myself with good works.

ALMA:
It's rather late to tell you how happy I am, and also how
proud. I almost feel as your father might have felt—if . . .
And—are you—happy now, John?

JOHN [*uncomfortably, not looking at her*]:
I've settled with life on fairly acceptable terms. Isn't that all
a reasonable person can ask for?

114

ALMA:

He can ask for much more than that. He can ask for the coming true of his most improbable dreams.

JOHN:

It's best not to ask for too much.

ALMA:

I disagree with you. I say, ask for all, but be prepared to get nothing! [*She springs up and crosses to the window. She continues.*] No, I haven't been well. I've thought many times of something you told me last summer, that I have a *doppelganger*. I looked that up and I found that it means another person inside me, another self, and I don't know whether to thank you or not for making me conscious of it!—I haven't been well. . . . For a while I thought I was dying, that that was the change that was coming.

JOHN:

When did you have that feeling?

ALMA:

August. September. But now the Gulf wind has blown that feeling away like a cloud of smoke, and I know now I'm not dying, that it isn't going to turn out to be that simple. . . .

JOHN:

Have you been anxious about your heart again? [*He retreats to a professional manner and takes out a silver watch, putting his fingers on her wrist.*]

ALMA:

And now the stethoscope? [*He removes the stethoscope from the table and starts to loosen her jacket. She looks down at his bent head. Slowly, involuntarily, her gloved hands lift and descend on the crown of his head. He gets up awkwardly. She suddenly leans toward him and presses her mouth to his.*] Why don't you say something? Has the cat got your tongue?

JOHN:

Miss Alma, what can I say?

ALMA:

You've gone back to calling me "Miss Alma" again.

JOHN:

We never really got past that point with each other.

ALMA:

Oh, yes, we did. We were so close that we almost breathed together!

JOHN [*with embarrassment*]:

I didn't know that.

ALMA:

No? Well, I did, I knew it. [*Her hand touches his face tenderly.*] You shave more carefully now? You don't have those little razor cuts on your chin that you dusted with gardenia talcum. . . .

JOHN:

I shave more carefully now.

ALMA:

So that explains it! [*Her fingers remain on his face, moving gently up and down it like a blind person reading Braille. He is intensely embarassed and gently removes her hands from him.*] Is it—impossible now?

JOHN:

I don't think I know what you mean.

ALMA:

You know what I mean, all right! So be honest with me. One time I said "no" to something. You may remember the time, and all that demented howling from the cock-fight? But now I have changed my mind, or the girl who said "no," she doesn't exist any more, she died last summer —suffocated in smoke from something on fire inside her. No, she doesn't live now, but she left me her ring— You see? This one you admired, the topaz ring set in pearls. . . . And she said to me when she slipped this ring on my finger—"Remember I died empty-handed, and so make sure that your hands have *something in them!*" [*She drops her gloves. She clasps his head again in her hands.*] I said, "But what about pride?"—She said, "Forget about pride whenever it stands between you and what you must have!" [*He takes hold of her wrists.*] And then I said, "But what if he doesn't want me?" I don't know what she said then. I'm not sure whether she said anything or not— her lips stopped moving—yes, I think she stopped breath-

116

ing! [*He gently removes her craving hands from his face.*]
No? [*He shakes his head in dumb suffering.*] Then the answer is "no"!

JOHN [*forcing himself to speak*]:
I have a respect for the truth, and I have a respect for you—
so I'd better speak honestly if you want me to speak. [*Alma
nods slightly.*] You've won the argument that we had between us.

ALMA:
What—argument?

JOHN:
The one about the chart.

ALMA:
Oh—the chart!

[*She turns from him and wanders across to the chart.
She gazes up at it with closed eyes, and her hands clasped
in front of her.*]

JOHN:
It shows that we're not a package of rose leaves, that every
interior inch of us is taken up with something ugly and
functional and no room seems to be left for anything else
in there.

ALMA:
No . . .

JOHN:
But I've come around to your way of thinking, that something else is in there, an immaterial something—as thin as
smoke—which all of those ugly machines combine to pro-
duce and that's their whole reason for being. It can't be seen
so it can't be shown on the chart. But it's there, just the
same, and knowing it's there—why, then the whole thing—
this—this unfathomable experience of ours—takes on a new
value, like some—some wildly romantic work in a labora-
tory! Don't you see?

[*The wind comes up very loud, almost like a choir of
voices. Both of them turn slightly, Alma raising a hand
to her plumed head as if she were outdoors.*]

ALMA:

Yes, I see! Now that you no longer want it to be otherwise you're willing to believe that a spiritual bond can exist between us two!

JOHN:

Can't you believe that I am sincere about it?

ALMA:

Maybe you are. But I don't want to be talked to like some incurably sick patient you have to comfort. [*A harsh and strong note comes into her voice.*] Oh, I suppose I am sick, one of those weak and divided people who slip like shadows among you solid strong ones. But sometimes, out of necessity, we shadowy people take on a strength of our own. I have that now. You needn't try to deceive me.

JOHN:

I wasn't.

ALMA:

You needn't try to comfort me. I haven't come here on any but equal terms. You said, let's talk truthfully. Well, let's do! Unsparingly, truthfully, even shamelessly, then! It's no longer a secret that I love you. It never was. I loved you as long ago as the time I asked you to read the stone angel's name with your fingers. Yes, I remember the long afternoons of our childhood, when I had to stay indoors to practice my music—and heard your playmates calling you, "Johnny, Johnny!" How it went through me, just to hear your name called! And how I—rushed to the window to watch you jump the porch railing! I stood at a distance, halfway down the block, only to keep in sight of your torn red sweater, racing about the vacant lot you played in. Yes, it had begun that early, this affliction of love, and has never let go of me since, but kept on growing. I've lived next door to you all the days of my life, a weak and divided person who stood in adoring awe of your singleness, of your strength. And that is my story! Now I wish *you* would tell *me*—why didn't it happen between us? Why did I fail? Why did you come almost close enough—and no closer?

JOHN:

Whenever we've gotten together, the three or four times that we have . . .

ALMA:

As few as that?

118

JOHN:
It's only been three or four times that we've—come face to face. And each of those times—we seemed to be trying to find something in each other without knowing what it was that we wanted to find. It wasn't a body hunger although— I acted as if I thought it might be the night I wasn't a gentleman—at the Casino—it wasn't the physical you that I really wanted!

ALMA:
I know, you've already . . .

JOHN:
You didn't have that to give me.

ALMA:
Not at that time.

JOHN:
You had something else to give.

ALMA:
What did I have?

[*John strikes a match. Unconsciously he holds his curved palm over the flame of the match to warm it. It is a long kitchen match and it makes a good flame. They both stare at it with a sorrowful understanding that is still perplexed. It is about to burn his fingers. She leans forward and blows it out, then she puts on her gloves.*]

JOHN:
You couldn't name it and I couldn't recognize it. I thought it was just a Puritanical ice that glittered like flame. But now I believe it *was* flame, mistaken for ice. I still don't understand it, but I know it was there, just as I know that your eyes and your voice are the two most beautiful things I've ever known—and also the warmest, although they don't seem to be set in your body at all. . . .

ALMA:
You talk as if my body had ceased to exist for you, John, in spite of the fact that you've just counted my pulse. Yes, that's it! You tried to avoid it, but you've told me plainly. The tables have turned, yes, the tables have turned with a vengeance! You've come around to my old way of thinking and I to yours like two people exchanging a call on each

other at the same time, and each one finding the other one gone out, the door locked against him and no one to answer the bell! [*She laughs.*] I came here to tell you that being a gentleman, doesn't seem so important to me any more, but you're telling me I've got to remain a lady. [*She laughs rather violently.*] The tables have turned with a vengeance! —The air in here smells of ether—It's making me dizzy . . .

JOHN:
I'll open a window.

ALMA:
Please.

JOHN:
There now.

ALMA:
Thank you, that's better. Do you remember those little white tablets you gave me? I've used them all up and I'd like to have some more.

JOHN:
I'll write the prescription for you. [*He bends to write.*]

[*Nellie is in the waiting room. They hear her voice.*]

ALMA:
Someone is waiting in the waiting room, John. One of my vocal pupils. The youngest and prettiest one with the least gift for music. The one that you helped wrap up this handkerchief for me. [*She takes it out and touches her eyes with it.*]

[*The door opens, first a crack. Nellie peers in and giggles. Then she throws the door wide open with a peal of merry laughter. She has holly pinned on her jacket. She rushes up to John and hugs him with childish squeals.*]

NELLIE:
I've been all over town just shouting, shouting!

JOHN:
Shouting what?

NELLIE:
Glad tidings!

[John looks at Alma over Nellie's shoulder.]

JOHN:
I thought we weren't going to tell anyone for a while.

NELLIE:
I couldn't stop myself. *[She wheels about.]* Oh, Alma, has he told *you?*

ALMA *[quietly]*:
He didn't need to, Nellie. I guessed . . . from the Christmas card with your two names written on it!

[Nellie rushes over to Alma and hugs her. Over Nellie's shoulder Alma looks at John. He makes a thwarted gesture as if he wanted to speak. She smiles desperately and shakes her head. She closes her eyes and bites her lips for a moment. Then she releases Nellie with a laugh of exaggerated gaiety.]

NELLIE:
So Alma you were really the first to know!

ALMA:
I'm proud of that, Nellie.

NELLIE:
See on my finger! This was the present I couldn't tell you about!

ALMA:
Oh, what a lovely, lovely solitaire! But solitaire is such a wrong name for it. Solitaire means single and this means *two!* It's blinding, Nellie! Why it . . . hurts my eyes!

[John catches Nellie's arm and pulls her to him. Almost violently Alma lifts her face; it is bathed in tears. She nods gratefully to John for releasing her from Nellie's attention. She picks up her gloves and purse.]

JOHN:
Excuse her, Miss Alma. Nellie's still such a child.

ALMA *[with a breathless laugh]*:
I've got to run along now.

JOHN:
Don't leave your prescription.

ALMA:
Oh, yes, where's my prescription?

JOHN:
On the table.

ALMA:
I'll take it to the drug store right away!

[*Nellie struggles to free herself from John's embrace which keeps her from turning to Alma.*]

NELLIE:
Alma, don't go! Johnny, let go of me, Johnny! You're hugging me so tight I can't breathe!

ALMA:
Goodbye.

NELLIE:
Alma! Alma, you know you're going to sing at the wedding! The very first Sunday in Spring!—which will be Palm Sunday! "The Voice that Breathed o'er Eden."

[*Alma has closed the door. John shuts his eyes tight with a look of torment. He rains kisses on Nellie's forehead and throat and lips. The scene dims out with music.*]

scene twelve

In the park near the angel of the fountain. About dusk.

Alma enters the lighted area and goes glowly up to the fountain and bends to drink. Then she removes a small white package from her pocketbook and starts to unwrap it. While she is doing this, a Young Man comes along. He is dressed in a checked suit and a derby. He pauses by the bench. They glance at each other.

A train whistles in the distance. The Young Man clears his throat. The train whistle is repeated. The Young Man crosses toward the fountain, his eyes on Alma. She hesitates, with the unwrapped package in her hand. Then she crosses toward the bench and stands hesitantly in front of it. He stuffs his hands in his pockets and whistles. He glances with an effect of unconcern back over his shoulder.

Alma pushes her veil back with an uncertain gesture. His whistle dies out. He sways back and forth on his heels as the train whistles again. He suddenly turns to the fountain and bends to drink. Alma slips the package back into her purse. As the young man straightens up, she speaks in a barely audible voice.

ALMA:
The water—is—cool.

THE YOUNG MAN [*eagerly*]:
Did you say something?

ALMA:
I said, the water is cool.

THE YOUNG MAN:
Yes, it sure is, it's nice and cool!

ALMA:
It's always cool.

THE YOUNG MAN:
Is it?

ALMA:
Yes. Yes, even in summer. It comes from deep underground.

THE YOUNG MAN:
That's what keeps it cool.

ALMA:
Glorious Hill is famous for its artesian springs.

THE YOUNG MAN:
I didn't know that.

[*The Young Man jerkily removes his hands from his pockets. She gathers confidence before the awkwardness of his youth.*]

ALMA:
Are you a stranger in town?

THE YOUNG MAN:
I'm a traveling salesman.

ALMA:
Ah, you're a salesman who travels! [*She laughs gently.*]
But you're younger than most of them are, and not so fat!

THE YOUNG MAN:
I'm just starting out. I travel for Red Goose shoes.

ALMA:
Ah! The Delt's your territory?

THE YOUNG MAN:
From the Peabody Lobby to Cat-Fish Row in Vicksburg.

[*Alma leans back and looks at him under half-closed lids,
perhaps a little suggestively.*]

ALMA:
The life of a traveling salesman is interesting . . . but lonely.

THE YOUNG MAN:
You're right about that. Hotel bedrooms are lonely.

[*There is a pause. Far away the train whistles again.*]

ALMA:
All rooms are lonely where there is only one person. [*Her
eyes fall shut.*]

THE YOUNG MAN [*gently*]:
You're tired, aren't you?

ALMA:
I? Tired? [*She starts to deny it; then laughs faintly and
confesses the truth.*] Yes . . . a little . . . But I shall rest
now. I've just now taken one of my sleeping tablets.

THE YOUNG MAN:
So early?

ALMA:
Oh, it won't put me to sleep. It will just quiet my nerves.

THE YOUNG MAN:
What are you nervous about?

ALMA:
I won an argument this afternoon.

THE YOUNG MAN:
That's nothing to be nervous over. You ought to be nervous if you *lost* one.

ALMA:
It wasn't the argument that I wanted to win. . . .

THE YOUNG MAN:
Well, I'm nervous too.

ALMA:
What over?

THE YOUNG MAN:
It's my first job and I'm scared of not making good.

[*That mysteriously sudden intimacy that sometimes occurs between strangers more completely than old friends or lovers moves them both. Alma hands the package of tablets to him.*]

ALMA:
Then you must take one of my tablets.

THE YOUNG MAN:
Shall I?

ALMA:
Please take one!

THE YOUNG MAN:
Yes, I shall.

ALMA:
You'll be surprised how infinitely merciful they are. The prescription number is 96814. I think of it as the telephone number of God! [*They both laugh. He places one of the tablets on his tongue and crosses to the fountain to wash it down.*]

THE YOUNG MAN [*to the stone figure*]:
Thanks, angel. [*He gives her a little salute, and crosses back to Alma.*]

ALMA:

Life is full of little mercies like that, not *big* mercies but comfortable *little* mercies. And so we are able to keep on going. . . . [*She has leaned back with half-closed eyes.*]

THE YOUNG MAN [*returning*]:
You're falling asleep.

ALMA:

Oh no, I'm not. I'm just closing my eyes. You know what I feel like now? I feel like a water-lily.

THE YOUNG MAN:
A water-lily?

ALMA:

Yes, I feel like a water-lily on a Chinese lagoon. Won't you sit down? [*The Young Man does.*] My name is Alma. Spanish for soul! What's yours?

THE YOUNG MAN:
Ha-ha! Mine's Archie Kramer. Mucho gusto, as they say in Spain.

ALMA:
Usted habla Espanol, senor?

THE YOUNG MAN:
Un poquito! Usted habla Espanol, senorita?

ALMA:
Me tambien. Un poquito!

THE YOUNG MAN [*delightedly*]:
Ha . . . ha . . . ha! Sometimes un poquito is plenty! [*Alma laughs . . . in a different way than she has ever laughed before, a little wearily, but quite naturally. The Young Man leans toward her confidentially.*] What's there to do in this town after dark?

ALMA:

There's not much to do in this town after dark, but there are resorts on the lake that offer all kinds of after-dark entertainment. There's one called Moon Lake Casino. It's under new management, now, but I don't suppose its character has changed.

THE YOUNG MAN:
What was its character?
126

ALMA:
Gay, very gay, Mr. Kramer. . . .

THE YOUNG MAN:
Then what in hell are we sitting here for? Vamonos!

ALMA:
Como no, senor!

THE YOUNG MAN:
Ha-ha-ha! [*He jumps up.*] I'll call a taxi. [*He goes off shouting "Taxi."*]

[*Alma rises from the bench. As she crosses to the fountain the grave mood of the play is reinstated with a phrase of music. She faces the stone angel and raises her gloved hand in a sort of valedictory salute. Then she turns slowly about toward the audience with her hand still raised in a gesture of wonder and finality as . . . the curtain falls.*]

ORPHEUS DESCENDING

For Marion Black Vaccaro

THE PAST, THE PRESENT
AND THE PERHAPS

One icy bright winter morning in the last week of 1940, my brave representative, Audrey Wood, and I were crossing the Common in Boston, from an undistinguished hotel on one side to the grandeur of the Ritz-Carlton on the other. We had just read the morning notices of *Battle of Angels,** which had opened at the Wilbur the evening before. As we crossed the Common there was a series of loud reports like gunfire from the street that we were approaching, and one of us said, "My God. they're shooting at us!"

We were still laughing, a bit hysterically, as we entered the Ritz-Carlton suite in which the big brass of the Theatre Guild and director Margaret Webster were waiting for us with that special air of gentle gravity that hangs over the demise of a play so much like the atmosphere that hangs over a home from which a living soul has been snatched by the Reaper.

Not present was little Miriam Hopkins, who was understandably shattered and cloistered after the events of the evening before, in which a simulated on-stage fire had erupted clouds of smoke so realistically over both stage and auditorium that a lot of Theatre Guild first-nighters had fled choking from the Wilbur before the choking star took her bows, which were about the quickest and most distracted that I have seen in a theatre.

It was not that morning that I was informed that the show must close. That morning I was only told that the play must be cut to the bone. I came with a rewrite of the final scene and I remember saying, heroically, "I will crawl on my belly through brimstone if you will substitute this!" The response was gently evasive. It was a few mornings later that I received the *coup de grace,* the announcement that the play would close at the completion of its run in Boston. On that occasion I made an equally dramatic statement, on a note of anguish. "You don't seem to see that I put my heart into this play!"

It was Miss Webster who answered with a remark I

*Originally published by New Directions in 1940, and republished by New Directions, with *Orpheus Descending,* in 1958.

have never forgotten and yet never heeded. She said, "You must not wear your heart on your sleeve for daws to peck at!" Someone else said, "At least you are not out of pocket." I don't think I had any answer for that one, any more than I had anything in my pocket to be out of.

Well, in the end, when the Boston run was finished, I was given a check for $200 and told to get off somewhere and rewrite the play. I squandered half of this subsidy on the first of four operations performed on a cataracted left eye, and the other half took me to Key West for the rewrite. It was a long rewrite. In fact, it is still going on, though the two hundred bucks are long gone.

Why have I stuck so stubbornly to this play? For seventeen years, in fact? Well, nothing is more precious to anybody than the emotional record of his youth, and you will find the trail of my sleeve-worn heart in this completed play that I now call Orpheus Descending. On its surface it was and still is the tale of a wild-spirited boy who wanders into a conventional community of the South and creates the commotion of a fox in a chicken coop.

But beneath that now familiar surface it is a play about unanswered questions that haunt the hearts of people and the difference between continuing to ask them, a difference represented by the four major protagonists of the play, and the acceptance of prescribed answers that are not answers at all, but expedient adaptations or surrender to a state of quandary.

Battle was actually my fifth long play, but the first to be given a professional production. Two of the others, *Candles to the Sun* and *Fugitive Kind*,* were produced by a brilliant, but semiprofessional group called The Mummers of St. Louis. A third one, called *Spring Storm,* was written for the late Prof. E. C. Mabie's seminar in playwriting at the University of Iowa, and I read it aloud, appropriately in the spring.

When I had finished reading, the good professor's eyes had a glassy look as though he had drifted into a state of trance. There was a long and all but unendurable silence. Everyone seemed more or less embarrassed. At last the professor pushed back his chair, thus dismissing the seminar, and remarked casually and kindly, "Well, we all

*This early play is not to be confused with the previous Signet edition nor the movie, *The Fugitive Kind.*

have to paint our nudes!" And this is the only reference that I can remember anyone making to the play. That is, in the playwriting class, but I do remember that the late Lemuel Ayers, who was a graduate student at Iowa that year, read it and gave me sufficient praise for its dialogue and atmosphere to reverse my decision to give up the theatre in favor of my other occupation of waiting on tables, or more precisely, handing out trays in the cafeteria of the State Hospital.

Then there was Chicago for a while and a desperate effort to get on the W. P. A. Writers' Project, which didn't succeed, for my work lacked "social content" or "protest" and I couldn't prove that my family was destitute and I still had, in those days, a touch of refinement in my social behavior which made me seem frivolous and decadent to the conscientiously rough-hewn pillars of the Chicago Project.

And so I drifted back to St. Louis, again, and wrote my fourth long play which was the best of the lot. It was called *Not About Nightingales* and it concerned prison life, and I have never written anything since then that could compete with it in violence and horror, for it was based on something that actually occurred along about that time, the literal roasting-alive of a group of intransigent convicts sent for correction to a hot room called "The Klondike."

I submitted it to The Mummers of St. Louis and they were eager to perform it but they had come to the end of their economic tether and had to disband at this point.

Then there was New Orleans and another effort, while waiting on tables in a restaurant where meals cost only two-bits, to get on a Writers' Project or the Theatre Project, again unsuccessful.

And then there was a wild and wonderful trip to California with a young clarinet player. We ran out of gas in El Paso, also out of cash, and it seemed for days that we would never go farther, but my grandmother was an "easy touch" and I got a letter with a $10 bill stitched neatly to one of the pages, and we continued westward.

In the Los Angeles area, in the summer of 1939, I worked for a while at Clark's Bootery in Culver City, within sight of the M-G-M studio and I lived on a pigeon ranch, and I rode between the two, a distance of ten miles, on a secondhand bicycle that I bought for $5.

Then a most wonderful thing happened. While in New Orleans I had heard about a play contest being conducted by the Group Theatre of New York. I submitted all four of the long plays I have mentioned that preceded *Battle of Angels,* plus a group of one-acts called *American Blues.* One fine day I received, when I returned to the ranch on my bike, a telegram saying that I had won a special award of $100 for the one-acts, and it was signed by Harold Clurman, Molly Day Thacher, who is the present Mrs. Elia Kazan, and that fine writer, Irwin Shaw, the judges of the contest.

I retired from Clark's Bootery and from picking squabs at the pigeon ranch. And the clarinet player and I hopped on our bicycles and rode all the way down to Tiajuana and back as far as Laguna Beach, where we obtained, rent free, a small cabin on a small ranch in return for taking care of the poultry.

We lived all that summer on the $100 from the Group Theatre and I think it was the happiest summer of my life. All the days were pure gold, the nights were starry, and I looked so young, or carefree, that they would sometimes refuse to sell me a drink because I did not appear to have reached 21. But toward the end of the summer, maybe only because it was the end of the summer as well as the end of the $100, the clarinet player became very moody and disappeared without warning into the San Bernardino Mountains to commune with his soul in solitude, and there was nothing left in the cabin in the canyon but a bag of dried peas.

I lived on stolen eggs and avocados and dried peas for a week, and also on a faint hope stirred by a letter from a lady in New York whose name was Audrey Wood, who had taken hold of all those plays that I had submitted to the Group Theatre contest, and told me that it might be possible to get me one of the Rockefeller Fellowships, or grants, of $1,000 which were being passed out to gifted young writers at that time. And I began to write *Battle of Angels,* a lyrical play about memories and the loneliness of them. Although my beloved grandmother was living on the pension of a retired minister (I believe it was only $85 a month in those days), and her meager earnings as a piano instructor, she once again stitched some bills to a page of a letter, and I took a bus to St. Louis.

Battle of Angels was finished late that fall and sent to Miss Wood.

One day the phone rang and, in a terrified tone, my mother told me that it was long distance, for me. The voice was Audrey Wood's. Mother waited, shakily, in the doorway. When I hung up I said, quietly, "Rockefeller has given me a $1,000 grant and they want me to come to New York." For the first time since I had known her, my mother burst into tears. "I am so happy," she said. It was all she could say.

And so you see it is a very old play that *Orpheus Descending* has come out of, but a play is never an old one until you quit working on it and I have never quit working on this one, not even now. It never went into the trunk, it always stayed on the work bench, and I am not presenting it now because I have run out of ideas or material for completely new work. I am offering it this season because I honestly believe that it is finally finished. About 75 per cent of it is new writing, but what is much more important, I believe that I have now finally managed to say in it what I wanted to say, and I feel that it now has in it a sort of emotional bridge between those early years described in this article and my present state of existence as a playwright.

So much for the past and present. The future is called "perhaps," which is the only possible thing to call the future. And the important thing is not to allow that to scare you.

Tennessee Williams

1957

Orpheus Descending was presented at the Martin Beck Theatre in New York on March 21, 1957, by the Producers Theatre. It was directed by Harold Clurman; the stage set was designed by Boris Aronson, the costumes by Lucinda Ballard, and the lighting by Feder. The cast was as follows:

DOLLY HAMMA	ELIZABETH EUSTIS
BEULAH BINNINGS	JANE ROSE
PEE WEE BINNINGS	WARREN KEMMERLING
DOG HAMMA	DAVID CLARKE
CAROL CUTRERE	LOIS SMITH
EVA TEMPLE	NELL HARRISON
SISTER TEMPLE	MARY FARRELL
UNCLE PLEASANT	JOHN MARRIOTT
VAL XAVIER	CLIFF ROBERTSON
VEE TALBOTT	JOANNA ROOS
LADY TORRANCE	MAUREEN STAPLETON
JABE TORRANCE	CRAHAN DENTON
SHERIFF TALBOTT	R. G. ARMSTRONG
MR. DUBINSKY	BEAU TILDEN
WOMAN	JANICE MARS
DAVID CUTRERE	ROBERT WEBBER
NURSE PORTER	VIRGILIA CHEW
FIRST MAN	ALBERT HENDERSON
SECOND MAN	CHARLES TYNER

SCENE: *The set represents in nonrealistic fashion a general drygoods store and part of a connecting "confectionery" in a small Southern town. The ceiling is high and the upper walls are dark, as if streaked with moisture and cobwebbed. A great dusty window upstage offers a view of disturbing emptiness that fades into late dusk. The action of the play occurs during a rainy season, late winter and early spring, and sometimes the window turns opaque but glistening silver with sheets of rain. "TORRANCE MERCANTILE STORE" is lettered on the window in gilt of old-fashioned design.*

Merchandise is represented very sparsely and it is not realistic. Bolts of pepperel and percale stand upright on large spools, the black skeleton of a dressmaker's dummy stands meaninglessly against a thin white column, and there is a motionless ceiling fan with strips of flypaper hanging from it.

There are stairs that lead to a landing and disappear above it, and on the landing there is a sinister-looking artificial palm tree in a greenish-brown jardiniere.

But the confectionery, which is seen partly through a wide arched door, is shadowy and poetic as some inner dimension of the play.

Another, much smaller, playing area is a tiny bedroom alcove which is usually masked by an Oriental drapery which is worn dim but bears the formal design of a gold tree with scarlet fruit and fantastic birds.

At the rise of the curtain two youngish middle-aged women, DOLLY *and* BEULAH, *are laying out a buffet supper on a pair of pink-and-gray-veined marble-topped tables with gracefully curved black-iron legs, brought into the main area from the confectionery. They are wives of small planters and tastelessly overdressed in a somewhat bizarre fashion.*

A train whistles in the distance and dogs bark in response from various points and distances. The women

11

*pause in their occupations at the tables and rush to the
archway, crying out harshly.*

DOLLY:
Pee Wee!

BEULAH:
Dawg!

DOLLY:
Cannonball is comin' into th' depot!

BEULAH:
You all git down to th' depot an' meet that train!
  [*Their husbands slouch through, heavy, red-faced
  men in clothes that are too tight for them or too
  loose, and mud-stained boots.*]

PEE WEE:
I fed that one-armed bandit a hunnerd nickles an' it
coughed up five.

DOG:
Must have hed indigestion.

PEE WEE:
I'm gonna speak to Jabe about them slots.
  [*They go out and a motor starts and pauses.*]

DOLLY:
I guess Jabe Torrance has got more to worry about than
the slot machines and pinball games in that confectionery.

BEULAH:
You're not tellin' a lie. I wint to see Dr. Johnny about
Dawg's condition. Dawg's got sugar in his urine again, an'
as I was leavin' I ast him what was the facks about Jabe
Torrance's operation in Mimphis. Well —

DOLLY:
What'd he tell you, Beulah?

BEULAH:
He said the worse thing a doctor ever can say.

DOLLY:
What's that, Beulah?

BEULAH:
Nothin' a-tall, not a spoken word did he utter! He just looked at me with those big dark eyes of his and shook his haid like this!

DOLLY [*with doleful satisfaction*]:
I guess he signed Jabe Torrance's death warrant with just that single silent motion of his haid.

BEULAH:
That's exactly what passed through my mind. I understand that they cut him open—
[*Pauses to taste something on the table.*]

DOLLY:
—An' sewed him right back up!—that's what I heard . . .

BEULAH:
I didn't know these olives had seeds in them!

DOLLY:
You thought they was stuffed?

BEULAH:
Uh-huh. Where's the Temple sisters?

DOLLY:
Where d'you think?

BEULAH:
Snoopin' aroun' upstairs. If Lady catches 'em at it she'll give those two old maids a touch of her tongue! She's not a Dago for nothin'!

DOLLY:
Ha, ha, no! You spoke a true word, honey . . .
[*Looks out door as car passes.*]
Well, I was surprised when I wint up myself!

BEULAH:
You wint up you'self?

13

DOLLY:
I did and so did you because I seen you, Beulah.

BEULAH:
I never said that I didn't. Curiosity is a human instinct.

DOLLY:
They got two separate bedrooms which are not even connectin'. At opposite ends of the hall, and everything is so dingy an' dark up there. Y'know what it seemed like to me? A county jail! I swear to goodness it didn't seem to me like a place for white people to live in!—that's the truth . . .

BEULAH [*darkly*]:
Well, I wasn't surprised. Jabe Torrance bought that woman.

DOLLY:
Bought her?

BEULAH:
Yais, he bought her, when she was a girl of eighteen! He bought her and bought her cheap because she'd been thrown over and her heart was broken by that—
        [*Jerks head toward a passing car, then continues:*]
—that Cutrere boy. . . . *Oh*, what a—*Mmmm*, what a—*beautiful* thing he was. . . . And those two met like you struck two stones together and made a fire!—yes—fire . . .

DOLLY:
What?

BEULAH:
Fire!—Ha . . .
        [*Strikes another match and lights one of the candelabra. Mandolin begins to fade in. The following monologue should be treated frankly as exposition, spoken to audience, almost directly, with a force that commands attention. DOLLY does not remain in the playing area, and after the first few sentences, there is no longer any pretense of a duologue.*]
—Well, that was a long time ago, before you and Dog moved into Two River County. Although you must have

14

heard of it. Lady's father was a Wop from the old country and when he first come here with a mandolin and a monkey that wore a little green velvet suit, ha ha.
—He picked up dimes and quarters in the saloons—this was before Prohibition. . . .
—People just called him The Wop, nobody knew his name, just called him 'The Wop,' ha ha ha. . . .

DOLLY [*Off, vaguely*]:
Anh-hannnh. . . .

> [BEULAH *switches in the chair and fixes the audience with her eyes, leaning slightly forward to compel their attention. Her voice is rich with nostalgia, and at a sign of restlessness, she rises and comes straight out to the proscenium, like a pitchman. This monologue should set the nonrealistic key for the whole production.*]

BEULAH:
Oh, my law, well, that was Lady's daddy! Then come Prohibition an' first thing ennyone knew, The Wop had took to bootleggin' like a duck to water! He picked up a piece of land cheap, it was on the no'th shore of Moon Lake which used to be the old channel of the river and people thought some day the river might swing back that way, and so he got it cheap. . . .
> [*Moves her chair up closer to proscenium.*]
He planted an orchard on it; he covered the whole no'th shore of the lake with grapevines and fruit trees, and then he built little arbors, little white wooden arbors with tables and benches to drink in and carry on in, ha ha! And in the spring and the summer, young couples would come out there, like me and Pee Wee, we used to go out there, an' court up a storm, ha ha, just court up a—storm! Ha ha!—The county was dry in those days, I don't mean dry like now, why, now you just walk a couple of feet off the highway and whistle three times like a jaybird and a nigger pops out of a bush with a bottle of corn!

DOLLY:
Ain't that the truth? Ha ha.

BEULAH:
But in those days the county was dry for true, I mean

bone dry except for The Wop's wine garden. So we'd go
out to The Wop's an' drink that Dago red wine an' cut up
an' carry on an' raise such cane in those arbors! Why, I
remember one Sunday old Doctor Tooker, Methodist minister then, he bust a blood vessel denouncing The Wop in
the pulpit!

DOLLY:
Lawd have mercy!

BEULAH:
Yes, ma'am!—Each of those white wooden arbors had a
lamp in it, and one by one, here and there, the lamps
would go out as the couples begun to make love . . .

DOLLY:
Oh—oh . . .

BEULAH:
What strange noises you could hear if you listened, calls,
cries, whispers, moans—giggles. . . .
        [*Her voice is soft with recollection.*]
—And then, one by one, the lamps would be lighted
again, and The Wop and his daughter would sing and
play Dago songs. . . .
        [*Bring up mandolin: voice under* 'Dicitencello Vuoi.']
But sometimes The Wop would look around for his
daughter, and all of a sudden Lady wouldn't be there!

DOLLY:
Where would she be?

BEULAH:
She'd be with David Cutrere.

DOLLY:
Awwwwww—ha ha . . .

BEULAH:
—Carol Cutrere's big brother, Lady and him would disappear in the orchard and old Papa Romano, The Wop,
would holler, "Lady, Lady!"—no answer whatsoever, no

matter how long he called and no matter how loud. . . .

DOLLY:
Well, I guess it's hard to shout back, "Here I am, Papa,"
when where you are is in the arms of your lover!

BEULAH:
Well, that spring, no, it was late that summer . . .
    [DOLLY *retires again from the playing area.*]
—Papa Romano made a bad mistake. He sold liquor to
niggers. The Mystic Crew took action.—They rode out
there, one night, with gallons of coal oil—it was a real dry
summer—and set that place on fire!—They burned the
whole thing up, vines, arbors, fruit trees.—Pee Wee and
me, we stood on the dance pavilion across the lake and
watched that fire spring up. Inside of tin minutes the
whole no'th shore of the lake was a mass of flames, a
regular sea of flames, and all the way over the lake we
could hear Lady's papa shouting, "Fire, fire, fire!"—as if
it was necessary to let people know, and the whole sky lit
up with it, as red as Guinea red wine!—Ha ha ha ha. . . .
Not a fire engine, not a single engine pulled out of a
station that night in Two River County!—The poor old
fellow, The Wop, he took a blanket and run up into the
orchard to fight the fire singlehanded—*and* burned *alive*.
. . . Uh-huh! *burned alive*. . . .
    [*Mandolin stops short.* DOLLY *has returned to the
    table to have her coffee.*]
You know what I sometimes wonder?

DOLLY:
No. What do you wonder?

BEULAH:
I wonder sometimes if Lady has any suspicion that her
husband, Jabe Torrance was the leader of the Mystic
Crew the night they burned up her father in his wine
garden on Moon Lake?

DOLLY:
Beulah Binnings, you make my blood run cold with such
a thought! How could she live in marriage twenty years

17

with a man if she knew he'd burned her father up in his wine garden?

[*Dog bays in distance.*]

BEULAH:
She could live with him in hate. People can live together in hate for a long time, Dolly. Notice their passion for money. I've always noticed when couples don't love each other they develop a passion for money. Haven't you seen that happen? Of course you have. Now there's not many couples that stay devoted forever. Why, some git so they just barely tolerate each other's existence. Isn't that true?

DOLLY:
You couldn't of spoken a truer word if you read it out loud from the Bible!

BEULAH:
Barely tolerate each other's existence, and some don't even do that. You know, Dolly Hamma, I don't think half as many married min have committed suicide in this county as the Coroner says has done so!

DOLLY [*with voluptuous appreciation of* BEULAH's *wit*]:
You think it's their wives that give them the deep six, honey?

BEULAH:
I don't think so, I know so. Why there's couples that loathe and despise the sight, smell and sound of each other before that round-trip honeymoon ticket is punched at both ends, Dolly.

DOLLY:
I hate to admit it but I can't deny it.

BEULAH:
But they hang on together.

DOLLY:
Yes, they hang on together.

BEULAH:
Year after year after year, accumulating property and

money, building up wealth and respect and position in the towns they live in and the counties and cities and the churches they go to, belonging to the clubs and so on and so forth and not a soul but them knowin' they have to go wash their hands after touching something the other one just put down! ha ha ha ha ha!—

DOLLY:
Beulah, that's an evil laugh of yours, that laugh of yours is evil!

BEULAH [*louder*]:
Ha ha ha ha ha!—But you know it's the truth.

DOLLY:
Yes, she's tellin' the truth!
    [*Nods to audience.*]

BEULAH:
Then one of them—gits—*cincer* or has a—*stroke* or somethin'?—The other one—

DOLLY:
—Hauls in the loot?

BEULAH:
That's right, hauls in the loot! Oh, my, then you should see how him or her blossoms out. New house, new car, new clothes. Some of 'em even change to a different church!—If it's a widow, she goes with a younger man, and if it's a widower, he starts courtin' some chick, ha ha ha ha ha!
And so I said, I said to Lady this morning before she left for Mamphis to bring Jabe home, I said, "Lady, I don't suppose you're going to reopen the confectionery till Jabe is completely recovered from his operation." She said, "It can't wait for anything that might take that much time." Those are her exact words. "It can't wait for anything that might take that much time. Too much is invested in it. It's going to be done over, redecorated, and opened on schedule, the Saturday before Easter this spring"—Why?—Because—she knows Jabe is dying and she wants to clean up quick!

19

DOLLY:
An awful thought. But a true one. Most awful thoughts are.

[*They are startled by sudden light laughter from the dim upstage area. The light changes on the stage to mark a division.*]

The women turn to see CAROL CUTRERE *in the archway between the store and the confectionery. She is past thirty and, lacking prettiness, she has an odd, fugitive beauty which is stressed, almost to the point of fantasy, by a style of makeup with which a dancer named Valli has lately made such an impression in the bohemian centers of France and Italy, the face and lips powdered white and the eyes outlined and exaggerated with black pencil and the lids tinted blue. Her family name is the oldest and most distinguished in the county.*

BEULAH:
Somebody don't seem to know that the store is closed.

DOLLY:
Beulah?

BEULAH:
What?

DOLLY:
Can you understand how anybody would deliberately make themselves look fantastic as that?

BEULAH:
Some people have to show off, it's a passion with them, anything on earth to get attention.

DOLLY:
I sure wouldn't care for that kind of attention. Not me. I wouldn't desire it. . . .
[*During these lines, just loud enough for her to hear them,* CAROL *has crossed to the pay-phone and deposited a coin.*]

CAROL:
I want Tulane 0370 in New Orleans. What? Oh. Hold on a minute.
[EVA TEMPLE *is descending the stairs, slowly, as if awed by* CAROL'S *appearance.* CAROL *rings open the*

21

cashbox and removes some coins; returns to deposit coins in phone.]

BEULAH:
She helped herself to money out of the cashbox.
[EVA *passes* CAROL *like a timid child skirting a lion cage.*]

CAROL:
Hello, Sister.

EVA:
I'm Eva.

CAROL:
Hello, Eva.

EVA:
Hello . . .
[*Then in a loud whisper to* BEULAH *and* DOLLY:]
She took money out of the cashbox.

DOLLY:
Oh, she can do as she pleases, she's a Cutrere!

BEULAH:
Shoot . . .

EVA:
What is she doin' barefooted?

BEULAH:
The last time she was arrested on the highway, they say that she was naked under her coat.

CAROL [*to operator*]:
I'm waiting.
[*Then to women:*]
—I caught the heel of my slipper in that rotten boardwalk out there and it broke right off.
[*Raises slippers in hand.*]
They say if you break the heel of your slipper in the morning it means you'll meet the love of your life before dark. But it was already dark when I broke the heel of

my slipper. Maybe that means I'll meet the love of my life before daybreak.

[*The quality of her voice is curiously clear and childlike.* SISTER TEMPLE *appears on stair landing bearing an old waffle iron.*]

SISTER:
Wasn't that them?

EVA:
No, it was Carol Cutrere!

CAROL [*at phone*]:
Just keep on ringing, please, he's probably drunk.

[SISTER *crosses by her as* EVA *did.*]

Sometimes it takes quite a while to get through the living-room furniture. . . .

SISTER:
—She a *sight?*

EVA:
Uh-huh!

CAROL:
Bertie?—Carol!—Hi, doll! Did you trip over something? I heard a crash. Well, I'm leaving right now, I'm already on the highway and everything's fixed, I've got my allowance back on condition that I remain forever away from Two River County! I had to blackmail them a little. I came to dinner with my eyes made up and my little black sequin jacket and Betsy Boo, my brother's wife, said, "Carol, you going out to a fancy dress ball?" I said, "Oh, no, I'm just going jooking tonight up and down the Dixie Highway between here and Memphis like I used to when I lived here." Why, honey, she flew so fast you couldn't see her passing and came back in with the ink still wet on the check! And this will be done once a month as long as I stay away from Two River County. . . .

[*Laughs gaily.*]

—How's Jackie? Bless his heart, give him a sweet kiss for me! Oh, honey, I'm driving straight through, not even stopping for pickups unless you need one! I'll meet you in the Starlite Lounge before it closes, or if I'm irresistibly

23

delayed, I'll certainly join you for coffee at the Morning
Call before the all-night places have closed for the day . . .
—I—Bertie? Bertie?

>[*Laughs uncertainly and hangs up.*]

—let's see, now. . . .

>[*Removes a revolver from her trench-coat pocket
and crosses to fill it with cartridges back of counter.*]

EVA:
What she looking for?

SISTER:
Ask her.

EVA [*advancing*]:
What're you looking for, Carol?

CAROL:
Cartridges for my revolver.

DOLLY:
She don't have a license to carry a pistol.

BEULAH:
She don't have a license to drive a car.

CAROL:
When I stop for someone I want to be sure it's someone
I want to stop for.

DOLLY:
Sheriff Talbott ought to know about this when he gits back
from the depot.

CAROL:
Tell him, ladies. I've already given him notice that if he
ever attempts to stop me again on the highway, I'll shoot
it out with him. . . .

BEULAH:
When anybody has trouble with the law—

>[*Her sentence is interrupted by a panicky scream
from* EVA, *immediately repeated by* SISTER. *The*
TEMPLE SISTERS *scramble upstairs to the landing.*

24

DOLLY *also cries out and turns, covering her face. A Negro* CONJURE MAN *has entered the store. His tattered garments are fantastically bedizened with many talismans and good-luck charms of shell and bone and feather. His blue-black skin is daubed with cryptic signs in white paint.*]

DOLLY:
Git him out, git him out, he's going to mark my baby!

BEULAH:
Oh, shoot, Dolly. . . .
[DOLLY *has now fled after the* TEMPLE SISTERS, *to the landing of the stairs. The* CONJURE MAN *advances with a soft, rapid, toothless mumble of words that sound like wind in dry grass. He is holding out something in his shaking hand.*]
It's just that old crazy conjure man from Blue Mountain. He cain't mark your baby.
[*Phrase of primitive music or percussion as* NEGRO *moves into light.* BEULAH *follows* DOLLY *to landing.*]

CAROL [*very high and clear voice*]:
Come here, Uncle, and let me see what you've got there. Oh, it's a bone of some kind. No, I don't want to touch it, it isn't clean yet, there's still some flesh clinging to it.
[*Women make sounds of revulsion.*]
Yes, I know it's the breastbone of a bird but it's still tainted with corruption. Leave it a long time on a bare rock in the rain and the sun till every sign of corruption is burned and washed away from it, and then it will be a good charm, a white charm, but now it's a black charm, Uncle. So take it away and do what I told you with it. . . .
[*The* NEGRO *makes a ducking obeisance and shuffles slowly back to the door.*]
Hey, Uncle Pleasant, give us the Choctaw cry.
[NEGRO *stops in confectionery.*]
He's part Choctaw, he knows the Choctaw cry.

SISTER TEMPLE:
Don't let him holler in *here!*

CAROL:
Come on, Uncle Pleasant, *you* know it!

[*She takes off her coat and sits on the R. window sill.
She starts the cry herself. The* NEGRO *throws back his
head and completes it: a series of barking sounds
that rise to a high sustained note of wild intensity.
The women on the landing retreat further upstairs.
Just then, as though the cry had brought him,* VAL
*enters the store. He is a young man, about 30, who
has a kind of wild beauty about him that the cry
would suggest. He does not wear Levi's or a T-shirt,
he has on a pair of dark serge pants, glazed from long
wear and not excessively tight-fitting. His remarkable
garment is a snakeskin jacket, mottled white, black
and gray. He carries a guitar which is covered with
inscriptions.*]

CAROL [*looking at the young man*]:
Thanks, Uncle . . .

BEULAH:
*Hey, old man, you! Choctaw! Conjure man! Nigguh! Will
you go out-a this sto'? So we can come back down stairs?*
[CAROL *hands* NEGRO *a dollar; he goes out right
cackling.* VAL *holds the door open for* VEE TALBOTT,
*a heavy, vague woman in her forties. She does primi-
tive oil paintings and carries one into the store, saying:*]

VEE:
I got m'skirt caught in th' door of the Chevrolet an' I'm
afraid I tore it.
[*The women descend into store: laconic greetings,
interest focused on* VAL.]
Is it dark in here or am I losin' my eyesight? I been painting all day, finished a picture in a ten-hour stretch, just
stopped a few minutes fo' coffee and went back to it again
while I had a clear vision. I think I got it this time. But
I'm so exhausted I could drop in my tracks. There's nothing more exhausting than that kind of work on earth, it's
not so much that it tires your body out, but it leaves you
drained inside. Y'know what I mean? Inside? Like you
was burned out by something? Well! Still!—You feel
you've accomplished something when you're through with
it, sometimes you feel—*elevated!* How are you, Dolly?

26

DOLLY:
All right, Mrs. Talbott.

VEE:
That's good. How are *you,* Beulah?

BEULAH:
Oh, I'm all right, I reckon.

VEE:
Still can't make out much. Who is that there?
  [*Indicates* CAROL's *figure by the window. A signifi-
  cant silence greets this question.* VEE *suddenly:*]
Oh! I thought her folks had got her out of the county . . .
  [CAROL *utters a very light, slightly rueful laugh, her
  eyes drifting back to* VAL *as she moves back into con-
  fectionery.*]
Jabe and Lady back yet?

DOLLY:
Pee Wee an' Dawg have gone to the depot to meet 'em.

VEE:
Aw. Well, I'm just in time. I brought my new picture with
me, the paint isn't dry on it yet. I thought that Lady might
want to hang it up in Jabe's room while he's convalescin'
from the operation, cause after a close shave with death,
people like to be reminded of spiritual things. Huh? Yes!
This is the Holy Ghost ascending. . . .

DOLLY [*looking at canvas*]:
You didn't put a head on it.

VEE:
The head was a blaze of light, that's all I saw in my vision.

DOLLY:
Who's the young man with yuh?

VEE:
Aw, excuse me, I'm too worn out to have manners. This
is Mr. Valentine Xavier, Mrs. Hamma and Mrs.—I'm
sorry, Beulah. I never *can* get y' last *name!*

27

BEULAH:
I fo'give you. My name is Beulah Binnings.

VAL:
What shall I do with this here?

VEE:
Oh, that bowl of sherbet. I thought that Jabe might need something light an' digestible so I brought a bowl of sherbet.

DOLLY:
What flavor is it?

VEE:
Pineapple.

DOLLY:
Oh, Goody, I love pineapple. Better put it in the icebox before it starts to melt.

BEULAH [*looking under napkin that covers bowl*]:
I'm afraid you're lockin' th' stable after the horse is gone.

DOLLY:
Aw, is it melted already?

BEULAH:
Reduced to juice.

VEE:
Aw, shoot. Well, put it on ice anyhow, it might thicken up.
　　　[*Women are still watching* VAL.]
Where's the icebox?

BEULAH:
In the confectionery.

VEE:
I thought that Lady had closed the confectionery.

BEULAH:
Yes, but the Frigidaire's still there.
　　　[VAL *goes out R. through confectionery.*]

VEE:
Mr. Xavier is a stranger in our midst. His car broke down in that storm last night and I let him sleep in the lockup. He's lookin' for work and I thought I'd introduce him to Lady an' Jabe because if Jabe can't work they're going to need somebody to help out in th' store.

BEULAH:
That's a good idea.

DOLLY:
Uh-huh.

BEULAH:
Well, come on in, you all, it don't look like they're comin' straight home from the depot anyhow.

DOLLY:
Maybe that wasn't the Cannonball Express.

BEULAH:
Or maybe they stopped off fo' Pee Wee to buy some liquor.

DOLLY:
Yeah . . . at Ruby Lightfoot's.
[*They move past* CAROL *and out of sight.* CAROL *has risen. Now she crosses into the main store area, watching* VAL *with the candid curiosity of one child observing another. He pays no attention but concentrates on his belt buckle which he is repairing with a pocketknife.*]

CAROL:
What're you fixing?

VAL:
Belt buckle.

CAROL:
Boys like you are always fixing something. Could you fix my slipper?

VEE:
What's wrong with your slipper?

29

CAROL:
Why are you pretending not to remember me?

VAL:
It's hard to remember someone you never met.

CAROL:
Then why'd you look so startled when you saw me?

VAL:
Did I?

CAROL:
I thought for a moment you'd run back out the door.

VAL:
The sight of a woman can make me walk in a hurry but I don't think it's ever made me run.—You're standing in my light.

CAROL [*moving aside slightly*]:
Oh, excuse me. Better?

VAL:
Thanks. . . .

CAROL:
Are you afraid I'll snitch?

VAL:
Do what?

CAROL:
Snitch? I wouldn't; I'm not a snitch. But I can prove that I know you if I have to. It was New Year's Eve in New Orleans.

VAL:
I need a small pair of pliers. . . .

CAROL:
You had on that jacket and a snake ring with a ruby eye.

VAL:
I never had a snake ring with a ruby eye.

CAROL:
A snake ring with an emerald eye?

VAL:
I never had a snake ring with any kind of an eye. . . .
   [*Begins to whistle softly, his face averted.*]

CAROL [*smiling gently*]:
Then maybe it was a dragon ring with an emerald eye or
a diamond or a ruby eye. You told us that it was a gift
from a lady osteopath that you'd met somewhere in your
travels and that any time you were broke you'd wire this
lady osteopath collect, and no matter how far you were
or how long it was since you'd seen her, she'd send you a
money order for twenty-five dollars with the same sweet
message each time. "I love you. When will you come
back?" And to prove the story, not that it was difficult to
believe it, you took the latest of these sweet messages
from your wallet for us to see. . . .
   [*She throws back her head with soft laughter. He
   looks away still further and busies himself with the
   belt buckle.*]
—We followed you through five places before we made
contact with you and I was the one that made contact. I
went up to the bar where you were standing and touched
your jacket and said, "What stuff is this made of?" and
when you said it was snakeskin, I said, "I wish you'd told
me before I touched it." And you said something not nice.
You said, "Maybe that will learn you to hold back your
hands." I was drunk by that time which was after midnight. Do you remember what I said to you? I said, "What
on earth can you do on this earth but catch at whatever
comes near you, with both your hands, until your fingers
are broken?" I'd never said that before, or even consciously thought it, but afterwards it seemed like the truest
thing that my lips had ever spoken, what on earth can
you do but catch at whatever comes near you with both
your hands until your fingers are broken. . . . You gave
me a quick, sober look. I think you nodded slightly, and
then you picked up your guitar and began to sing. After
singing you passed the kitty. Whenever paper money was
dropped in the kitty you blew a whistle. My cousin Bertie
and I dropped in five dollars, you blew the whistle five
times and then sat down at our table for a drink, Schen-

ley's with Seven Up. You showed us all those signatures on your guitar . . . Any correction so far?

VAL:
Why are you so anxious to prove I know you?

CAROL:
Because I want to know you better and better! I'd like to go out jooking with you tonight.

VAL:
What's jooking?

CAROL:
Oh, don't you know what that is? That's where you get in a car and drink a little and drive a little and stop and dance a little to a juke box and then you drink a little more and drive a little more and stop and dance a little more to a juke box and then you stop dancing and you just drink and drive and then you stop driving and just drink, and then, finally, you stop drinking. . . .

VAL:
—What do you do, then?

CAROL:
That depends on the weather and who you're jooking with. If it's a clear night you spread a blanket among the memorial stones on Cypress Hill, which is the local bone orchard, but if it's not a fair night, and this one certainly isn't, why, usually then you go to the Idlewild cabins between here and Sunset on the Dixie Highway. . . .

VAL:
—That's about what I figured. But I don't go that route. Heavy drinking and smoking the weed and shacking with strangers is okay for kids in their twenties but this is my thirtieth birthday and I'm all through with that route.
    [Looks up with dark eyes.]
I'm not young any more.

CAROL:
You're young at thirty—I hope so! I'm twenty-nine!

VAL:
Naw, you're not young at thirty if you've been on a Goddam party since you were fifteen!
[*Picks up his guitar and sings and plays "Heavenly Grass." CAROL has taken a pint of bourbon from her trench-coat pocket and she passes it to him.*]

CAROL:
Thanks. That's lovely. Many happy returns of your birthday, Snakeskin.
[*She is very close to him. VEE enters and says sharply:*]

VEE:
Mr. Xavier don't drink.

CAROL:
Oh, ex-cuse *me!*

VEE:
And if you behaved yourself better your father would not be paralyzed in bed!
[*Sound of car out front. Women come running with various cries. LADY enters, nodding to the women, and holding the door open for her husband and the men following him. She greets the women in almost toneless murmurs, as if too tired to speak. She could be any age between thirty-five and forty-five, in appearance, but her figure is youthful. Her face taut. She is a woman who met with emotional disaster in her girlhood; verges on hysteria under strain. Her voice is often shrill and her body tense. But when in repose, a girlish softness emerges again and she looks ten years younger.*]

LADY:
Come in, Jabe. We've got a reception committee here to meet us. They've set up a buffet supper.
[*JABE enters. A gaunt, wolfish man, gray and yellow. The women chatter idiotically.*]

BEULAH:
Well, look who's here!

DOLLY:
Well, *Jabe!*

BEULAH:
I don't think he's been sick. I think he's been to Miami.
Look at that wonderful color in his face!

DOLLY:
I never seen him look better in my life!

BEULAH:
Who does he think he's foolin'? Ha ha ha!—not *me!*

JABE:
Whew, Jesus—I'm mighty—tired. . . .
 [*An uncomfortable silence, everyone staring greedily
 at the dying man with his tense, wolfish smile and
 nervous cough.*]

PEE WEE:
Well, Jabe, we been feedin' lots of nickles to those one-
arm bandits in there.

DOG:
An' that pinball machine is hotter'n a pistol.

PEE WEE:
Ha ha.
 [*EVA TEMPLE appears on stairs and screams for her
 sister.*]

EVA:
Sistuh! Sistuh! Sistuh! Cousin Jabe's here!
 [*A loud clatter upstairs and shrieks.*]

JABE:
Jesus. . . .
 [*EVA rushing at him—stops short and burst into
 tears.*

LADY:
Oh, cut that out, Eva Temple!—What were you doin' upstairs?

EVA:
I can't help it, it's so good to see him, it's so wonderful to see our cousin again, oh, Jabe, *blessed!*

SISTER:
Where's Jabe, where's precious Jabe? Where's our precious cousin?

EVA:
Right here, Sister!

SISTER:
Well, bless your old sweet life, and lookit the color he's got in his face, will you?

BEULAH:
I just told him he looks like he's been to Miami and got a Florida suntan, haha ha!
[*The preceding speeches are very rapid, all overlapping.*]

JABE:
I ain't been out in no sun an' if you all will excuse me I'm gonna do my celebratin' upstairs in bed because I'm kind of—worn out.
[*Goes creakily to foot of steps while* EVA *and* SISTER *sob into their handkerchiefs behind him.*]
—I see they's been some changes made here. Uh-huh. Uh-huh. How come the shoe department's back here now?
[*Instant hostility as if habitual between them.*]

LADY:
We always had a problem with light in this store.

JABE:
So you put the shoe department farther away from the window? That's sensible. A very intelligent solution to the problem, Lady.

LADY:
Jabe, you know I told you we got a fluorescent tube coming to put back here.

35

JABE:
Uh-huh. Uh-huh. Well. Tomorrow I'll get me some niggers to help me move the shoe department back front.

LADY:
You do whatever you want to, it's your store.

JABE:
Uh-huh. Uh-huh. I'm glad you reminded me of it.
[LADY *turns sharply away. He starts up stairs.* PEE WEE *and* DOG *follow him up. The women huddle and whisper in the store.* LADY *sinks wearily into chair at table.*]

BEULAH:
That man will never come down those stairs again!

DOLLY:
Never in this world, honey.

BEULAH:
He has th' death sweat on him! Did you notice that death sweat on him?

DOLLY:
An' yellow as butter, just as yellow as—
[SISTER *sobs.*]

EVA:
Sister, Sister!

BEULAH [*crossing to* LADY]:
Lady, I don't suppose you feel much like talking about it right now but Dog and me are so worried.

DOLLY:
Pee Wee and me are worried sick about it.

LADY:
—About what?

BEULAH:
Jabe's operation in Memphis. Was it successful?

36

DOLLY:
Wasn't it successful?
[LADY *stares at them blindly. The women, except* CAROL, *close avidly about, tense with morbid interest.*]

SISTER:
Was it too late for surgical interference?

EVA:
Wasn't it successful?
[*A loud, measured knock begins on the floor above.*]

BEULAH:
Somebody told us it had gone past the knife.

DOLLY:
We do hope it ain't hopeless.

EVA:
We hope and pray it ain't hopeless.
[*All their faces wear faint, unconscious smiles.* LADY *looks from face to face; then utters a slight, startled laugh and springs up from the table and crosses to the stairs.*]

LADY [*as if in flight*]:
Excuse me, I have to go up, Jabe's knocking for me.
[LADY *goes upstairs. The women gaze after her.*]

CAROL [*suddenly and clearly, in the silence*]:
Speaking of knocks, I have a knock in my engine. It goes knock, knock, and I say who's there. I don't know whether I'm in communication with some dead ancestor or the motor's about to drop out and leave me stranded in the dead of night on the Dixie Highway. Do you have any knowledge of mechanics? I'm sure you do. Would you be sweet and take a short drive with me? So you could hear that knock?

VAL:
I don't have time.

37

CAROL:
What have you go to do?

VAL:
I'm waiting to see about a job in this store.

CAROL:
I'm offering you a job.

VAL:
I want a job that pays.

CAROL:
I expect to pay you.
    [*Women whisper loudly in the background.*]

VAL:
Maybe sometime tomorrow.

CAROL:
I can't stay here overnight; I'm not allowed to stay overnight in this county.
    [*Whispers rise. The word "corrupt" is distinguished.*]
    [*Without turning, smiling very brightly:*]
What are they saying about me? Can you hear what those women are saying about me?

VAL:
—Play it cool. . . .

CAROL:
I don't like playing it cool! What are they saying about me? That I'm corrupt?

VAL:
If you don't want to be talked about, why do you make up like that, why do you—

CAROL:
To show off!

VAL:
What?

38

CAROL:
I'm an exhibitionist! I want to be noticed, seen, heard, felt! I want them to know I'm alive! Don't you want them to know you're alive?

VAL:
I want to live and I don't care if they know I'm alive or not.

CAROL:
Then why do you play a guitar?

VAL:
Why do you make a Goddam show of yourself?

CAROL:
That's right, for the same reason.

VAL:
We don't go the same route. . . .
   [*He keeps moving away from her; she continually follows him. Her speech is compulsive.*]

CAROL:
I used to be what they called a Christ-bitten reformer. You know what that is?—A kind of benign exhibitionist. . . . I delivered stump speeches, wrote letters of protest about the gradual massacre of the colored majority in the county. I thought it was wrong for pellagra and slow starvation to cut them down when the cotton crop failed from army worm or boll weevil or too much rain in summer. I wanted to, tried to, put up free clinics, I squandered the money my mother left me on it. And when that Willie McGee thing came along—he was sent to the chair for having improper relations with a white whore—
   [*Her voice is like a passionate incantation.*]
I made a fuss about it. I put on a potato sack and set out for the capitol on foot. This was in winter. I walked barefoot in this burlap sack to deliver a personal protest to the Governor of the State. Oh, I suppose it was partly exhibitionism on my part, but it wasn't completely exhibitionism; there was something else in it, too. You know how far I got? Six miles out of town—hooted, jeered at, even spit

on!—every step of the way—and then arrested! Guess
what for? Lewd vagrancy! Uh-huh, that was the charge,
"lewd vagrancy," because they said that potato sack I had
on was not a respectable garment. . . . Well, all that was
a pretty long time ago, and now I'm not a reformer any
more. I'm just a "lewd vagrant." And I'm showing the
"S.O.B.S." how lewd a "lewd vagrant" can be if she puts
her whole heart in it like I do mine! All right. I've told
you my story, the story of an exhibitionist. Now I want
you to do something for me. Take me out to Cypress Hill
in my car. And we'll hear the dead people talk. They do
talk there. They chatter together like birds on Cypress
Hill, but all they say is one word and that one word is
"live," they say "Live, live, live, live, live!" It's all they've
learned, it's the only advice they can give.—Just live. . . .
   [*She opens the door.*]
Simple!—a very simple instruction. . . .
   [*Goes out. Women's voices rise from the steady, indistinct murmur, like hissing geese.*]

WOMEN'S VOICES:
—No, not liquor! Dope!

—Something not normal all right!

—Her father and brother were warned by the Vigilantes
to keep her out of this county.

—She's absolutely degraded!

—Yes, corrupt!

—Corrupt! (Etc., etc.)
   [*As if repelled by their hissing voices,* VAL *suddenly
   picks up his guitar and goes out of the store as—*VEE
   TALBOTT *appears on the landing and calls down to
   him.*]

VEE:
Mr. Xavier! Where is Mr. Xavier?

BEULAH:
Gone, honey.

DOLLY:
You might as fell face it, Vee. This is one candidate for salvation that you have lost to the opposition.

BEULAH:
He's gone off to Cypress Hill with the Cutrere girl.

VEE [*descending*]:
—If some of you older women in Two River County would set a better example there'd be more decent young people!

BEULAH:
What was that remark?

VEE:
I mean that people who give drinkin' parties an' get so drunk they don't know which is their husband and which is somebody else's and people who serve on the altar guild and still play cards on Sundays—

BEULAH:
Just stop right there! Now I've discovered the source of that dirty gossip!

VEE:
I'm only repeating what I've been told by others. I never been to these parties!

BEULAH:
No, and you never will! You're a public kill-joy, a professional hypocrite!

VEE:
I try to build up characters! You and your drinkin' parties are only concerned with tearin' characters down! I'm goin' upstairs, I'm goin' back upstairs!
    [*Rushes upstairs.*]

BEULAH:
Well, I'm glad I said what I said to that woman. I've got no earthly patience with that sort of hypocriticism. Dolly, let's put this perishable stuff in the Frigidaire and leave here. I've never been so thoroughly disgusted!

DOLLY:
Oh, my Lawd.
[*Pauses at stairs and shouts:*]
PEE WEE!
[*Goes off with the dishes.*]

SISTER:
Both of those wimmen are as common as dirt.

EVA:
Dolly's folks in Blue Mountain are nothin' at all but the poorest kind of white trash. Why, Lollie Tucker told me the old man sits on the porch with his shoes off drinkin' beer out of a bucket!—Let's take these flowers with us to put on the altar.

SISTER:
Yes, we can give Jabe credit in the parish notes.

EVA:
I'm going to take these olive-nut sandwiches, too. They'll come in handy for the Bishop Adjutant's tea.
[DOLLY *and* BEULAH *cross through.*]

DOLLY:
We still have time to make the second show.

BEULAH [*shouting*]:
Dog!

DOLLY:
Pee Wee!
[*They rush out of store.*]

EVA:
Sits on the porch with his shoes off?

SISTER:
Drinkin' beer out of a bucket!
[*They go out with umbrellas, etc. Men descend stairs.*]

SHERIFF TALBOTT:
Well, it looks to me like Jabe will more than likely go under before the cotton comes up.

PEE WEE:
He never looked good.

DOG:
Naw, but now he looks worse.
   [*They cross to door.*]

SHERIFF:
Vee!

VEE [*from landing*]:
Hush that bawling. I had to speak to Lady about that boy and I couldn't speak to her in front of Jabe because he thinks he's gonna be able to go back to work himself.

SHERIFF:
Well, move along, quit foolin'.

VEE:
I think I ought to wait till that boy gits back.

SHERIFF:
I'm sick of you making a Goddam fool of yourself over every stray bastard that wanders into this county.
   [*Car horn honks loudly.* VEE *follows her husband out. Sound of cars driving off. Dogs bay in distance as lights dim to indicate short passage of time.*]

A couple of hours later that night. Through the great window the landscape is faintly luminous under a scudding moonlit sky. Outside a girl's laughter, CAROL'S, *rings out high and clear and is followed by the sound of a motor, rapidly going off.*

VAL enters the store before the car sound quite fades out and while a dog is still barking at it somewhere along the highway. He says "Christ" under his breath, goes to the buffet table and scrubs lipstick stain off his mouth and face with a paper napkin, picks up his guitar which he had left on a counter.

Footsteps descending: LADY *appears on the landing in a flannel robe, shivering in the cold air; she snaps her fingers impatiently for the old dog,* BELLA, *who comes limping down beside her. She doesn't see* VAL, *seated on the shadowy counter, and she goes directly to the phone near the stairs. Her manner is desperate, her voice harsh and shrill.*

LADY:
Ge' me the drugstore, will you? I know the drugstore's closed, this is Mrs. Torrance, my store's closed, too, but I got a sick man here, just back from the hospital, yeah, yeah, an emergency, wake up Mr. Dubinsky, keep ringing till he answers, it's an emergency!
  [*Pause: she mutters under her breath:*]
—*Porca la miseria!*—I wish I was dead, dead, dead. . . .

VAL [*quietly*]:
No, you don't Lady.
  [*She gasps, turning and seeing him, without leaving the phone, she rings the cashbox open and snatches out something.*]

LADY:
What're you doin' here? You know this store is closed!

VAL:
I seen a light was still on and the door was open so I come back to—

44

LADY:
You see what I got in my hand?
[*Raises revolver above level of counter.*]

VAL:
You going to shoot me?

LADY:
You better believe it if you don't get out of here, mister!

VAL:
That's all right, Lady, I just come back to pick up my guitar.

LADY:
To pick up your guitar?
[*He lifts it gravely.*]
—Huh. . . .

VAL:
Miss Talbott brought me here. I was here when you got back from Memphis, don't you remember?

LADY:
—Aw. Aw, yeah. . . . You been here all this time?

VAL:
No. I went out and come back.

LADY [*into the phone*]:
I told you to keep ringing till he answers! Go on, keep ringing, keep ringing!
[*Then to* VAL:]
You went out and come back?

VAL:
Yeah.

LADY:
What for?

VAL:
You know that girl that was here?

45

LADY:
Carol Cutrere?

VAL:
She said she had car trouble and could I fix it.

LADY:
—Did you fix it?

VAL:
She didn't have no car trouble, that wasn't her trouble, oh, she had trouble, all right, but *that* wasn't it. . . .

LADY:
What was her trouble?

VAL:
She made a mistake about me.

LADY:
What mistake?

VAL:
She thought I had a sign "Male at Stud" hung on me.

LADY:
She thought you—?
[Into phone suddenly:]
Oh, Mr. Dubinsky, I'm sorry to wake you up but I just brought my husband back from the Memphis hospital and I left my box of luminal tablets in the—I got to have some! I ain't slep' for three nights, I'm going to pieces, you hear me, I'm going to pieces, I ain't slept in three nights, I got to have some tonight. Now you look here, if you want to keep my trade, you send me over some tablets. Then bring them yourself, God damn it, excuse my French! Because I'm going to pieces right this minute!
[Hangs up violently.]
—*Mannage la miseria!*—Christ. . . . I'm shivering!—It's cold as a Goddam ice-plant in this store, I don't know why, it never seems to hold heat, the ceiling's too high or something, it don't hold heat at all.—Now what do you want? I got to go upstairs.

46

VAL:
Here. Put this on you.

> [*He removes his jacket and hands it to her. She doesn't take it at once, stares at him questioningly and then slowly takes the jacket in her hands and examines it, running her fingers curiously over the snakeskin.*]

LADY:
What is this stuff this thing's made of? It looks like it was snakeskin.

VAL:
Yeah, well, that's what it is.

LADY:
What're you doing with a snakeskin jacket?

VAL:
It's a sort of a trademark; people call me Snakeskin.

LADY:
Who calls you Snakeskin?

VAL:
Oh, in the bars, the sort of places I work in—but I've quit that. I'm through with that stuff now. . . .

LADY:
You're a—entertainer?

VAL:
I sing and play the guitar.

LADY:
—Aw?

> [*She puts the jacket on as if to explore it.*]

It feels warm all right.

VAL:
It's warm from my body, I guess. . . .

LADY:
You must be a warm-blooded boy. . . .

VAL:
That's right. . . .

LADY:
Well, what in God's name are you lookin' for around
here?

VAL:
—Work.

LADY:
Boys like you don't work.

VAL:
What d'you mean by boys like me?

LADY:
Ones that play th' guitar and go around talkin' about how
warm they are. . . .

VAL:
That happens t' be the truth. My temperature's always
a couple degrees above normal the same as a dog's, it's
normal for me the same as it is for a dog, that's the
truth. . . .

LADY:
—Huh!

VAL:
You don't believe me?

LADY:
I have no reason to doubt you, but what about it?

VAL:
—Why—nothing. . . .
    [LADY *laughs softly and suddenly;* VAL *smiles slowly
    and warmly.*]

LADY:
You're a peculiar somebody all right, you sure are! How
did you get around here?

VAL:
I was driving through here last night and an axle broke on my car, that stopped me here, and I went to the county jail for a place to sleep out of the rain. Mizz Talbott took me in and give me a cot in the lockup and said if I hung around till you got back that you might give me a job in the store to help out since your husband was tooken sick.

LADY:
—Uh-huh. Well—she was wrong about that. . . . If I took on help here it would have to be local help, I couldn't hire no stranger with a—snakeskin jacket and a guitar ... and that runs a temperature as high as a dog's!
  [*Throws back her head in another soft, sudden laugh and starts to take off the jacket.*]

VAL:
Keep it on.

LADY:
No, I got to go up now and you had better be going ...

VAL:
I got nowhere to go.

LADY:
Well, everyone's got a problem and that's yours.

VAL:
—What nationality are you?

LADY:
Why do you ask me that?

VAL:
You seem to be like a foreigner.

LADY:
I'm the daughter of a Wop bootlegger burned to death in his orchard!—Take your jacket. . . .

VAL:
What was that you said about your father?

LADY:
Why?

VAL:
—A "Wop bootlegger"?

LADY:
—They burned him to death in his orchard! What about
it? The story's well known around here.
[JABE *knocks on ceiling.*]
I got to go up, I'm being called for.
[*She turns out light over counter and at the same
moment he begins to sing softly with his guitar:
"Heavenly Grass." He suddenly stops short and says
abruptly:*]

VAL:
I do electric repairs.
[*Lady stares at him softly.*]
I can do all kinds of odd jobs. Lady, I'm thirty today and
I'm through with the life that I've been leading.
[*Pause. Dog bays in distance.*]
I lived in corruption but I'm not corrupted. Here is why.
[*Picks up his guitar.*]
My life's companion! It washes me clean like water when
anything unclean has touched me. . . .
[*Plays softly, with a slow smile.*]

LADY:
What's all that writing on it?

VAL:
Autographs of musicians I run into here and here.

LADY:
Can I see it?

VAL:
Turn on that light above you.
[*She switches on green-shaded bulb over counter.
VAL holds the instrument tenderly between them as
if it were a child; his voice is soft, intimate, tender.*]
See this name? Leadbelly?

50

LADY:
Leadbelly?

VAL:
Greatest man ever lived on the twelve-string guitar! Played
it so good he broke the stone heart of a Texas governor
with it and won himself a pardon out of jail. . . . And see
this name Oliver? King Oliver? That name is immortal,
Lady. Greatest man since Gabriel on a horn. . . .

LADY:
What's this name?

VAL:
Oh. That name? That name is also immortal. The name
Bessie Smith is written in the stars!—Jim Crow killed her,
John Barleycorn and Jim Crow killed Bessie Smith but
that's another story. . . . See this name here? That's an-
other immortal!

LADY:
Fats Waller? Is his name written in the stars, too?

VAL:
Yes, his name is written in the stars, too. . . .
    [*Her voice is also intimate and soft: a spell of soft-
    ness between them, their bodies almost touching, only
    divided by the guitar.*]

LADY:
You had any sales experience?

VAL:
All my life I been selling something to someone.

LADY:
So's everybody. You got any character reference on you?

VAL:
I have this—letter.
    [*Removes a worn, folded letter from a wallet, drop-
    ping a lot of snapshots and cards of various kinds on
    the floor. He passes the letter to her gravely and*]

51

crouches to collect the dropped articles while she
peruses the character reference.]

LADY [*reading slowly aloud*]:
"This boy worked for me three months in my auto repair
shop and is a real hard worker and is good and honest
but is a peculiar talker and that is the reason I got to let
him go but would like to—
  [*Holds letter closer to light.*]
—would like to—keep him. Yours truly."
  [VAL *stares at her gravely, blinking a little.*]
Huh!—Some reference!

VAL:
—Is that what it says?

LADY:
Didn't you know what it said?

VAL:
No.—The man sealed the envelope on it.

LADY:
Well, that's not the sort of character reference that will
do you much good, boy.

VAL:
Naw. I guess it ain't.

LADY:
—However. . . .

VAL:
—What?

LADY:
What people say about you don't mean much. Can you
read shoe sizes?

VAL:
I guess so.

LADY:
What does 75 David mean?

52

[VAL *stares at her, shakes head slowly*.]
75 means seven and one half long and David mean "D"
wide. You know how to make change?

VAL:
Yeah, I could make change in a store.

LADY:
Change for better or worse? Ha ha!—Well—
    [*Pause.*]
Well—you see that other room there, through that arch
there? That's the confectionery; it's closed now but it's
going to be reopened in a short while and I'm going to
compete for the night life in this county, the after-the-
movies trade. I'm going to serve setups in there and I'm
going to redecorate. I got it all planned.
    [*She is talking eagerly now, as if to herself.*]
Artificial branches of fruit trees in flower on the walls and
ceilings!—It's going to be like an orchard in the spring!—
My father, he had an orchard on Moon Lake. He made a
wine garden of it. We had fifteen little white arbors with
tables in them and they were covered with—grapevines
and—we sold Dago red wine an' bootleg whiskey and
beer.—They burned it up! My father was burned up in
it. . . .
    [JABE *knocks above more loudly and a hoarse voice
    shouts "Lady!" Figure appears at the door and calls:
    "Mrs. Torrance?"*]
Oh, that's the sandman with my sleeping tablets.
    [*Crosses to door.*]
Thanks, Mr. Dubinsky, sorry I had to disturb you, sorry
I—
    [*Man mutters something and goes. She closes the
    door.*]
Well, go to hell, then, old bastard. . . .
    [*Returns with package.*]
—You ever have trouble sleeping?

VAL:
I can sleep or not sleep as long or short as I want to.

LADY:
Is that right?

VAL:
I can sleep on a concrete floor or go without sleeping, without even feeling sleepy, for forty-eight hours. And I can hold my breath three minutes without blacking out; I made ten dollars betting I could do it and I did it! And I can go a whole day without passing water.

LADY [*startled*]:
Is *that* a fact?

VAL [*very simply as if he'd made an ordinary remark*]:
That's a fact. I served time on a chain gang for vagrancy once and they tied me to a post all day and I stood there all day without passing water to show the sons of bitches that I could do it.

LADY:
—I see what that auto repair man was talking about when he said this boy is a peculiar talker! Well—what else can you do? Tell me some more about your self-control!

VAL [*grinning*]:
Well, they say that a woman can burn a man down. But I can burn down a woman.

LADY:
Which woman?

VAL:
Any two-footed woman.

LADY [*throws back her head in sudden friendly laughter as he grins at her with the simple candor of a child*]:
—Well, there's lots of two-footed women round here that might be willin' to test the truth of that statement.

VAL:
I'm saying I could. I'm not saying I would.

LADY:
Don't worry, boy. I'm one two-footed woman that you don't have to convince of your perfect controls.

VAL:
No, I'm done with all that.

LADY:
What's the matter? Have they tired you out?

VAL:
I'm not tired. I'm disgusted.

LADY:
Aw, you're disgusted, huh?

VAL:
I'm telling you, Lady, there's people bought and sold in this world like carcasses of hogs in butcher shops!

LADY:
You ain't tellin' me nothin' I don't know.

VAL:
You might think there's many and many kinds of people in this world but, Lady, there's just two kinds of people, the ones that are bought and the buyers! No—there's one other kind . . .

LADY:
What kind's that?

VAL:
The kind that's never been branded.

LADY:
You will be, man.

VAL:
They got to catch me first.

LADY:
Well, then, you better not settle down in this county.

VAL:
You know they's a kind of bird that don't have legs so it can't light on nothing but has to stay all its life on its wings in the sky? That's true. I seen one once, it had died and fallen to earth and it was light-blue colored and its body was tiny as your little finger, that's the truth, it had a body as tiny as your little finger and so light on the

55

palm of your hand it didn't weigh more than a feather, but its wings spread out this wide but they was transparent, the color of the sky and you could see through them. That's what they call protection coloring. Camouflage, they call it. You can't tell those birds from the sky and that's why the hawks don't catch them, don't see them up there in the high blue sky near the sun!

LADY:
How about in gray weather?

VAL:
They fly so high in gray weather the Goddam hawks would get dizzy. But those little birds, they don't have no legs at all and they live their whole lives on the wing, and they sleep on the wind, that's how they sleep at night, they just spread their wings and go to sleep on the wind like other birds fold their wings and go to sleep on a tree. . . .
    [*Music fades in.*]
—They sleep on the wind and . . .
    [*His eyes grow soft and vague and he lifts his guitar and accompanies the very faint music.*]
—never light on this earth but one time when they die!

LADY:
—I'd like to be one of those birds.

VAL:
So'd I like to be one of those birds; they's lots of people would like to be one of those birds and never be—corrupted!

LADY:
If one of those birds ever dies and falls on the ground and you happen to find it, I wish you would show it to me because I think maybe you just imagine there is a bird of that kind in existence. Because I don't think nothing living has ever been that free, not even nearly. Show me one of them birds and I'll say, Yes, God's made one perfect creature!—I sure would give this mercantile store and every bit of stock in it to be that tiny bird the color of the sky . . . for one night to sleep on the wind and— float!—around under th'—stars . . .

56

[JABE *knocks on floor.* LADY'S *eyes return to* VAL.]
—Because I sleep with a son of a bitch who bought me
at a fire sale, and not in fifteen years have I had a single
good dream, not one—oh!—*Shit* . . . I don't know why
I'm—telling a stranger—this. . . .
[*She rings the cashbox open.*]
Take this dollar and go eat at the Al-Nite on the highway
and come back here in the morning and I'll put you to
work. I'll break you in clerking here and when the new
confectionery opens, well, maybe I can use you in there.—
That door locks when you close it!—But let's get one
thing straight.

VAL:
What thing?

LADY:
I'm not interested in your perfect functions, in fact you
don't interest me no more than the air that you stand in.
If that's understood we'll have a good working relation,
but otherwise trouble!—Of course I know you're crazy,
but they's lots of crazier people than you are still running
loose and some of them in high positions, too. Just remember. No monkey business with me. Now go. Go eat,
you're hungry.

VAL:
Mind if I leave this here? My life's companion?
   [*He means his guitar.*]

LADY:
Leave it here if you want to.

VAL:
Thanks, Lady.

LADY:
Don't mention it.
   [*He crosses toward the door as a dog barks with
   passionate clarity in the distance. He turns to smile
   back at her and says:*]

VAL:
I don't know nothing about you except you're nice but

57

you are just about the nicest person that I have ever run into! And I'm going to be steady and honest and hard-working to please you and any time you have any more trouble sleeping, I know how to fix that for you. A lady osteopath taught me' how to make little adjustments in the neck and spine and give you sound, natural sleep. Well, g'night, now.

[*He goes out. Count five. Then she throws back her head and laughs as lightly and gaily as a young girl. Then she turns and wonderingly picks up and runs her hands tenderly over his guitar as the curtain falls.*]

SCENE ONE

The store, afternoon, a few weeks later. The table and chair are back in the confectionery. LADY *is hanging up the phone.* VAL *is standing just outside the door. He turns and enters. Outside on the highway a mule team is laboring to pull a big truck back on the icy pavement. A Negro's voice shouts: "Hyyyyyyyyy-up."*

VAL [*moving to R. window*]:
One a them big Diamond T trucks an' trailers gone off the highway last night and a six mule team is tryin' t' pull it back on. . . .
[*He looks out window.*]

LADY [*coming from behind to R. of counter*]:
Mister, we just now gotten a big fat complaint about you from a woman that says if she wasn't a widow her husband would come in here and beat the tar out of you.

VAL [*taking a step toward her*]:
Yeah?—Is this a small pink-headed woman?

LADY:
Pin-headed woman did you say?

VAL:
Naw, I said, "Pink!"—A little pink-haired woman, in a checkered coat with pearl buttons this big on it.

LADY:
I talked to her on the phone. She didn't go into such details about her appearance but she did say you got familiar. I said, "How? by his talk or behavior?" And she said, "Both!"—Now I was afraid of this when I warned you last week, "No monkey business here, boy!"

VAL:
This little pink-headed woman bought a valentine from

me and all I said is my *name* is Valentine to her. Few minutes later a small colored boy come in and delivered the valentine to me with something wrote on it an' I believe I still got it. . . .

> [*Finds and shows it to* LADY *who goes to him.* LADY *reads it, and tears it fiercely to pieces. He lights a cigarette.*]

LADY:
Signed it with a lipstick kiss? You didn't show up for this date?

VAL:
No, ma'am. That's why she complained.
> [*Throws match on floor.*]

LADY:
Pick that match up off the floor.

VAL:
Are you bucking for sergeant, or something?
> [*He throws match out the door with elaborate care. Her eyes follow his back.* VAL *returns lazily toward her.*]

LADY:
Did you walk around in front of her that way?

VAL [*at counter*]:
What way?

LADY:
Slew-foot, slew-foot!
> [*He regards her closely with good-humored perplexity.*]

Did you stand in front of her like that? That close? In that, that—*position?*

VAL:
What position?

LADY:
Ev'rything you do is suggestive!

60

VAL:
Suggestive of what?

LADY:
Of what you said you was through with—somethin'—
Oh, shoot, you know what I mean.—Why'd 'ya think I
give you a plain, dark business suit to work in?

VAL [*sadly*]:
Un-hun. . . .
    [*Sighs and removes his blue jacket.*]

LADY:
Now what're you takin' that off for?

VAL:
I'm giving the suit back to you. I'll change my pants in
the closet.
    [*Gives her the jacket and crosses into alcove.*]

LADY:
Hey! I'm sorry! You hear me? I didn't sleep well last night.
Hey! I said I'm sorry! You hear me?
    [*She enters alcove and returns immediately with* VAL'S
    guitar and crosses to D.R. He follows.]

VAL:
Le' me have my guitar, Lady. You find too many faults
with me and I tried to do good.

LADY:
I told you I'm sorry. You want me to get down and lick
the dust off your shoes?

VAL:
Just give me back my guitar.

LADY:
I ain't dissatisfied with you. I'm pleased with you, sincerely!

VAL:
You sure don't show it.

LADY:
My nerves are all shot to pieces.
>[*Extends hand to him.*]

Shake.

VAL:
You mean I ain't fired, so I don't have to quit?
>[*They shake hands like two men. She hands him
guitar—then silence falls between them.*]

LADY:
You see, we don't know each other, we're, we're—just
gettin'—acquainted.   .

VAL:
That's right, like a couple of animals sniffin' around each
other. . . .
>[*The image embarrasses her. He crosses to counter,
leans over and puts guitar behind it.*]

LADY:
Well, not exactly like that, but—!

VAL:
We don't know each other. How do people get to know
each other? I used to think they did it by touch.

LADY:
By what?

VAL:
By touch, by touchin' each other.

LADY [*moving up and sitting on shoe-fitting chair which
has been moved to R. window*]:
Oh, you mean by close—contact!

VAL:
But later it seemed like that made them more strangers
than ever, uhh, huh, more strangers than ever. . . .

LADY:
Then how d'you think they get to know each other?

VAL [*sitting on counter*]:
Well, in answer to your last question, I would say this:
Nobody ever gets to know *no body!* We're all of us sentenced to solitary confinement inside our own skins, for life! You understand me, Lady?—I'm tellin' you it's the truth; we got to face it, we're under a life-long sentence to solitary confinement inside our own lonely skins for as long as we live on this earth!

LADY [*rising and crossing to him*]:
Oh, no, I'm not a big optimist but I cannot agree with something as sad as that statement!
    [*They are sweetly grave as two children; the store is somewhat dusky. She sits in chair R. of counter.*]

VAL:
Listen!—When I was a kid on Witches' Bayou? After my folks all scattered away like loose chicken's feathers blown around by the wind?—I stayed there alone on the bayou, hunted and trapped out of season and hid from the law!—*Listen!*—All that time, all that lonely time, I felt I was—waiting for something!

LADY:
What for?

VAL:
What does anyone wait for? For something to happen, for anything to happen, to make things make more sense.
. . . It's hard to remember what that feeling was like because I've lost it now, but I was waiting for something like if you ask a question you wait for someone to answer, but you ask the wrong question or you ask the wrong person and the answer don't come.
Does everything stop because you don't get the answer? No, it goes right on as if the answer was given, day comes after day and night comes after night, and you're still waiting for someone to answer the question and going right on as if the question was answered. And then—well—then. . . .

LADY:
Then what?

VAL:
You get the make-believe answer.

LADY:
What answer is that?

VAL:
Don't pretend you don't know because you do!

LADY:
—Love?

VAL [*placing hand on her shoulder*]:
That's the make-believe answer. It's fooled many a fool besides you an' me, that's the God's truth, Lady, and you had better believe it.

    [LADY *looks reflectively at* VAL *and he goes on speaking and sits on stool below counter.*]
—I met a girl on the bayou when I was fourteen. I'd had a feeling that day that if I just kept poling the boat down the bayou a little bit further I would come bang into whatever it was I'd been so long expecting!

LADY:
Was she the answer, this girl that you met on the bayou?

VAL:
She made me think that she was.

LADY:
How did she do that?

VAL:
By coming out on the dogtrot of a cabin as naked as I was in that flat-bottom boat! She stood there a while with the daylight burning around her as bright as heaven as far as I could see. You seen the inside of a shell, how white that is, pearly white? Her naked skin was like that.—Oh, God, I remember a bird flown out of the moss and its wings made a shadow on her, and then it sung a single, high clear note, and as if she was waiting for that as a kind of a signal to catch me, she turned and smiled, and walked on back in the cabin. . . .

LADY:
You followed?

VAL:
Yes, I followed, I followed, like a bird's tail follows a bird, I followed!
I thought that she gave me the answer to the question, I'd been waiting for, but afterwards I wasn't sure that was it, but from that time the question wasn't much plainer than the answer and—

LADY:
—What?

VAL:
At fifteen I left Witches' Bayou. When the dog died I sold my boat and the gun. . . . I went to New Orleans in this snakeskin jacket. . . . It didn't take long for me to learn the score.

LADY:
What did you learn?

VAL:
I learned that I had something to sell besides snakeskins and other wild things' skins I caught on the bayou. I was corrupted! That's the answer. . . .

LADY:
Naw, that ain't the answer!

VAL:
Okay, *you* tell me the answer!

LADY:
I don't know the answer, I just know corruption ain't the answer. I know that much. If I thought that was the answer I'd take Jabe's pistol or his morphine tablets and—
        [*A woman bursts into store.*]

WOMAN:
I got to use your pay-phone!

LADY:
Go ahead. Help yourself.

[*Woman crosses to phone, deposits coin.* LADY *crosses to confectionery. To* VAL:]
Get me a Coke from the cooler.
  [VAL *crosses and goes out R. During the intense activity among the choral women,* LADY *and* VAL *seem bemused as if they were thinking back over their talk before. For the past minute or two a car horn has been heard blowing repeatedly in the near distance.*]

WOMAN [*at phone*]:
Cutrere place, get me the Cutrere place, will yuh? David Cutrere or his wife, whichever comes to the phone!
  [BEULAH *rushes in from the street to R.C.*]

BEULAH:
Lady, Lady, where's Lady! Carol Cutrere is——!

WOMAN:
Quiet, please! I am callin' her brother about her!
  [LADY *sits at table in confectionery.*]
  [*At phone:*]
Who's this I'm talking to? Good! I'm calling about your sister, Carol Cutrere. She is blowing her car horn at the Red Crown station, she is blowing and blowing her car horn at the Red Crown station because my husband give the station attendants instructions not to service her car, and she is blowing and blowing and blowing on her horn, drawing a big crowd there and, Mr. Cutrere, I thought that you and your father had agreed to keep that girl out of Two River County for good, that's what we all understood around here.
  [*Car horn.*]

BEULAH [*Listening with excited approval*]:
Good! Good! Tell him that if——
  [DOLLY *enters.*]

DOLLY:
She's gotten out of the car and——

BEULAH:
Shhh!

WOMAN:
Well, I just wanted to let you know she's back here in

66

town makin' another disturbance and my husband's on the phone now at the Red Crown station—

[DOLLY *goes outside and looks off.*]

trying to get the Sheriff, so if she gits picked up again by th' law, you can't say I didn't warn you, Mr. Cutrere.

[*Car horn.*]

DOLLY [*coming back in*]:
Oh, good! Good!

BEULAH:
Where is she, where's she gone now?

WOMAN:
You better be quick about it. Yes, I do. I sympathize with you and your father and with Mrs. Cutrere, but Carol cannot demand service at our station, we just refuse to wait on her, she's not—Hello? Hello?

[*She jiggles phone violently.*]

BEULAH:
What's he doin'? Comin' to pick her up?

DOLLY:
Call the Sheriff's office!

[BEULAH *goes outside again.* VAL *comes back with a bottle of Coca-Cola—hands it to* LADY *and leans on juke box.*]

What's goin' on now?

BEULAH [*outside*]:
Look, look, they're pushing her out of the station driveway.

[*They forget* LADY *in this new excitement. Ad libs continual. The short woman from the station charges back out of the store.*]

DOLLY:
Where is Carol?

BEULAH:
Going into the White Star Pharmacy!

[DOLLY *rushes back in to the phone.*]

BEULAH [*crossing to* LADY]:
Lady, I want you to give me your word that if that Cutrere girl comes in here, you won't wait on her! You hear me?

LADY:
No.

BEULAH:
—What? Will you refuse to wait on her?

LADY:
I can't refuse to wait on anyone in this store.

BEULAH:
Well, I'd like to know why you can't.

DOLLY:
Shhh! I'm on the phone!

BEULAH:
Who you phonin' Dolly?

DOLLY:
That White Star Pharmacy! I want to make sure that Mr. Dubinsky refuses to wait on that girl!
   [*Having found and deposited coin.*]
I want the White Far Starmacy. I mean the—
   [*Stamps foot.*]
—White Star Pharmacy!—I'm so upset my tongu~'s twisted!
   [LADY *hands Coke to* VAL. BEULAH *is at the window.*]
I'm getting a busy signal. Has she come out yet?

BEULAH:
No, she's still in the White Star!

DOLLY:
Maybe they're not waiting on her.

BEULAH:
Dubinsky'd wait on a purple-bottom baboon if it put a dime on th' counter an' pointed at something!

DOLLY:
I know she sat at a table in the Blue Bird Café half'n

hour last time she was here and the waitresses never came near her!

BEULAH:
That's different. They're not foreigners there!
   [DOLLY *crosses to counter*.]
You can't ostracize a person out of this county unless everybody cooperates. Lady just told me that she was going to wait on her if she comes here.

DOLLY:
Lady wouldn't do that.

BEULAH:
Ask her! She told *me* she would!

LADY [*rising and turning at once to the women and shouting at them*]:
Oh, for God's sake, no! I'm not going to refuse to wait on her because you all don't like her! Besides I'm delighted that wild girl is givin' her brother so much trouble!
   [*After this outburst she goes back of the counter*.]

DOLLY [*at phone*]:
Hush! Mr. Dubinsky! This is Dolly Hamma, Mr. "Dog" Hamma's wife!
   [CAROL *quietly enters the front door*.]
I want to ask you, is Carol Cutrere in your drugstore?

BEULAH [*warningly*]:
Dolly!

CAROL:
No. She isn't.

DOLLY:
—What?

CAROL:
She's here.
   [BEULAH *goes into confectionery*. CAROL *moves toward* VAL *to D.R.C.*]

DOLLY:
—Aw!—Never mind, Mr. Dubinsky, I—

69

[Hangs up furiously and crosses to door.]

[A silence in which they all stare at the girl from various positions about the store. She has been on the road all night in an open car: her hair is blown wild, her face flushed and eyes bright with fever. Her manner in the scene is that of a wild animal at bay, desperate but fearless.]

LADY [*finally and quietly*]:
Hello, Carol.

CAROL:
Hello, Lady.

LADY [*defiantly cordial*]:
I thought that you were in New Orleans, Carol.

CAROL:
Yes, I was. Last night.

LADY:
Well, you got back fast.

CAROL:
I drove all night.

LADY:
In that storm?

CAROL:
The wind took the top off my car but I didn't stop.
[She watches VAL steadily; he steadily ignores her; turns away and puts bottles of Coca-Cola on a table.]

LADY [*with growing impatience*]:
Is something wrong at home, is someone sick?

CAROL [*absently*]:
No. No, not that I know of, I wouldn't know if there was, they—may I sit down?

LADY:
Why, sure.

CAROL [*crossing to chair at counter and sitting*]:
—They pay me to stay away so I wouldn't know. . . .
[*Silence.* VAL *walks deliberately past her and goes into alcove.*]
—I think I have a fever, I feel like I'm catching pneumonia, everything's so far away. . . .
[*Silence again except for the faint, hissing whispers of* BEULAH *and* DOLLY *at the back of the store.*]

LADY [*with a touch of exasperation*]:
Is there something you want?

CAROL:
Everything seems miles away. . . .

LADY:
Carol, I said is there anything you want here?

CAROL:
Excuse me!—yes. . . .

LADY:
Yes, what?

CAROL:
Don't bother now. I'll wait.
[VAL *comes out of alcove with the blue jacket on.*]

LADY:
Wait for what, what are you waiting for? You don't have to wait for nothing, just say what you want and if I got it in stock I'll give it to you!
[*Phone rings once.*]

CAROL [*vaguely*]:
—Thank you,—no. . . .

LADY [*to* VAL]:
Get that phone, Val.
[DOLLY *crosses and hisses something inaudible to* BEULAH.]

BEULAH [*rising*]:
I just want to wait here to see if she does or she don't.

DOLLY:
She just said she would!

BEULAH:
Just the same, I'm gonna wait!!

VAL [at phone]:
Yes, sir, she is.—I'll tell her
　　[Hangs up and speaks to LADY:]
Her brother's heard she's here and he's coming to pick her up.

LADY:
David Cutrere is not coming in this store!

DOLLY:
Aw-aw!

BEULAH:
David Cutrere used to be her lover.

DOLLY:
I remember you told me.

LADY [wheels about suddenly toward the women]:
Beulah! Dolly! Why're you back there hissing together like geese?
　　[Coming from behind counter to R.C.]
Why don't you go to th'—Blue Bird and—have some hot coffee—talk there!

BEULAH:
It looks like we're getting what they call the bum's rush.

DOLLY:
I never stay where I'm not wanted and when I'm not wanted somewhere I never come back!
　　[They cross out and slam door.]

LADY [after a pause]:
What did you come here for?

CAROL:
To deliver a message.

LADY:
To me?

CAROL:
No.

LADY:
Then who?
[CAROL *stares at* LADY *gravely a moment, then turns slowly to look at* VAL.]
—Him?—Him?
[CAROL *nods slowly and slightly.*]
OK, then, give him the message, deliver the message to him.

CAROL:
It's a private message. Could I speak to him alone, please?
[LADY *gets a shawl from a hook.*]

LADY:
Oh, for God's sake! Your brother's plantation is ten minutes from here in that sky-blue Cadillac his rich wife give him. Now look, he's on his way here but I won't let him come in, I don't even want his hand to touch the doorhandle. I know your message, this boy knows your message, there's nothing private about it. But I tell you, that this boy's not for sale in my store!—Now—I'm going out to watch for the sky-blue Cadillac on the highway. When I see it, I'm going to throw this door open and holler and when I holler, I want you out of this door like a shot from a pistol!—that fast! Understand?
[NOTE: *Above scene is overextended. This can be remedied by a very lively performance. It might also help to indicate a division between the Lady-Val scene and the group scene that follows.*]
[LADY *slams door behind her. The loud noise of the door-slam increases the silence that follows.* VAL's *oblivious attitude is not exactly hostile, but deliberate. There's a kind of purity in it; also a kind of refusal to concern himself with a problem that isn't his own. He holds his guitar with a specially tender concentration, and strikes a soft chord on it. The girl stares at* VAL; *he whistles a note and tightens a guitar string to the pitch of the whistle, not looking at the girl.*]

*Since this scene is followed by the emotional scene
between* LADY *and* DAVID, *it should be keyed somewhat lower than written; it's important that* VAL
should not seem brutal in his attitude toward CAROL;
*there should be an air between them of two lonely
children.*]

VAL [*in a soft preoccupied tone*]:
You told the lady I work for that you had a message for
me. Is that right, Miss? Have you got a message for me?

CAROL [*she rises, moves a few steps toward him, hesitantly.*
VAL *whistles, plucks guitar string, changes pitch*]:
You've spilt some ashes on your new blue suit.

VAL:
Is that the message?

CAROL [*moves away a step*]:
No. No, that was just an excuse to touch you. The message is—

VAL:
What?
      [*Music fades in—guitar.*]

CAROL:
—I'd love to hold something the way you hold your guitar,
that's how I'd love to hold something, with such—*tender
protection!* I'd love to hold *you* that way, with that same
—*tender protection!*
      [*Her hand has fallen onto his knee, which he has
      drawn up to rest a foot on the counter stool.*]
—*Because you hang the moon for me!*

VAL [*he speaks to her, not roughly but in a tone that holds
a long history that began with a romantic acceptance of
such declarations as she has just made to him, and that
turned gradually to his present distrust. He puts guitar
down and goes to her*]:
Who're you tryin' t' fool besides you'self? You couldn't
stand the weight of a man's body on you.
      [*He casually picks up her wrist and pushes the sleeve
      back from it.*]

74

What's this here? A human wrist with a bone? It feels like a twig I could snap with two fingers. . . .

[Gently, negligently, pushes collar of her trench coat back from her bare throat and shoulders. Runs a finger along her neck tracing a vein.]

Little girl, you're transparent, I can see the veins in you. A man's weight on you would break you like a bundle of sticks. . . .

[Music fades out.]

CAROL [gazes at him, startled by his perception]:
Isn't it funny! You've hit on the truth about me. The act of love-making is almost unbearably painful, and yet of course, I do bear it, because to be not alone, even for a few moments, is worth the pain and the danger. It's dangerous for me because I'm not built for childbearing.

VAL:
Well, then, fly away, little bird, fly away before you—get broke.

[He turns back to his guitar.]

CAROL:
Why do you dislike me?

VAL [turning back]:
I never dislike nobody till they interfere with me.

CAROL:
How have I interfered with you? Did I snitch when I saw my cousin's watch on you?

VAL [beginning to remove his watch]:
—You won't take my word for a true thing I told you. I'm thirty years old and I'm done with the crowd you run with and the places you run to. The Club Rendezvous, the Starlite Lounge, the Music Bar, and all the night places. Here—

[Offers watch.]

—take this Rolex Chronometer that tells the time of the day and the day of the week and the month and all the crazy moon's phases. I never stole nothing before. When I stole that I known it was time for me to get off the party, so take it back, now, to Bertie. . . .

75

*[He takes her hand and tries to force the watch into
her fist. There is a little struggle, he can't open her
fist. She is crying, but staring fiercely into his eyes.
He draws a hissing breath and hurls watch violently
across the floor.]*

—That's my message to you and the pack you run with!

CAROL *[flinging coat away]*:
I RUN WITH NOBODY!—I hoped I could run with
you. . . .

[Music stops short.]

You're in danger here, Snakeskin. You've taken off the
jacket that said: "I'm wild, I'm alone!" and put on the
nice blue uniform of a convict! . . . Last night I woke up
thinking about you again. I drove all night to bring you
this warning of danger. . . .

[Her trembling hand covers her lips.]

—The message I came here to give you was a warning
of danger! I hoped you'd hear me and let me take you
away before it's—too late.

[Door bursts open. LADY rushes inside, crying out:]

LADY:
Your brother's coming, go out! He can't come in!

*[CAROL picks up coat and goes into confectionery,
sobbing. VAL crosses toward door.]*

Lock that door! Don't let him come in my store!

*[CAROL sinks sobbing at table. LADY runs up to the
landing of the stairs as DAVID CUTRERE enters the
store. He is a tall man in hunter's clothes. He is
hardly less handsome now than he was in his youth
but something has gone: his power is that of a cap-
tive who rules over other captives. His face, his eyes,
have something of the same desperate, unnatural
hardness that LADY meets the world with.]*

DAVID:
Carol?

VAL:
She's in there.

*[He nods toward the dim confectionery into which
the girl has retreated.]*

DAVID [crossing]:
Carol!
> [She rises and advances a few steps into the lighted area of the stage.]

You broke the agreement.
> [CAROL nods slightly, staring at VAL.]

[Harshly:] All right. I'll drive you back. Where's your coat?
> [CAROL murmurs something inaudible, staring at VAL.]

Where is her coat, where is my sister's coat?
> [VAL crosses below and picks up the coat that CAROL has dropped on the floor and hands it to DAVID. He throws it roughly about CAROL's shoulders and propels her forcefully toward the store entrance. VAL moves away to D.R.]

LADY [suddenly and sharply]:
Wait, please!
> [DAVID looks up at the landing; stands frozen as LADY rushes down the stairs.]

DAVID [softly, hoarsely]:
How—are you, Lady?

LADY [turning to VAL]:
Val, go out.

DAVID [to CAROL]:
Carol, will you wait for me in my car?
> [He opens the door for his sister; she glances back at VAL with desolation in her eyes. VAL crosses quickly though the confectionery. Sound of door closing in there. CAROL nods slightly as if in sad response to some painful question and goes out of the store. Pause.]

LADY:
I told you once never to come in this store.

DAVID:
I came for my sister. . . .
> [He turns as if to go.]

LADY:
No, wait!

DAVID:
I don't dare leave my sister alone on the road.

LADY:
I have something to tell you I never told you before.
    [*She crosses to him.* DAVID *turns back to her, then
    moves away to D.R.C.*]
—I—carried your child in my body the summer you
quit me.
    [*Silence.*]

DAVID:
—I—didn't know.

LADY:
No, no, I didn't write you no letter about it; I was proud
then; I had pride. But I had your child in my body the
summer you quit me, that summer they burned my father
in his wine garden, and you, you washed your hands
clean of any connection with a Dago bootlegger's daughter
and—
    [*Her breathless voice momentarily falters and she
    makes a fierce gesture as she struggles to speak.*]
—took that—society girl that—restored your homeplace
and give you such—
    [*Catches breath.*]
—wellborn children. . . .

DAVID:
—I—didn't know.

LADY:
Well, now you do know, you know now. I carried your
child in my body the summer you quit me but I had it cut
out of my body, and they cut my heart out with it!

DAVID:
—I—didn't know.

LADY:
I wanted death after that, but death don't come when you
want it, it comes when you don't want it! I wanted death,
then, but I took the next best thing. *You* sold *yourself*. I

sold *my* self. *You* was bought. *I* was bought. You made whores of us both!

DAVID:
—I—didn't know. . . .
　　[*Mandolin, barely audible,* "Dicitincello Vuoi."]

LADY:
But that's all a long time ago. Some reason I drove by there a few nights ago; the shore of the lake where my father had his wine garden? You remember? You remember the wine garden of my father?
　　[DAVID *stares at her. She turns away.*]
No, you don't? You don't remember it even?

DAVID:
—Lady, I don't—remember—anything else. . . .

LADY:
The mandolin of my father, the songs that I sang with my father in my father's wine garden?

DAVID:
Yes, I don't remember anything else. . . .

LADY:
Core Ingrata! Come Le Rose! And we disappeared and he would call, "*Lady? Lady?*"
　　[*Turns to him.*]
How could I answer him with two tongues in my mouth!
　　[*A sharp hissing intake of breath, eyes opened wide, hand clapped over her mouth as if what she said was unendurable to her. He turns instantly, sharply away.*]
　　[*Music stops short.* JABE *begins to knock for her on the floor above. She crosses to stairs, stops, turns.*]
I hold hard feelings!—Don't ever come here again. If your wild sister comes here, send somebody else for her, not you, not you. Because I hope never to feel this knife again in me.
　　[*Her hand is on her chest; she breathes with difficulty.*]
　　[*He turns away from her; starts toward the door. She takes a step toward him.*]

79

And don't pity me neither. I haven't gone down so terribly far in the world. I got a going concern in this mercantile store, in there's the confectionery which'll reopen this spring, it's being done over to make it the place that all the young people will come to, it's going to be like—

[*He touches the door, pauses with his back to her.*]

—the wine garden of my father, those wine-drinking nights when you had something better than anything you've had since!

DAVID:
Lady—*That's*—

LADY:
—*What?*

DAVID:
—*True!*
[*Opens door.*]

LADY:
Go now. I just wanted to tell you my life ain't over.
[*He goes out as* JABE *continues knocking. She stands, stunned, motionless till* VAL *quietly re-enters the store. She becomes aware of his return rather slowly; then she murmurs:*]
I made a fool of myself. . . .

VAL:
What?
[*She crosses to stairs.*]

LADY:
I made a fool of myself!
[*She goes up the stairs with effort as the lights change slowly to mark a division of scenes.*]

Sunset of that day. VAL *is alone in the store, as if preparing to go. The sunset is fiery. A large woman opens the door and stands there looking dazed. It is* VEE TALBOTT.

VAL [*turning*]:
Hello, Mrs. Talbott.

VEE:
Something's gone wrong with my eyes. I can't see nothing.

VAL [*going to her*]:
Here, let me help you. You probably drove up here with that setting sun in your face.
[*Leading her to shoe-fitting chair at R. window.*]
There now. Set down right here.

VEE:
Thank you—so—much. . . .

VAL:
I haven't seen you since that night you brought me here to ask for this job. '

VEE:
Has the minister called on you yet? Reverend Tooker? I made him promise he would. I told him you were new around here and weren't affiliated to any church yet. I want you to go to ours.

VAL:
—That's—mighty kind of you.

VEE:
The Church of the Resurrection, it's Episcopal.

VAL:
Uh, huh.

VEE:
Unwrap that picture, please.

VAL:
Sure.
[*He tears paper off canvas.*]

VEE:
It's the Church of the Resurrection. I give it a sort of imaginative treatment. You know, Jabe and Lady have never darkened a church door. I thought it ought to be hung where Jabe could look at it, it might help to bring that poor dying man to Jesus. . . .
[*VAL places it against chair R. of counter and crouches before the canvas, studying it long and seriously. VEE coughs nervously, gets up, bends to look at the canvas, sits uncertainly back down. VAL smiles at her warmly, then back to the canvas.*]

VAL [*at last*]:
What's this here in the picture?

VEE:
The steeple.

VAL:
Aw—Is the church steeple red?

VEE:
Why—no, but—

VAL:
Why'd you paint it red, then?

VEE:
Oh, well, you see, I—
[*Laughs nervously, childlike in her growing excitement.*]
—I just, just *felt* it that way! I paint a thing how I feel it instead of always the way it actually is. Appearances are misleading, nothing is what it looks like to the eyes. You got to have—*vision—to see!*

VAL:
—Yes. Vision. Vision!—to see. . . .

82

[*Rises, nodding gravely, emphatically.*]

VEE:
I paint from vision. They call me a visionary.

VAL:
Oh.

VEE [*with shy pride*]:
That's what the New Orleans and Memphis newspaper people admire so much in my work. They call it a primitive style, the work of a visionary. One of my pictures is hung on the exhibition in Audubon Park and they have asked for others. I can't turn them out fast enough!—I have to wait for—visions, no, I—I can't paint without—visions . . . I couldn't *live* without visions!

VAL:
Have you always had visions?

VEE:
No, just since I was born, I—
    [*Stops short, started by the absurdity of her answer. Both laughs suddenly, then she rushes on, her great bosom heaving with curious excitement, twisting in her chair, gesturing with clenched hands.*]
I was born, I was born with a caul! A sort of thing like a veil, a thin, thin sort of a web was over my eyes. They call that a caul. It's a sign that you're going to have visions, and I did, I had them!
    [*Pauses for breath; light fades.*]
—When I was little my baby sister died. Just one day old, she died. They had to baptize her at midnight to save her soul.

VAL:
Uh-huh.
    [*He sits opposite her, smiling, attentive.*]

VEE:
The minister came at midnight, and after the baptism service, he handed the bowl of holy water to me and told me, "Be sure to empty this out on the ground"—I didn't. I was scared to go out at midnight, with, with—death! in

83

the—house and—I sneaked into the kitchen; I emptied
the holy water into the kitchen sink—thunder struck!—
the kitchen sink turned black, the kitchen sink turned
absolutely black!

[SHERIFF TALBOTT *enters the front door*.]

TALBOTT:
Mama! What're you doin'?

VEE:
Talkin'.

TALBOTT:
I'm gonna see Jabe a minute, you go out and wait in
th' car.

[*He goes up. She rises slowly, picks up canvas and
moves to counter*.]

VEE:
—Oh, I—tell you!—since I got into this painting, my
whole outlook is different. I can't explain how it is, the
difference to me.

VAL:
You don't have to explain. I know what you mean. Before
you started to paint, it didn't make sense.

VEE:
—What—what didn't?

VAL:
Existence!

VEE [*slowly and softly*]:
No—no, it didn't . . . existence didn't make sense. . . .

[*She places canvas on guitar on counter and sits in
chair*.]

VAL [*rising and crossing to her*]:
You lived in Two River County, the wife of the county
Sheriff. You saw awful things take place.

VEE:
Awful! Things!

84

VAL:
Beatings!

VEE:
Yes!

VAL:
Lynchings!

VEE:
Yes!

VAL:
Runaway convicts torn to pieces by hounds!
     [*This is the first time she could express this horror.*]

VEE:
Chain-gang dogs!

VAL:
Yeah?

VEE:
Tear fugitives!

VAL:
Yeah?

VEE:
—to *pieces.* . . .
     [*She had half risen: now sinks back faintly.* VAL *looks
     beyond her in the dim store, his light eyes have a
     dark gaze. It may be that his speech is too articulate:
     counteract this effect by groping, hesitations.*]

VAL [*moving away a step*]:
But violence ain't quick always. Sometimes it's slow. Some
tornadoes are slow. Corruption—rots men's hearts and—
rot is slow. . . .

VEE:
—How do you—?

VAL:
Know? I been a witness, I know!

VEE:
I been a witness! *I* know!

VAL:
We seen these things from seats down front at the show.
[*He crouches before her and touches her hands in
her lap. Her breath shudders.*]
And so you begun to paint your visions. Without no plan,
no training, you started to paint as if God touched your
fingers.
[*He lifts her hands slowly, gently from her soft lap.*]
You made some beauty out of this dark country with
these two, soft, woman hands. . . .
[TALBOTT *appears on the stair landing, looks down,
silent.*]
Yeah, you made some beauty!
[*Strangely, gently, he lifts her hands to his mouth.
She gasps.* TALBOTT *calls out:*]

TALBOTT:
Hey!
[VEE *springs up, gasping.*]
[*Descending*] Cut this crap!
[VAL *moves away to R.C*]
[*To* VEE:] Go out. Wait in the car.
[*He stares at* VAL *till* VEE *lumbers out as if dazed.
After a while:*]
Jabe Torrance told me to take a good look at you.
[*Crosses to* VAL].
Well, now, I've taken that look.
[*Nods shortly. Goes out of store. The store is now
very dim. As door closes on* TALBOTT, VAL *picks up
painting; he goes behind counter and places it on a
shelf, then picks up his guitar and sits on counter.
Lights go down to mark a division as he signs and
plays "Heavenly Grass."*]

SCENE THREE

As VAL *finishes the sing,* LADY *descends the stair. He rises and turns on a green-shaded light bulb.*

VAL [*to* LADY]:
You been up there along time.

LADY:
—I gave him morphine. He must be out of his mind. He says such awful things to me. He says I want him to die.

VAL:
You sure you don't?

LADY:
I don't want no one to die. Death's terrible, Val.
  [*Pause. She wanders to the front window R. He takes his guitar and crosses to the door.*]
You gotta go now?

VAL:
I'm late.

LADY:
Late for what? You got a date with somebody?

VAL:
—No. . . .

LADY:
Then stay a while. Play something. I'm all unstrung. . . .
  [*He crosses back and leans against counter; the guitar is barely audible, under the speeches.*]
I made a terrible fool of myself down here today with—

VAL:
—That girl's brother?

LADY:
Yes, I—threw away—pride. . . .

VAL:
His sister said she'd come here to give me a warning. I wonder what of?

LADY [*sitting in shoe-fitting chair*]:
—I said things to him I should of been too proud to say. . . .
[*Both are pursuing their own reflections; guitar continues softly.*]

VAL:
Once or twice lately I've woke up with a fast heart, shouting something, and had to pick up my guitar to calm myself down. . . . Somehow or other I can't get used to this place, I don't feel safe in this place, but I—want to stay. . . .
[*Stops short; sound of wild baying.*]

LADY:
The chain-gang dogs are chasing some runaway convict. . . .

VAL:
Run boy! Run fast, brother! If they catch you, you never will run again! That's—
[*He has thrust his guitar under his arm on this line and crossed to the door.*]
—for sure. . . .
[*The baying of the dogs changes, becomes almost a single savage note.*]
—Uh-huh—the dogs've got him. . . .
[*Pause.*]
They're tearing him to pieces!
[*Pause. Baying continues. A shot is fired. The baying dies out. He stops with his hand on the door; glances back at her; nods; draws the door open. The wind sings loud in the dusk.*]

LADY:
Wait!

VAL:
—Huh?

88

LADY:
—Where do you stay?

VAL:
—When?

LADY:
Nights.

VAL:
I stay at the Wildwood cabins on the highway.

LADY:
You like it there?

VAL:
Uh-huh.

LADY:
—Why?

VAL:
I got a comfortable bed, a two-burner stove, a shower and icebox there.

LADY:
You want to save money?

VAL:
I never could in my life.

LADY:
You could if you stayed on the place.

VAL:
What place?

LADY:
This place.

VAL:
Whereabouts on this place?

LADY [*pointing to alcove*]:
Back of that curtain.

VAL:
—Where they try on clothes?

LADY:
There's a cot there. A nurse slept on it when Jabe had his first operation, and there's a washroom down here and I'll get a plumber to put in a hot an' cold shower! I'll— fix it up nice for you. . . .
[*She rises, crosses to foot of stairs. Pause. He lets the door shut, staring at her.*]

VAL [*moving D.C.*]:
—I—don't like to be—obligated.

LADY:
There wouldn't be no obligation, you'd do me a favor. I'd feel safer at night with somebody on the place. I would; it would cost you nothing! And you could save up that money you spend on the cabin. How much? Ten a week? Why, two or three months from now you'd—save enough money to—
[*Makes a wide gesture with a short laugh as if startled.*]
Go on! Take a look at it! See if it don't suit you!— All right. . . .
[*But he doesn't move; he appears reflective.*]

LADY [*shivering, hugging herself*]:
Where does heat go in this building?

VAL [*reflectively*]:
—Heat rises. . . .

LADY:
You with your dog's temperature, don't feel cold, do you? I do! I turn blue with it!

VAL:
—Yeah. . . .
[*The wait is unendurable to* LADY.]

LADY:
Well, aren't you going to look at it, the room back there, and see if it suits you or not?!

90

VAL:
—I'll go and take a look at it. . . .
[*He crosses to the alcove and disappears behind the curtain. A light goes on behind it, making its bizarre pattern translucent: a gold tree with scarlet fruit and white birds in it, formally designed. Truck roars; lights sweep the frosted window.* LADY *gasps aloud; takes out a pint bottle and a glass from under the counter, setting them down with a crash that makes her utter a startled exclamation: then a startled laugh. She pours a drink and sits in chair R. of counter. The lights turn off behind the alcove curtain and* VAL *comes back out. She sits stiffly without looking at him as he crosses back lazily, goes behind counter, puts guitar down. His manner is gently sad as if he had met with a familiar, expected disappointment. He sits down quietly on edge of counter and takes the pint bottle and pours himself a shot of the liquor with a reflective sigh. Boards creak loudly, contracting with the cold.* LADY'S *voice is harsh and sudden, demanding:*]

LADY:
Well, is it okay or—what!

VAL:
I never been in a position where I could turn down something I got for nothing in my life. I like that picture in there. That's a famous picture, that "September Morn" picture you got on the wall in there. Ha ha! I might have trouble sleeping in a room with that picture. I might keep turning the light on to take another look at it! The way she's cold in that water and sort of crouched over in it, holding her body like that, that—might—ha ha! sort of keep me awake . . .

LADY:
Aw, you with your dog's temperature and your control of all functions, it would take more than a picture to keep you awake!

VAL:
I was just kidding.

LADY:
I was just kidding too.

VAL:
But you know how a single man is. He don't come home every night with just his shadow.
     [*Pause. She takes a drink.*]

LADY:
You bring girls home nights to the Wildwood cabins, do you?

VAL:
I ain't so far. But I would like to feel free to. That old life is what I'm used to. I always worked nights in cities and if you work nights in cities you live in a different city from those that work days.

LADY:
Yes. I know, I—imagine. . . .

VAL:
The ones that work days in cities and the ones that work nights in cities, they live in different cities. The cities have the same name but they are different cities. As different as night and day. There's something wild in the country that only the night people know. . . .

LADY:
Yeah, I know!

VAL:
I'm thirty years old!—but sudden changes don't work, it takes—

LADY:
—Time—yes. . . .
     [*Slight pause which she finds disconcerting. He slides off counter and moves around below it.*]

VAL:
You been good to me, Lady.—Why d'you want me to stay here?

LADY [*defensively*]:
I told you why.

VAL:
For company nights?

LADY:
Yeah, to, to!—*guard the store*, nights!

VAL:
To be a night watchman?

LADY:
Yeah, to be a night *watchman*.

VAL:
You feel nervous alone here?

LADY:
Naturally now!—Jabe sleeps with a pistol next to him but
if somebody broke in the store, he couldn't git up and all
I could do is holler!—Who'd *hear* me? They got a telephone girl on the night shift with—sleepin' sickness, I
think! Anyhow, why're you so suspicious? You look at me
like you thought I was *plottin'*.—Kind people *exist:* Even
me!

[*She sits up rigid in chair, lips and eyes tight closed,
drawing in a loud breath which comes from a tension
both personal and vicarious.*]

VAL:
I understand, Lady, but. . . . Why're you sitting up so stiff
in that chair?

LADY:
Ha!

[*Sharp laugh; she leans back in chair.*]

VAL:
You're still unrelaxed.

LADY:
I know.

93

VAL:
Relax.
> [*Moving around close to her.*]

I'm going to show you some tricks I learned from a lady osteopath that took me in, too.

LADY:
What tricks?

VAL:
How to manipulate joints and bones in a way that makes you feel like a loose piece of string.
> [*Moves behind her chair. She watches him.*]

Do you trust me or don't you?

LADY:
Yeah, I trust you completely, but—

VAL:
Well then, lean forward a little and raise your arms up and turn sideways in the chair.
> [*She follows these instructions.*]

Drop your head.
> [*He manipulates her head and neck.*]

Now the spine, Lady.
> [*He places his knee against the small of her backbone and she utters a sharp, startled laugh as he draws her backbone hard against his kneecap.*]

LADY:
Ha, ha!—That makes a sound like, like, like!—boards contracting with cold in the building, ha, ha!
> [*He relaxes.*]

VAL:
Better?

LADY:
Oh, yes!—much . . . thanks. . . .

VAL [*stroking her neck*]:
Your skin is like silk. You're light skinned to be Italian.

LADY:
Most people in this country think Italian people are dark.
Some are but not all are! Some of them are fair . . . very
fair. . . . My father's people were dark but my mother's
people were fair. Ha ha!

> [*The laughter is senseless. He smiles understandingly
> at her as she chatters to cover confusion. He turns
> away, then goes above and sits on the counter close
> to her.*]

My mother's mother's sister—come here from Monte
Cassino, to die, with relations!—but I think people always
die alone . . . with or without relations. I was a little girl
then and I remember it took her such a long, long time to
die we almost forgot her.—And she was so quiet . . .
in a corner. . . . And I remember asking her one time,
Zia Teresa, how does it feel to die?—Only a little girl
would ask such a question, ha ha! Oh, and I remember
her answer. She said—"It's a lonely feeling."
I think she wished she had stayed in Italy and died in a
place that she knew. . . .

> [*Looks at him directly for the first time since men-
> tioning the alcove.*]

Well, there is a washroom, and I'll get the plumber to put
in a hot and cold shower! Well—

> [*Rises, retreats awkwardly from the chair. His inter-
> est seems to have wandered from her.*]

I'll go up and get some clean linen and make up that
bed in there.

> [*She turns and walks rapidly, almost running, to
> stairs. He appears lost in some private reflection but
> as soon as she has disappeared above the landing, he
> says something under his breath and crosses directly
> to the cashbox. He coughs loudly to cover the sound
> of ringing it open; scoops out a fistful of bills and
> coughs again to cover the sound of slamming drawer
> shut. Picks up his guitar and goes out the front door
> of store. LADY returns downstairs, laden with linen.
> The outer darkness moans through the door left
> open. She crosses to the door and a little outside it,
> peering both ways down the dark road. Then she
> comes in furiously, with an Italian curse, shutting
> the door with her foot or shoulder, and throws the*

95

linen down on counter. She crosses abruptly to cash-box, rings it open and discovers theft. Slams drawer violently shut.]

Thief! Thief!

[*Turns to phone, lifts receiver. Holds it a moment, then slams it back into place. Wanders desolately back to the door, opens it and stands staring out into the starless night as the scene dims out. Music: blues —guitar.*]

Late that night. VAL *enters the store, a little unsteadily, with his guitar; goes to the cashbox and rings it open. He counts some bills off a big wad and returns them to the cashbox and the larger wad to the pocket of his snakeskin jacket. Sudden footsteps above; light spills onto stair landing. He quickly moves away from the cashbox as* LADY *appears on the landing in a white sateen robe; she carries a flashlight.*

LADY:
Who's that?
    [*Music fades out.*]

VAL:
—Me.
    [*She turns the flashlight on his figure.*]

LADY:
Oh, my God, how you scared me!

VAL:
You didn't expect me?

LADY:
How'd I know it was you I heard come in?

VAL:
I thought you give me a room here.

LADY:
You left without letting me know if you took it or not.
    [*She is descending the stairs into store, flashlight still on him.*]

VAL:
Catch me turning down something I get for nothing.

LADY:
Well, you might have said something so I'd expect you or not.

VAL:
I thought you took it for granted.

LADY:
I don't take nothing for granted.
[*He starts back to the alcove.*]
Wait!—I'm coming downstairs. . . .
[*She descends with the flashlight beam on his face.*]

VAL:
You're blinding me with that flashlight.
[*He laughs. She keeps the flashlight on him. He starts back again toward the alcove.*]

LADY:
The bed's not made because I didn't expect you.

VAL:
That's all right.

LADY:
I brought the linen downstairs and you'd cut out.

VAL:
—Yeah, well—
[*She picks up linen on counter.*]
Give me that stuff. I can make up my own rack. Tomorrow you'll have to get yourself a new clerk.
[*Takes it from her and goes again toward alcove.*]
I had a lucky night.
[*Exhibits a wad of bills.*]

LADY:
Hey!
[*He stops near the curtain. She goes and turns on green-shaded bulb over cashbox.*]
—Did you just open this cashbox?

VAL:
—Why you ask that?

LADY:
I thought I heard it ring open a minute ago, that's why I come down here.

VAL:
—In your—white satin—kimona?

LADY:
Did you just open the cashbox?!

VAL:
—I wonder who did if I didn't. . . .

LADY:
Nobody did if you didn't, but somebody did!
[*Opens cashbox and hurriedly counts money. She is
trembling violently.*]

VAL:
How come you didn't lock the cash up in the safe this
evening, Lady?

LADY:
Sometimes I forget to.

VAL:
That's careless.

LADY:
—Why'd you open the cashbox when you come in?

VAL:
I opened it twice this evening, once before I went out and
again when I come back. I borrowed some money and put
it back in the box an' got all this left over!
[*Shows her the wad of bills.*]
I beat a blackjack dealer five times straight. With this
much loot I can retire for the season. . . .
[*He returns money to pocket.*]

LADY:
Chicken-feed!—I'm sorry for you.

VAL:
You're sorry for me?

LADY:
I'm sorry for you because nobody can help you. I was

touched by your—strangeness, your strange talk.—That thing about birds with no feet so they have to sleep on the wind?—I said to myself, "This boy is a bird with no feet so he has to sleep on the wind," and that softened my fool Dago heart and I wanted to help you. . . . Fool, me!— I got what I should of expected. You robbed me while I was upstairs to get sheets to make up your bed!

[*He starts out toward the door.*]

I guess I'm a fool to even feel disappointed.

VAL [*stopping C. and dropping linen on counter*]:
You're disappointed in me. I was disappointed in you.

LADY [*coming from behind counter*]:
—How did I disappoint you?

VAL:
There wasn't no cot behind that curtain before. You put it back there for a purpose.

LADY:
It was back there!—folded behind the mirror.

VAL:
It wasn't back of no mirror when you told me three times to go and—

LADY [*cutting in*]:
I left that money in the cashbox on purpose, to find out if I could trust you.

VAL:
You got back th' . . .

LADY:
No, no, no, I can't trust you, now I know I can't trust you, I got to trust anybody or I don't want him.

VAL:
That's OK, I don't expect no character reference from you.

LADY:
I'll give you a character reference. I'd say this boy's a

100

peculiar talker! But I wouldn't say a real hard worker or honest. I'd say a peculiar slew-footer that sweet talks you while he's got his hand in the cashbox.

VAL:
I took out less than you owed me.

LADY:
Don't mix up the issue. I see through you, mister!

VAL:
I see through you, Lady.

LADY:
What d'you see through me?

VAL:
You sure you want me to tell?

LADY:
I'd love for you to.

VAL:
—A not so young and not so satisfied woman, that hired a man off the highway to do double duty without paying overtime for it. . . . I mean a store clerk days and a stud nights, and—

LADY:
God, no! You—!
    [She raises her hand as if to strike at him.]
Oh, God no . . . you cheap little—
    [Invectives fail her so she uses her fists, hammering at him with them. He seizes her wrists. She struggles a few moments more, then collapses, in chair, sobbing. He lets go of her gently.]

VAL:
It's natural. You felt—lonely. . . .
    [She sobs brokenly against the counter.]

LADY:
Why did you come back here?

101

VAL:
To put back the money I took so you wouldn't remember
me as not honest or grateful—

[*He picks up his guitar and starts to the door nodding gravely. She catches her breath; rushes to intercept him, spreading her arms like a crossbar over
the door.*]

LADY:
NO, NO, DON'T GO . . . I NEED YOU!!!

[*He faces her for five beats. The true passion of her
outcry touches him then, and he turns about and
crosses to the alcove. . . . As he draws the curtain
across it he looks back at her.*]

TO LIVE. . . . TO GO ON LIVING!!!

[*Music fades in—"Lady's Love Song"—guitar. He
closes the curtain and turns on the light behind it,
making it translucent. Through an opening in the
alcove entrance, we see him sitting down with his
guitar.* LADY *picks up the linen and crosses to the
alcove like a spellbound child. Just outside it she
stops, frozen with uncertainty, a conflict of feelings,
but then he begins to whisper the words of a song so
tenderly that she is able to draw the curtain open and
enter the alcove. He looks up gravely at her from his
guitar. She closes the curtain behind her. Its bizarre
design, a gold tree with white birds and scarlet fruit
in it, is softly translucent with the bulb lighted behind
it. The guitar continues softly for a few moments;
stops; the stage darkens till only the curtain of the
alcove is clearly visible.*]

CURTAIN

An early morning. The Saturday before Easter. The sleeping alcove is lighted. VAL is smoking, half dressed, on the edge of the cot. LADY comes running, panting downstairs, her hair loose, in dressing robe and slippers and calls out in a panicky, shrill whisper.

LADY:
Val! Val, he's comin' downstairs!

VAL [*hoarse with sleep*]:
Who's—what?

LADY:
Jabe!

VAL:
Jabe?

LADY:
I swear he is, he's coming downstairs!

VAL:
What of it?

LADY:
Jesus, will you get up and put some clothes on? The damned nurse told him that he could come down in the store to check over the stock! You want him to catch you half dressed on that bed there?

VAL:
Don't he know I sleep here?

LADY:
Nobody knows you sleep here but you and me.
    [*Voices above.*]
Oh, God!—they've started.

103

NURSE:
Don't hurry now. Take one step at a time.

[*Footsteps on stairs, slow, shuffling. The professional, nasal cheer of a nurse's voice.*]

LADY [*panicky*]:
Get your shirt on! Come out!

NURSE:
That's right. One step at a time, one step at a time, lean on my shoulder and take one step at a time.

[*VAL rises, still dazed from sleep. LADY gasps and sweeps the curtain across the alcove just a moment before the descending figures enter the sight-lines on the landing. LADY breathes like an exhausted runner as she backs away from the alcove and assumes a forced smile. JABE and the nurse, MISS PORTER, appear on the landing of the stairs and at the same moment scudding clouds expose the sun. A narrow window on the landing admits a brilliant shaft of light upon the pair. They have a bizarre and awful appearance, the tall man, his rusty black suit hanging on him like an empty sack, his eyes burning malignantly from his yellow face, leaning on a stumpy little woman with bright pink or orange hair, clad all in starched white, with a voice that purrs with the faintly contemptuous cheer and sweetness of those hired to care for the dying.*]

NURSE:
Aw, now, just look at that, that nice bright sun comin' out.

LADY:
Miss Porter? It's—it's cold down here!

JABE:
What's she say?

NURSE:
She says it's cold down here.

LADY:
The—the—the air's not warm enough yet, the air's not heated!

104

NURSE:
He's determined to come right down, Mrs. Torrance.

LADY:
I know but—

NURSE:
Wild horses couldn't hold him a minute longer.

JABE [exhausted]:
—Let's—rest here a minute. . . .

LADY [eagerly]:
Yes! Rest there a minute!

NURSE:
Okay. We'll rest here a minute. . . .
    [They sit down side by side on a bench under the
    artificial palm tree in the shaft of light. JABE glares
    into the light like a fierce dying old beast. There are
    sounds from the alcove. To cover them up, LADY
    keeps making startled, laughing sounds in her throat,
    half laughing, half panting, chafing her hands together
    at the foot of the stairs, and coughing falsely.]

JABE:
Lady, what's wrong? Why are you so excited?

LADY:
It seems like a miracle to me.

JABE:
What seems like a miracle to you?

LADY:
You coming downstairs.

JABE:
You never thought I would come downstairs again?

LADY:
Not this quick! Not as quick as this, Jabe! Did you think
he would pick up as quick as this, Miss Porter?
    [JABE rises.]

NURSE:
Ready?

JABE:
Ready.

NURSE:
He's doing fine, knock wood.

LADY:
Yes, knock wood, knock wood!
[*Drums counter loudly with her knuckles.* VAL *steps silently from behind the alcove curtain as the* NURSE *and* JABE *resume their slow, shuffling descent of the stairs.*]
[*Moving back to D.R.C.*] You got to be careful not to overdo. You don't want another setback. Ain't that right, Miss Porter?

NURSE:
Well, it's my policy to mobilize the patient.

LADY [*to* VAL *in a shrill whisper*]:
Coffee's boiling, take the Goddam coffee pot off the burner!
[*She gives* VAL *a panicky signal to go in the alcove.*]

JABE:
Who're you talking to, Lady?

LADY:
To—to—to Val, the clerk! I told him to—get you a—chair!

JABE:
Who's that?

LADY:
Val, Val, the clerk, you know Val!

JABE:
Not yet. I'm anxious to meet him. Where is he?

LADY:
Right here, right here, here's Val!

[VAL *returns from the alcove.*]

JABE:
He's here bright and early.

LADY:
The early bird catches the worm!

JABE:
That's right. Where is the worm?

LADY [*loudly*]:
Ha ha!

NURSE:
Careful! One step at a time, Mr. Torrance.

LADY:
Saturday before Easter's our biggest sales-day of the year,
I mean second biggest, but sometimes it's even bigger
than Christmas Eve! So I told Val to get here a half
hour early.
    [JABE *misses his step and stumbles to foot of stairs.*
    LADY *screams.* NURSE *rushes down to him.* VAL *ad-*
    vances and raises the man to his feet.]

VAL:
Here. Here.

LADY:
Oh, my God.

NURSE:
Oh, oh!

JABE:
I'm all right.

NURSE:
Are you sure?

LADY:
Are you sure?

JABE:
Let me go!
[*He staggers to lean against counter, panting, glaring, with a malignant smile.*]

LADY:
Oh, my God. Oh, my—God. . . .

JABE:
This is the boy that works here?

LADY:
Yes, this is the clerk I hired to help us out, Jabe.

JABE:
How is he doing?

LADY:
Fine, fine.

JABE:
He's mighty good-looking. Do women give him much trouble?

LADY:
When school lets out the high-school girls are thick as flies in this store!

JABE:
How about older women? Don't he attract older women? The older ones are the buyers, they got the money. They sweat it out of their husbands and throw it away! What's your salary, boy, how much do I pay you?

LADY:
Twenty-two fifty a week.

JABE:
You're getting him cheap.

VAL:
I get—commissions.

JABE:
Commissions?

VAL:
Yes. One percent of all sales.

JABE:
Oh? Oh? I didn't know about that.

LADY:
I knew he would bring in trade and he brings it in.

JABE:
I bet.

LADY:
Val, get Jabe a chair, he ought to sit down.

JABE:
No, I don't want to sit down. I want to take a look at the new confectionery.

LADY:
Oh, yes, yes! Take a look at it! Val, Val, turn on the lights in the confectionery! I want Jabe to see the way I done it over! I'm—real—*proud!*
> [VAL *crosses and switches on light in confectionery. The bulbs in the arches and the juke box light up.*]
Go in and look at it, Jabe. I am real proud of it!
> [*He stares at* LADY *a moment; then shuffles slowly into the spectral radiance of the confectionery.* LADY *moves D.C. At the same time a calliope becomes faintly audible and slowly but steadily builds* MISS PORTER *goes with the patient, holding his elbow.*]

VAL [*returning to* LADY]:
He looks like death.

LADY [MOVING *away from him*]:
Hush!
> [VAL *goes up above counter and stands in the shadows.*]

NURSE:
Well, isn't this artistic.

JABE:
Yeh. Artistic as hell.

NURSE:
I never seen anything like it before.

JABE:
Nobody else did either.

NURSE [*coming back to U.R.C.*]:
Who done these decorations?

LADY [*defiantly*]:
I did them, all by myself!

NURSE:
What do you know. It sure is something artistic.
  [*Calliope is now up loud.*]

JABE [*coming back to D.R.*]:
Is there a circus or carnival in the county?

LADY:
What?

JABE:
That sounds like a circus calliope on the highway.

LADY:
That's no circus calliope. It's advertising the gala opening
of the Torrance Confectionery tonight!

JABE:
Doing what did you say?

LADY:
It's announcing the opening of our confectionery, it's going all over Glorious Hill this morning and all over Sunset
and Lyon this afternoon. Hurry on here so you can see it
go by the store.
  [*She rushes excitedly to open the front door as the
  ragtime music of the calliope approaches.*]

JABE:
I married a live one, Miss Porter. How much does that
damn thing cost me?

LADY:
You'll be surprised how little.
[*She is talking with an hysterical vivacity now.*]
I hired it for a song!

JABE:
How much of a song did you hire it for?

LADY [*closing door*]:
Next to nothing, seven-fifty an hour! And it covers three towns in Two River County!
[*Calliope fades out.*]

JABE [*with a muted ferocity*]:
Miss Porter, I married a live one! Didn't I marry a live one?
[*Switches off lights in confectionery.*]
Her daddy "The Wop" was just as much of a live one till he burned up.
[*LADY gasps as if struck.*]
[*With a slow, ugly grin:*] He had a wine garden on the north shore of Moon Lake. The new confectionery sort of reminds me of it. But he made a mistake, he made a bad mistake, one time, selling liquor to niggers. We burned him out. We burned him out, house and orchard and vines and "The Wop" was burned up trying to fight the fire.
[*He turns.*]
I think I better go up.

LADY:
—Did you say "WE"?

JABE:
—I have a kind of a cramp. . . .

NURSE [*taking his arm*]:
Well, let's go up.

JABE:
—Yes, I better go up. . . .
[*They cross to stairs. Calliope fades in.*]

LADY [*almost shouting as she moves D.C.*]:
Jabe, did you say "WE" did it, did you say "WE" did it?

111

JABE [*at foot of stairs, stops, turns*]:
Yes, I said *"We"* did it. You heard me, Lady.

NURSE:
One step at a time, one step at a time, take it easy.
[*They ascend gradually to the landing and above.
The calliope passes directly before the store and a
clown is seen, or heard, shouting through mega-
phone.*]

CLOWN:
Don't forget tonight, folks, the gala opening of the Torrance Confectionery, free drinks and free favors, don't
forget it, the gala opening of the confectionery.
[*Fade.* JABE *and the* NURSE *disappear above the
landing. Calliope gradually fades. A hoarse cry
above. The* NURSE *runs back downstairs, exclaiming:*]

NURSE:
He's bleeding, he's having a hemm'rhage!
[*Runs to phone.*]
Dr. Buchanan's office!
[*Turns again to* LADY.]
Your husband is having a hemm'rhage!
[*Calliope is loud still.* LADY *appears not to hear. She
speaks to* VAL:]

LADY:
Did you hear what he said? He said "We" did it, "WE"
burned—house—vines—orchard—"The Wop" burned
fighting the fire. . . .
[*The scene dims out; calliope fades out.*]

Sunset of the same day. At rise VAL *is alone. He is standing stock-still down center stage, almost beneath the pro-
scenium, in the tense, frozen attitude of a wild animal
listening to something that warns it of danger, his head
turned as if he were looking off stage left, out over the
house, frowning slightly, attentively. After a moment he
mutters something sharply, and his body relaxes; he takes
out a cigarette and crosses to the store entrance, opens the
door and stands looking out. It has been raining steadily
and will rain again in a while, but right now it is clearing:
the sun breaks through, suddenly, with great brilliance;
and almost at the same instant, at some distance, a woman
cries out a great hoarse cry of terror and exaltation; the
cry is repeated as she comes running nearer.*

VEE TALBOTT *appears through the window as if blind
and demented, stiff, groping gestures, shielding her eyes
with one arm as she feels along the store window for the
entrance, gasping for breath.* VAL *steps aside, taking hold
of her arm to guide her into the store. For a few moments
she learns weakly, blindly panting for breath against the
oval glass of the door, then calls out.*

VEE:
I'm—*struck blind!*

VAL:
You can't see?

VEE:
—No! Nothing. . . .

VAL [*assisting her to stool below counter*]:
Set down here, Mrs. Talbott.

VEE:
—Where?

VAL [*pushing her gently*]:
Here.
    [VEE *sinks moaning onto stool.*]

113

What hurt your eyes, Mrs. Talbott, what happened to your eyes?

VEE [drawing a long, deep breath]:
The vision I waited and prayed for all my life long!

VAL:
You had a vision?

VEE:
I saw the eyes of my Saviour!—They struck me blind.
[Leans forward, clasping her eyes in anguish.]
Ohhhh, they burned out my eyes!

VAL:
Lean back.

VEE:
Eyeballs burn like fire. . . .

VAL [going off R.]:
I'll get you something cold to put on your eyes.

VEE:
I knew a vision was coming, oh, I had many signs!

VAL [in confectionery]:
It must be a terrible shock to have a vision. . . .
[He speaks gravely, gently, scooping chipped ice from the soft-drink cooler and wrapping it in his handkerchief.]

VEE [with the naïveté of a child, as VAL comes back to her]:
I thought I would see my Saviour on the day of His passion, which was yesterday, Good Friday, that's when I expected to see Him. But I was mistaken, I was—disappointed. Yesterday passed and nothing, nothing much happened but—today—
[VAL places handkerchief over her eyes.]
—this afternoon, somehow I pulled myself together and walked outdoors and started to go to pray in the empty church and meditate on the Rising of Christ tomorrow.

114

Along the road as I walked, thinking about the mysteries of Easter, veils!

[*She makes a long shuddering word out of "veils."*]
—seemed to drop off my eyes! Light, oh light! I never have seen such brilliance! It *PRICKED* my eyeballs like *NEEDLES!*

VAL:
—Light?

VEE:
Yes, yes, light. YOU know, you know we live in light and shadow, that's, that's what we *live* in, a world of—*light* and—*shadow.* . . .

VAL:
Yes. In light and shadow.
[*He nods with complete understanding and agreement. They are like two children who have found life's meaning, simply and quietly, along a country road.*]

VEE:
A world of light and shadow is what we live in, and—it's—confusing. . . .
[*A man is peering in at store window.*]

VAL:
Yeah, they—*do* get—*mixed.* . . .

VEE:
Well, and then—
[*Hesitates to recapture her vision.*]
—I heard this clap of thunder! Sky!—Split open!—And there in the split-open sky, I saw, I tell you, I *saw the* TWO HUGE BLAZING EYES OF JESUS CHRIST RISEN!—Not crucified but Risen! I mean Crucified and *then* RISEN!—The blazing eyes of Christ Risen! And then a great—
[*Raises both arms and makes a great sweeping motion to describe an apocalyptic disturbance of the atmosphere.*]
—His hand!—*Invisible!*—I didn't *see* his hand!—But it touched me—*here!*

[*She seizes* VAL'S *hand and presses it to her great heaving bosom.*]

TALBOTT [*appearing R. in confectionery, furiously*]:
VEE!

[*She starts up, throwing the compress from her eyes. Utters a sharp gasp and staggers backward with terror and blasted ecstasy and dismay and belief, all confused in her look.*]

VEE:
You!

TALBOTT:
VEE!

VEE:
You!

TALBOTT [*advancing*]:
VEE!

VEE [*making two syllables of the word "eyes"*]:
The Ey—es!
[*She collapsed forward, falls to her knees, her arms thrown about* VAL. *He seizes her to lift her. Two or three men are peering in at the store window.*]

TALBOTT [*pushing* VAL *away*]:
Let go of her, don't put your hands on my wife!
[*He seizes her roughly and hauls her to the door.* VAL *moves up to help* VEE.]
Don't move.
[*At door, to* VAL:]
I'm coming back.

VAL:
I'm not goin' nowhere.

TALBOTT [*to* DOG, *as he goes off L. with* VEE]:
Dog, go in there with that boy.

VOICE [*outside*]:
Sheriff caught him messin' with his wife.

116

aphs of musicians dead and living.
Men read aloud the names printed on the guitar: essie Smith, Leadbelly, Woody Guthrie, Jelly Roll Morton, etc. They bend close to it, keeping the open nife blades pointed at VAL's body; DOG touches neck f guitar, draws it toward him. VAL suddenly springs with catlike agility, onto the counter. He runs along t, kicking at their hands as they catch at his legs. The NURSE runs down to the landing.]

PORTER:
's going on?

OTT [at the same time]:
that!
[JABE calls hoarsely above.]

PORTER [excitedly, all in one breath, as JABE calls]:
re's Mrs. Torrance? I got a very sick man up there his wife's disappeared.
[JABE calls out again.]
en on a whole lot of cases but never seen one where a showed no concern for a—
[JABE cries out again. Her voice fades out as she returns above.]

BOTT [overlapping NURSE's speech]:
! Pee Wee! You all stand back from that counter. , why don't you an' Pee Wee go up an' see Jabe. ve me straighten this boy out, go on, go on up.

WEE:
on, Dawg. . . .
[They go up. VAL remains panting on counter.]

BOTT [sits in shoe chair at R. window. In TALBOTT'S nner there is a curious, half-abashed gentleness, when ne with the boy, as if he recognized the purity in him I was, truly, for the moment, ashamed of the sadism licit in the occurrence]:

[Repeat: ANOTHER VOICE at a distance. "DOG" HAMMA enters and stands silently beside the door while there is a continued murmur of excited voices on the street. The following scene should be underplayed, played almost casually, like the performance of some familiar ritual.]

VAL:
What do you want?

[DOG says nothing but removes from his pocket and opens a spring-blade knife and moves to D.R. PEE WEE enters. Through the open door—voices.]

VOICES [outside]:
—Son of a low-down bitch foolin' with—

—That's right, ought to be—

—Cut the son of a—

VAL:
What do you—?
[PEE WEE closes the door and silently stands beside it, opening a spring-blade knife. VAL looks from one to the other.]
—It's six o'clock. Store's closed.
[Men chuckle like dry leaves rattling, VAL crosses toward the door; is confronted by TALBOTT; stops short.]

TALBOTT:
Boy, I said stay here.

VAL:
I'm not—goin' nowhere. . . .

TALBOTT:
Stand back under that light.

VAL:
Which light?

TALBOTT:
That light.

[*Points.* VAL *goes behind counter.*]
I want to look at you while I run through some photos of men wanted.

VAL:
I'm not wanted.

TALBOTT:
A good-looking boy like you is always wanted.
[*Men chuckle.* VAL *stands in hot light under green-shaded bulb.* TALBOTT *shuffles through photos he has removed from his pocket.*]
—How tall are you, boy?

VAL:
Never measured.

TALBOTT:
How much do you weigh?

VAL:
Never weighed.

TALBOTT:
Got any scars or marks of identification on your face or body?

VAL:
No, sir.

TALBOTT:
Open your shirt.

VAL:
What for?
[*He doesn't.*]

TALBOTT:
Opens his shirt for him, Dog.
[DOG *steps quickly forward and rips shirt open to waist.* VAL *starts forward; men point knives; he draws back.*]
That's right, stay there, boy. What did you do before?
[PEE WEE *sits on stairs.*]

118

VAL:
Before—what?

TALBOTT:
Before you come here?

VAL:
—Traveled and—played. . . .

TALBOTT:
Played?

DOG [*advancing to C.*]:
What?

PEE WEE:
With wimmen?
[DOG *laughs.*]

VAL:
No. Played guitar—and sang. . . .
[VAL *touches guitar on counter.*]

TALBOTT:
Let me see that guitar.

VAL:
Look at it. But don't touch it. I don't let musicians touch it.
[*Men come close.*]

DOG:
What're you smiling for, boy?

PEE WEE:
He ain't smiling, his mouth's just twitching chicken's foot.
[*They laugh.*]

TALBOTT:
What is all that writing on the guitar?

VAL:
—Names. . . .

119

Awright, boy. Git on down off th' counter, I ain't gonna touch y'r guitar.

[VAL *jumps off counter*.]

But I'm gonna tell you something. They's a certain county I know of which has a big sign at the county line that says, "Nigger, don't let the sun go down on you in this county." That's all it says, it don't threaten nothing, it just says, "Nigger, don't let the sun go down on you in this county!"

[*Chuckles hoarsely. Rises and takes a step toward* VAL.]

Well, son! You ain't a nigger and this is not that county, but, son, I want you to just imagine that you seen a sign that said to you: "Boy, don't let the sun rise on you in this county." I said "rise," not "go down" because it's too close to sunset for you to git packed an' move on before that. But I think if you value that instrument in your hands as much as you seem to, you'll simplify my job by not allowing the sun tomorrow to rise on you in this county. 'S that understood, now, boy?

[VAL *stares at him, expressionless, panting*.]

[*Crossing to door*] I *hope* so. I don't like *violence*.

[*He looks back and nods at* VAL *from the door. Then goes outside in the fiery afterglow of the sunset. Dogs bark in the distance. Music fades in: "Dog Howl Blues"—minor—guitar. Pause in which* VAL *remains motionless, cradling guitar in his arms. Then* VAL's *faraway, troubled look is resolved in a slight, abrupt nod of his head. He sweeps back the alcove curtain and enters the alcove and closes the curtain behind him. Lights dim down to indicate a division of scenes*.]

SCENE THREE

Half an hour later. The lighting is less realistic than in the previous scenes of the play. The interior of the store is so dim that only the vertical lines of the pillars and such selected items as the palm tree on the stair landing and the ghostly paper vineyard of the confectionery are plainly visible. The view through the great front window has virtually become the background of the action: A singing wind sweeps clouds before the moon so that the witchlike country brightens and dims and brightens again. The Marshal's hounds are restless: their baying is heard now and then. A lamp outside the door sometimes catches a figure that moves past with mysterious urgency, calling out softly and raising an arm to beckon, like a shade in the under kingdom.

At rise, or when the stage is lighted again, it is empty but footsteps are descending the stairs as DOLLY *and* BEULAH *rush into the store and call out, in soft shouts:*

DOLLY:
Dawg?

BEULAH:
Pee Wee?

EVA TEMPLE [*appearing on landing and calling down softly in the superior tone of a privileged attendant in a sick-chamber*]:
Please don't shout!—Mr. Binnings and Mr. Hamma [*Names of the two husbands*] are upstairs sitting with Jabe. . . .

> [*She continues her descent. Then* EVA TEMPLE *appears, sobbing, on landing.*]
—Come down carefully, Sister.

SISTER:
Help me, I'm all to pieces. . . .

> [EVA *ignores this request and faces the two women.*]

BEULAH:
Has the bleedin' quit yit?

EVA:
The hemorrhage seems to have stopped. Sister, Sister, pull yourself together, we all have to face these things sometime in life.

DOLLY:
Has he sunk into a coma?

EVA:
No. Cousin Jabe is conscious. Nurse Porter says his pulse is remarkably strong for a man that lost so much blood. Of course he's had a transfusion.

SISTER:
Two of 'em.

EVA [*crossing to* DOLLY]:
Yais, an' they put him on glucose. His strength came back like magic.

BEULAH:
She up there?

EVA:
Who?

BEULAH:
Lady!

EVA:
No! When last reported she had just stepped into the Glorious Hill Beauty Parlor.

BEULAH:
You don't mean it.

EVA:
Ask Sister!

SISTER:
She's planning to go ahead with—!

EVA:
—The gala opening of the confectionery. Switch on the lights in there, Sister.

[SISTER *crosses and switches on lights and moves off*
R. The decorated confectionery is lighted. DOLLY *and*
BEULAH *exclaim in awed voices.*]

—Of course it's not normal behavior; it's downright
lunacy, but still that's no excuse for it! And when she
called up at five, about one hour ago, it wasn't to ask
about Jabe, oh, no, she didn't mention his name. She
asked if Ruby Lightfoot had delivered a case of Seagram's.
Yais, she just shouted that question and hung up the
phone, before I could—
    [*She crosses and goes off R.*]

BEULAH [*going into confectionery*]:
Oh, I understand, now! Now I see what she's up to!
Electric moon, cut-out silver-paper stars and artificial
vines? Why, it's her father's wine garden on Moon Lake
she's turned this room into!

DOLLY [*suddenly as she sits in shoe chair*]:
Here she comes, here she comes!
    [*The* TEMPLE SISTERS *retreat from view in confec-*
    tionery as LADY *enters the store. She wears a hooded*
    rain-cape and carries a large paper shopping bag and
    paper carton box.]

LADY:
Go on, ladies, don't stop, my ears are burning!

BEULAH [*coming in to U.R.C.*]:
—Lady, oh, Lady, Lady. . . .

LADY:
Why d'you speak my name in that pitiful voice? Hanh?
    [*Throws back hood of cape, her eyes blazing, and*
    places bag and box on counter.]
Val? Val! Where is that boy that works here?
    [DOLLY *shakes her head.*]
I guess he's havin' a T-bone steak with French fries and
coleslaw fo' ninety-five cents at the Blue Bird. . . .
    [*Sounds in confectionery.*]
Who's in the confectionery, is that you, Val?
    [TEMPLE SISTERS *emerge and stalk past her.*]
Going, girls?
    [*They go out of store.*]

Yes, gone!
[*She laughs and throws off rain-cape, onto counter, revealing a low-cut gown, triple strand of pearls and a purple satin-ribboned corsage.*]

BEULAH [*sadly*]:
How long have I known you, Lady?

LADY [*going behind counter, unpacks paper hats and whistles*]:
A long time, Beulah. I think you remember when my people come here on a banana boat from Palermo, Sicily, by way of Caracas, Venezuela, yes, with a grind-organ and a monkey my papa had bought in Venezuela. I was not much bigger than the monkey, ha ha! You remember the monkey? The man that sold Papa the monkey said it was a very young monkey, but he was a liar, it was a very old monkey, it was on its last legs, ha ha ha! But it was a well-dressed monkey.
[*Coming around to R. of counter.*]
It had a green velvet suit and a little red cap that it tipped and a tambourine that it passed around for money, ha ha ha. . . . The grind-organ played and the monkey danced in the sun, ha ha!—"*O Sole Mio, Da Da Da daaa . . . !*"
[*Sits in chair at counter.*]
—One day, the monkey danced too much in the sun and it was a very old monkey and it dropped dead. . . . My Papa, he turned to the people, he made them a bow and he said, "The show is over, the monkey is dead." Ha ha!
[*Slight pause. Then* DOLLY *pipes up venomously:*]

DOLLY:
Ain't it wonderful Lady can be so brave?

BEULAH:
Yaiss, wonderful! Hanh. . . .

LADY:
For me the show is not over, the monkey is not dead yet!
[*Then suddenly:*]
Val, is that you Val?
[*Someone has entered the confectionery door, out of sight, and the draught of air has set the wind-chimes tinkling wildly.* LADY *rushes forward but stops short*

as CAROL *appears. She wears a trench coat and a white sailor's cap with a turned-down brim, inscribed with the name of a vessel and a date, past or future, memory or anticipation.*]

DOLLY:
Well, here's your first customer, Lady.

LADY [*going behind counter*]:
—Carol, that room ain't open.

CAROL:
There's a big sign outside that says "Open Tonite!"

LADY:
It ain't open to you.

CAROL:
I have to stay here a while. They stopped my car, you see, I don't have a license; my license has been revoked and I have to find someone to drive me across the river.

LADY:
You can call a taxi.

CAROL:
I heard that the boy that works for you is leaving tonight and I—

LADY:
Who said he's leaving?

CAROL [*crossing to counter*]:
Sheriff Talbott. The County Marshal suggested I get him to drive me over the river since he'd be crossing it too.

LADY:
You got some mighty wrong information!

CAROL:
Where is he? I don't see him?

LADY:
Why d'you keep coming back here bothering that boy?

126

He's not interested in you! Why would he be leaving here tonight?

[*Door opens off as she comes from behind counter.*]
Val, is that you, Val?

[CONJURE MAN *enters through confectionery, mumbling rapidly, holding out something.* BEULAH *and* DOLLY *take flight out the door with cries of revulsion.*]

No conjure stuff, go away!

[*He starts to withdraw.*]

CAROL [*crossing to U.R.C.*]:
Uncle! The Choctaw cry! I'll give you a dollar for it.

[LADY *turns away with a gasp, with a gesture of refusal. The* NEGRO *nods, then throws back his turkey neck and utters a series of sharp barking sounds that rise to a sustained cry of great intensity and wildness. The cry produces a violent reaction in the building.* BEULAH *and* DOLLY *run out of the store.* LADY *does not move but she catches her breath.* DOG *and* PEE WEE *run down the stairs with ad libs and hustle the* NEGRO *out of the store, ignoring* LADY, *as their wives call:* "PEE WEE!" *and* "DAWG!" *outside on the walk.* VAL *sweeps back the alcove curtain and appears as if the cry were his cue. Above, in the sick room, hoarse, outraged shouts that subside with exhaustion.* CAROL *crosses downstage and speaks to the audience and to herself:*]

CAROL:
Something is still wild in the country! This country used to be wild, the men and women were wild and there was a wild sort of sweetness in their hearts, for each other, but now it's sick with neon, it's broken out sick, with neon, like most other places. . . . I'll wait outside in my car. It's the fastest thing on wheels in Two River County!

[*She goes out of the store R.* LADY *stares at* VAL *with great asking eyes, a hand to her throat.*]

LADY [*with false boldness*]:
Well, ain't you going with her?

VAL:
I'm going with no one I didn't come here with. And I come here with no one.

127

LADY:
Then get into your white jacket. I need your services in that room there tonight.

[VAL *regards her steadily for several beats*.]

[*Clapping her hands together twice*.] Move, move, stop goofing! The Delta Brilliant lets out in half'n hour and they'll be driving up here. You got to shave ice for the setups!

VAL [*as if he thought she'd gone crazy*]:
"Shave ice for the setups"?

[*He moves up to counter*.]

LADY:
Yes, an' call Ruby Lightfoot, tell her I need me a dozen more half-pints of Seagram's. They all call for Seven-and-Sevens. You know how t' sell bottle goods under a counter? It's OK. We're gonna git paid for protection.

[*Gasps, touching her diaphragm*.]

But one thing you gotta watch out for is sellin' to minors. Don't serve liquor to minors. Ask for his driver's license if they's any doubt. Anybody born earlier than—let's see, twenty-one from—oh, I'll figure it later. Hey! Move! Move! Stop goofing!

VAL [*placing guitar on counter*]:
—You're the one that's goofing, not me, Lady.

LADY:
Move, I said, *move!*

VAL:
What kick are you on, are you on a benny kick, Lady? 'Ve you washed down a couple of bennies with a pot of black coffee t' make you come on strong for th' three o'clock show?

[*His mockery is gentle, almost tender, but he has already made a departure; he is back in the all-night bars with the B-girls and raffish entertainers. He stands at counter as she rushes about. As she crosses between the two rooms, he reaches out to catch hold of her bare arm and he pulls her to him and grips her arms.*]

128

LADY:
Hey!

VAL:
Will you quit thrashin' around like a hooked catfish?

LADY:
Go git in y'r white jacket an'—

VAL:
Sit down. I want to talk to you.

LADY:
I don't have time.

VAL:
I got to reason with you.

LADY:
It's not possible to.

VAL:
You can't open a night-place here this night.

LADY:
You bet your sweet life I'm *going* to!

VAL:
Not *me*, not *my* sweet life!

LADY:
I'm betting *my* life on it! Sweet or *not* sweet, I'm—

VAL:
Yours is yours, mine is mine. . . .
   [*He releases her with a sad shrug.*]

LADY:
You don't get the point, huh? There's a man up there that set fire to my father's wine garden and I lost my life in it, yeah, I lost my life in it, *three* lives was lost in it, two *born* lives and *one*—*not*. . . . I was made to commit a *murder* by him up there!
   [*Has frozen momentarily.*]

129

—I want that man to see the wine garden come open again when he's dying! I want him to hear it coming open again here tonight! While he's dying. It's necessary, no power on earth can stop it. Hell, I don't even want it, it's just necessary, it's just something's got to be done to square things away, to, to, to—be *not defeated! You get me? Just to be not defeated!* Ah, oh, I won't be defeated, not again, in my life!

[*Embraces him.*]

Thank you for staying here with me!—God bless you for it. . . . Now please go and get in your white jacket . . .

[VAL *looks at her as if he were trying to decide between a natural sensibility of heart and what his life's taught him since he left Witches' Bayou. Then he sighs again, with the same slight, sad shrug, and crosses into alcove to put on a jacket and remove from under his cot a canvas-wrapped package of his belongings.* LADY *takes paper hats and carnival stuff from counter, crosses into confectionery and puts them on the table, then starts back but stops short as she sees* VAL *come out of alcove with his snakeskin jacket and luggage.*]

LADY:
That's not your white jacket, that's that snakeskin jacket you had on when you come here.

VAL:
I come and I go in this jacket.

LADY:
Go, did you say?

VAL:
Yes, ma'am, I did, I said go. All that stays to be settled is a little matter of wages.

[*The dreaded thing's happened to her. This is what they call "the moment of truth" in the bull ring, when the matador goes in over the horns of the bull to plant the mortal sword-thrust.*]

LADY:
—So you're—cutting out, are you?

130

VAL:
My gear's all packed. I'm catchin' the southbound bus.

LADY:
Uh-huh, in a pig's eye. You're not conning me, mister.
She's waiting for you outside in her high-powered car and
you're—
> [*Sudden footsteps on stairs. They break apart,* VAL
> *puts suitcase down, drawing back into shadow, as*
> NURSE PORTER *appears on the stair landing.*]

NURSE PORTER:
Miss Torrance, are you down there?

LADY [*crossing to foot of stairs*]:
Yeah. I'm here. I'm back.

NURSE PORTER:
Can I talk to you up here about Mr. Torrance?

LADY [*shouting to* NURSE]:
I'll be up in a minute.
> [*Door closes above.* LADY *turns to* VAL:]
OK, now, mister. You're scared about something, ain't
you?

VAL:
I been threatened with violence if I stay here.

LADY:
I got paid for protection in this county, plenty paid for it,
and it covers you too.

VAL:
No, ma'am. My time is up here.

LADY:
Y' say that like you'd served a sentence in jail.

VAL:
I got in deeper than I meant to, Lady.

LADY:
Yeah, and how about me?

VAL [*going to her*]:
I would of cut out before you got back to the store, but I
wanted to tell you something I never told no one before.
   [*Places hands on her shoulder.*]
I feel a true love for you, Lady!
   [*He kisses her.*]
I'll wait for you out of this county, just name the time
and the . . .

LADY [*moving back*]:
Oh, don't talk about love, not to me. It's easy to say
"Love, Love!" with fast and free transportation waiting
right out the door for you!

VAL:
D'you remember something I told you about me the
night we met here?

LADY [*crossing to R.C.*]:
Yeah, many things. Yeah, temperature of a dog. And
some bird, oh, yeah, without legs so it had to sleep on
the wind!

VAL [*through her speech*]:
Naw, not that; not that.

LADY:
And how you could burn down a woman? I said "Bull!"
I take that back. You can! You can burn down a woman
and stamp on her ashes to make sure the fire is put out!

VAL:
I mean what I said about gettin' away from . . .

LADY:
How long've you held this first steady job in your life?

VAL:
Too long, too long!

LADY:
Four months and five days, mister. All right! How much
pay have you took?

VAL:
I told you to keep out all but—

LADY:
Y'r living expenses. I can give you the figures to a dime. Eighty-five bucks, no, ninety! Chicken-feed, mister! Y'know how much you got coming? IF you get it? I don't need paper to figure, I got it all in my head. You got five hundred and eighty-six bucks coming to you, not, not chicken-feed, that. But, mister.
  [*Gasps for breath.*]
—If you try to walk out on me, now, tonight, without notice!—You're going to get just nothing! A great big zero. . . .
  [*Somebody hollers at door off R.: "Hey! You open?" She rushes toward it shouting, "CLOSED! CLOSED! GO AWAY!"—*VAL *crosses to the cashbox. She turns back toward him, gasps:*]
Now you watch your next move and I'll watch mine. You open that cashbox and I swear I'll throw open that door and holler, clerk's robbing the store!

VAL:
—Lady?

LADY [*fiercely*]:
Hanh?

VAL:
—Nothing, you've—

LADY:
—Hanh?

VAL:
Blown your stack. I will go without pay.

LADY [*coming to C.*]:
Then you ain't understood me! With or without pay, you're staying!

VAL:
I've got my gear.
  [*Picks up suitcase. She rushes to seize his guitar.*]

LADY:
Then I'll go up and git mine! And take this with me, just
t'make sure you wait till I'm—
> [*She moves back to R.C. He puts suitcase down.*]

VAL [*advancing toward her*]:
Lady, what're you—?

LADY [*entreating with guitar raised*]:
Don't—!

VAL:
—Doing with—

LADY:
—*Don't!*

VAL:
—my guitar!

LADY:
Holding it for security while I—

VAL:
Lady, you been a lunatic since this morning!

LADY:
Longer, longer than morning! I'm going to keep hold of
your "life companion" while I pack! I am! I am goin' to
pack an' go, if you go, where you go!
> [*He makes a move toward her. She crosses below
> and around to counter.*]
You didn't think so, you actually didn't think so? What
was I going to do, in your opinion? What, in your opinion,
would I be doing? Stay on here in a store full of bottles
and boxes while you go far, while you go fast and far,
without me having your—forwarding address!—even?

VAL:
I'll—give you a forwarding address. . . .

LADY:
Thanks, oh, thanks! Would I take your forwarding address

back of that curtain? "Oh, dear forwarding address, hold me, kiss me, be faithful!"

> [*Utters grotesque, stifled cry; presses fist to mouth.*]
> [*He advances cautiously, hand stretched toward the guitar. She retreats above to U.R.C., biting lip, eyes flaring.* JABE *knocks above.*]

Stay back! You want me to smash it!

VAL [*D.C.*]:
He's—knocking for you. . . .

LADY:
I know! Death's knocking for me! Don't you think I hear him, knock, knock, knock? It sounds like what it is! Bones knocking bones. . . . Ask me how it felt to be coupled with death up there, and I can tell you. My skin crawled when he touched me. But I endured it. I guess my heart knew that somebody must be coming to take me out of this hell! You did. You came. Now look at me! I'm alive once more!

> [*Convulsive sobbing controlled: continues more calmly and harshly:*]

—*I won't wither in dark!* Got that through your skull? Now. Listen! Everything in this rotten store is yours, not just your pay, but everything Death's scraped together down here!—but Death has got to die before we can go. . . . You got that memorized, now?—Then get into your white jacket!—*Tonight is the gala opening*—

> [*Rushes through confectionery.*]

—*of the confectionery*—

> [VAL *runs and seizes her arm holding guitar. She breaks violently free.*]

Smash me against a rock and I'll smash your guitar! I will, if you—

> [*Rapid footsteps on stairs.*]

Oh, Miss Porter!

> [*She motions* VAL *back. He retreats into alcove.* LADY *puts guitar down beside juke-box.* MISS PORTER *is descending the stairs.*]

NURSE PORTER [*descending watchfully*]:
You been out a long time.

LADY [*moving U.R.C.*]:
Yeah, well, I had lots of—

[*Her voice expires breathlessly. She stares fiercely, blindly, into the other's hard face.*]

NURSE PORTER:
—Of what?

LADY:
Things to—things to—take care of. . . .
    [*Draws a deep, shuddering breath, clenched fist to her bosom.*]

NURSE PORTER:
Didn't I hear you shouting to someone just now?

LADY:
—Uh-huh. Some drunk tourist made a fuss because I wouldn't sell him no—liquor. . . .

NURSE [*crossing to the door*]:
Oh. Mr. Torrance is sleeping under medication.

LADY:
That's good.
    [*She sits in a shoe-fitting chair.*]

NURSE:
I gave him a hypo at five.

LADY:
—Don't all that morphine weaken the heart, Miss Porter?

NURSE:
Gradually, yes.

LADY:
How long does it usually take for them to let go?

NURSE:
It varies according to the age of the patient and the condition his heart's in. Why?

LADY:
Miss Porter, don't people sort of help them let go?

NURSE:
How do you mean, Mrs. Torrance?

LADY:
Shorten their suffering for them?

NURSE:
Oh, I see what you mean.
[*Snaps her purse shut.*]
—I see what you mean, Mrs. Torrance. But killing is
killing, regardless of circumstances.

LADY:
Nobody said killing.

NURSE:
You said "shorten their suffering."

LADY:
Yes, like merciful people shorten an animal's suffering
when he's. . . .

NURSE:
A human being is not the same as an animal, Mrs. Torrance. And I don't hold with what they call—

LADY [*overlapping*]:
Don't give me a sermon, Miss Porter. I just wanted to
know if—

NURSE [*overlapping*]:
I'm not giving a sermon. I just answered your question.
If you want to get somebody to shorten your husband's
life—

LADY [*jumping up; overlapping*]:
Why, how dare you say that I—

NURSE:
I'll be back at ten-thirty.

LADY:
Don't!

NURSE:
What?

LADY [crossing behind counter]:
Don't come back at ten-thirty, don't come back.

NURSE:
I'm always discharged by the doctors on my cases.

LADY:
This time you're being discharged by the patient's wife.

NURSE:
That's something we'll have to discuss with Dr. Buchanan.

LADY:
I'll call him myself about it. I don't like you. I don't think
you belong in the nursing profession, you have cold eyes;
I think you like to watch pain!

NURSE:
I know why you don't like my eyes.
      [Snaps purse shut.]
You don't like my eyes because you know they see clear.

LADY:
Why are you staring at *me*?

NURSE:
I'm not staring at you, I'm staring at the curtain. There's
something burning in there, smoke's coming out.
      [Starts toward alcove.]
Oh.

LADY:
Oh, no, you don't.
      [Seizes her arm.]

NURSE [pushes her roughly aside and crosses to the curtain. VAL rises from cot, opens the curtain and faces her
coolly]:
Oh, excuse me!
      [She turns to LADY.]
—The moment I looked at you when I was called on this

138

case last Friday morning I knew that you were pregnant.
[LADY *gasps.*]
I also knew the moment I looked at your husband it
wasn't by him.
[*She stalks to the door.* LADY *suddenly cries out:*]

LADY:
Thank you for telling me what I hoped for is true.

MISS PORTER:
You don't seem to have any shame.

LADY [*exalted*]:
No. I don't have shame. I have—great—joy!

MISS PORTER [*venomously*]:
Then why don't you get the calliope and the clown to
make the announcement?

LADY:
You do it for me, save me the money! Make the announcement, all over!
[NURSE *goes out.* VAL *crosses swiftly to the door and
locks it. Then he advances toward her, saying:*]

VAL:
Is it true what she said?
[LADY *moves as if stunned to the counter; the stunned
look gradually turns to a look of wonder. On the
counter is a heap of silver and gold paper hats and
trumpets for the gala opening of the confectionery.*]

VAL [*in a hoarse whisper*]:
Is it true or not true, what that woman told you?

LADY:
You sound like a scared little boy.

VAL:
She's gone out to tell.
[*Pause.*]

LADY:
You gotta go now—it's dangerous for you to stay here.

. . . Take your pay out of the cashbox, you can go. Go, go, take the keys to my car, cross the river into some other county. You've done what you came here to do. . . .

VAL:
—It's true then, it's—?

LADY [*sitting in chair of counter*]:
True as God's word! I have life in my body, this dead tree, my body, has burst in flower! You've given me life, you can go!
[*He crouches down gravely opposite her, gently takes hold of her knotted fingers and draws them to his lips, breathing on them as if to warm them. She sits bolt upright, tense, blind as a clairvoyant.*]

VAL:
—Why didn't you tell me before?

LADY:
—When a woman's been childless as long as I've been childless, it's hard to believe that you're still able to bear!
—We used to have a little fig tree between the house and the orchard. It never bore any fruit, they said it was barren. Time went by it, spring after useless spring, and it almost started to—die. . . . Then one day I discovered a small green fig on the tree they said wouldn't bear!
[*She is clasping a gilt paper horn.*]
I ran through the orchard. I ran through the wine garden shouting, "Oh, Father, it's going to bear, the fig tree is going to bear!"—It seemed such a wonderful thing, after those ten barren springs, for the little fig tree to bear, it called for a celebration—I ran to a closet, I opened a box that we kept Christmas ornaments in!—I took them out, glass bells, glass birds, tinsel, icicles, stars. . . . And I hung the little tree with them, I decorated the fig tree with glass bells and glass birds, and silver icicles and stars, because it won the battle and it would bear!
[*Rises, ecstatic.*]
Unpack the box! Unpack the box with the Christmas ornaments in it, put them on me, glass bells and glass birds and stars and tinsel and snow!
[*In a sort of delirium she thrusts the conical gilt*]

*paper hat on her head and runs to the foot of the
stairs with the paper horn. She blows the horn over
and over, grotesquely mounting the stairs, as* VAL
*tries to stop her. She breaks away from him and runs
up to the landing, blowing the paper horn and crying
out:*]

I've won, I've won, Mr. Death, I'm going to bear!

[*Then suddenly she falters, catches her breath in a
shocked gasp and awkwardly retreats to the stairs.
Then turns screaming and runs back down them, her
cries dying out as she arrives at the floor level. She
retreats haltingly as a blind person, a hand stretched
out to* VAL, *as slow, clumping footsteps and hoarse
breathing are hard on the stairs. She moans:*]

—Oh, God, oh—God. . . .

[JABE *appears on the landing, by the artificial palm
tree in its dully lustrous green jardiniere, a stained
purple robe hangs loosely about his wasted yellowed
frame. He is death's self, and malignancy, as he
peers, crouching, down into the store's dimness to
discover his quarry.*]

JABE:
Buzzards! Buzzards!

[*Clutching the trunk of the false palm tree, he raises
the other hand holding a revolver and fires down into
the store.* LADY *screams and rushes to cover* VAL'S
motionless figure with hers. JABE *scrambles down a
few steps and fires again and the bullet strikes her,
expelling her breath in a great "Hah!" He fires again;
the great "Hah!" is repeated. She turns to face him,
still covering* VAL *with her body, her face with all the
passions and secrets of life and death in it now, her
fierce eyes blazing, knowing, defying and accepting.
But the revolver is empty; it clicks impotently and*
JABE *hurls it toward them; he descends and passes
them, shouting out hoarsely:*]

I'll have you burned! I burned her father and I'll have you
burned!

[*He opens the door and rushes out onto the road,
shouting hoarsely:*]

The clerk is robbing the store, he shot my wife, the clerk
is robbing the store, he killed my wife!

VAL:
—Did it—?

LADY:
—Yes!—it did. . . .
[A curious, almost formal, dignity appears in them
both. She turns to him with the sort of smile that
people offer in apology for an awkward speech, and
he looks back at her gravely, raising one hand as if to
stay her. But she shakes her head slightly and points
to the ghostly radiance of her make-believe orchard
and she begin to move a little unsteadily toward it.
Music. LADY enters the confectionery and looks about
it as people look for the last time at a loved place
they are deserting.]
The show is over. The monkey is dead . . .
[Music rises to cover whatever sound Death makes in
the confectionery. It halts abruptly. Figures appear
through the great front window of the store, pocket-
lamps stare through the glass and someone begins to
force the front door open. VAL cries out:]

VAL:
Which way!
[He turns and runs through the dim radiance of the
confectionery, out of our sight. Something slams.
Something cracks open. Men are in the store and the
dark is full of hoarse, shouting voices.]

VOICES OF MEN [shouting]:
—Keep to the walls! He's armed!

—Upstairs, Dog!

—Jack, the confectionery!

[Wild cry back of store.]

Got him. GOT HIM!

—They got him!

—Rope, git rope!

142

—Git rope from th' hardware section!

—I got something better than rope!

—What've you got?

—What's that, what's he got?

—A BLOWTORCH!

—Christ. . . .

[*A momentary hush.*]

—Come on, what in hell are we waiting for?

—Hold on a minute, I wanta see if it works!

—Wait, Wait!

—LOOK here!

[*A jet of blue flame stabs the dark. It flickers on*
CAROL'S *figure in the confectionery. The men cry out
together in hoarse passion crouching toward the fierce
blue jet of fire, their faces lit by it like the faces of
demons.*]

—Christ!

—It works!

[*They rush out. Confused shouting behind. Motors
start. Fade quickly. There is almost silence, a dog
bays in the distance. Then—the* CONJURE MAN
*appears with a bundle of garments which he ex-
amines, dropping them all except the snakeskin jacket, which he holds up with a toothless mumble of
excitement.*]

CAROL [*quietly, gently*]:
What have you got there, Uncle? Come here and let me
see.

143

[*He crosses to her.*]
Oh yes, his snakeskin jacket. I'll give you a gold ring
for it.

> [*She slowly twists ring off her finger. Somewhere
> there is a cry of anguish. She listens attentively till it
> fades out, then nods with understanding.*]

—Wild things leave skins behind them, they leave clean
skins and teeth and white bones behind them, and these
are tokens passed from one to another, so that the fugitive
kind can always follow their kind. . . .

> [*The cry is repeated more terribly than before. It
> expires again. She draws the jacket about her as if
> she were cold, nods to the old* NEGRO, *handing him
> the ring. Then she crosses toward the door, pausing
> halfway as* SHERIFF TALBOTT *enters with his pocket-
> lamp.*]

SHERIFF:
Don't no one move, don't move!

> [*She crosses directly past him as if she no longer saw
> him, and out the door. He shouts furiously:*]

Stay here!

> [*Her laughter rings outside. He follows the girl,
> shouting:*]

Stop! Stop!

> [*Silence. The* NEGRO *looks up with a secret smile as
> the curtain falls slowly.*]

SUDDENLY
LAST SUMMER

To Anne Meacham

Suddenly Last Summer, with *Something Unspoken*, were presented together under the collective title of *Garden District* at the York Theatre on First Avenue in New York on January 7, 1958 by John C. Wilson and Warner Le Roy. It was directed by Herbert Machiz; the stage set was designed by Robert Soule and the costumes by Stanley Simmons. Lighting was by Lee Watson and the incidental music was by Ned Rorem. *Something Unspoken* was published in the latest edition of 27 *Wagons Full of Cotton and Other Plays*.

CAST OF CHARACTERS

MRS. VENABLE	HORTENSE ALDEN
DR. CUKROWICZ	ROBERT LANSING
MISS FOXHILL	DONNA CAMERON
MRS. HOLLY	ELEANOR PHELPS
GEORGE HOLLY	ALAN MIXON
CATHERINE HOLLY	ANNE MEACHAM
SISTER FELICITY	NANON-KIAM

Scene One

*The set may be as un-
realistic as the decor of
a dramatic ballet. It rep-
resents part of a mansion of Victorian Gothic style in
the Garden District of New Orleans on a late afternoon, between late summer and early fall. The interior
is blended with a fantastic garden which is more like
a tropical jungle, or forest, in the prehistoric age of
giant fern-forests when living creatures had flippers
turning to limbs and scales to skin. The colors of this
jungle-garden are violent, especially since it is steaming with heat after rain. There are massive tree-flowers
that suggest organs of a body, torn out, still blistening
with undried blood; there are harsh cries and sibilant
hissings and thrashing sounds in the garden as if it
were inhabited by beasts, serpents and birds, all of
savage nature. . . .*

*The jungle tumult continues a few moments after the
curtain rises; then subsides into relative quiet, which
is occasionally broken by a new outburst.*

*A lady enters with the assistance of a silver-knobbed
cane. She has light orange or pink hair and wears a
lavender lace dress, and over her withered bosom is
pinned a starfish of diamonds.*

She is followed by a young blond Doctor, all in

9

*white, glacially brilliant, very, very good-looking,
and the old lady's manner and eloquence indicate her
undeliberate response to his icy charm.*

MRS. VENABLE:
Yes, this was Sebastian's garden. The Latin names of
the plants were printed on tags attached to them but
the print's fading out. Those ones there—[*She draws
a deep breath*]—are the oldest plants on earth, survi-
vors from the age of the giant fern-forests. Of course
in this semitropical climate—[*She takes another deep
breath*]—some of the rarest plants, such at the Venus
flytrap—you know what this is, Doctor? The Venus
flytrap?

DOCTOR:
An insectivorous plant?

MRS. VENABLE:
Yes, it feeds on insects. It has to be kept under glass
from early fall to late spring and when it went under
glass, my son, Sebastian, had to provide it with fruit
flies flown in at great expense from a Florida lab-
oratory that used fruit flies for experiments in gen-
etics. Well, I can't do that, Doctor. [*She takes a deep
breath.*] I can't, I just can't do it! It's not the expense
but the—

DOCTOR:
Effort.

MRS. VENABLE:
Yes. So goodbye, Venus flytrap!—like so much else . . .
Whew! . . . [*She draws breath.*]—I don't know why,
but—! I already feel I can lean on your shoulder,
Doctor—Cu?—Cu?

DOCTOR:
Cu-kro-wicz. It's a Polish word that mean sugar, so
let's make it simple and call me Doctor Sugar.
[*He returns her smile.*]

MRS. VENABLE:
Well, now, Doctor Sugar, you've seen Sebastian's
garden.
[*They are advancing slowly to the patio area.*]

DOCTOR:
It's like a well-groomed jungle. . . .

MRS. VENABLE:
That's how he meant it to be, nothing was accidental,
everything was planned and designed in Sebastian's
life and his—[*She dabs her forehead with her handkerchief which she had taken from her reticule*]—
work!

DOCTOR:
What was your son's work, Mrs. Venable?—besides
this garden?

MRS. VENABLE:
As many times as I've had to answer that question!
D'you know it still shocks me a little?—to realize that
Sebastian Venable, the poet it still unknown outside
of a small coterie of friends, including his mother.

DOCTOR:
Oh.

MRS. VENABLE:
You see, strictly speaking, his *life* was his occupation.

DOCTOR:
I see.

MRS. VENABLE:

No, you *don't* see, yet, but before I'm through, you will.—Sebastian was a poet! That's what I meant when I said his life was his work because the work of a poet is the life of a poet and—vice versa, the life of a poet is the work of a poet, I mean you can't separate them, I mean—well, for instance, a salesman's work is one thing and his life is another—or can be. The same thing's true of—doctor, lawyer, merchant, *thief*!— But a poet's life is his work and his work is his life in a special sense because—oh, I've already talked myself breathless and dizzy.

[*The Doctor offers his arm.*]

Thank you.

DOCTOR:

Mrs. Venable, did your doctor okay this thing?

MRS. VENABLE [*breathless*]:

What thing?

DOCTOR:

Your meeting this girl that you think is responsible for your son's death?

MRS. VENABLE:

I've waited months to face her because I couldn't get to St. Mary's to face her—I've had her brought here to my house. I won't collapse! She'll collapse! I mean her lies will collapse—not my truth—not the truth. . . . *Forward march, Doctor Sugar!*

[*He conducts her slowly to the patio.*]

Ah, we've *made* it, *ha ha*! I didn't know that I was so weak on my pins! Sit down, Doctor. I'm not afraid of using every last ounce and inch of my little, left-

over strength in doing just what I'm doing. I'm devoting all that's left of my life, Doctor, to the defense
of a dead poet's reputation. Sebastian had no public
name as a poet, he didn't want one, he refused to have
one. He *dreaded, abhorred!*—false values that come
from being publicly known, from fame, from personal
—exploitation. . . . Oh, he'd say to me: "Violet?
Mother?—You're going to outlive me!!"

DOCTOR:
What made him think that?

MRS. VENABLE:
Poets are always clairvoyant!—And he had rheumatic
fever when he was fifteen and it affected a heart-valve
and he wouldn't stay off horses and out of water and
so forth. . . . "Violet? Mother? You're going to live
longer than me, and then, when I'm gone, it will be
yours, in your hands, to do whatever you please
with!"—Meaning, of course, his future recognition!—
That he *did* want, he wanted it after his death when
it couldn't disturb him; then he did want to offer his
work to the world. All right. Have I made my point,
Doctor? Well, here is my son's work, Doctor, here's
his life going *on!*

[*She lifts a thin gilt-edged volume from the patio
table as if elevating the Host before the altar. Its
gold leaf and lettering catch the afternoon sun. It
says* Poem of Summer. *Her face suddenly has a
different look, the look of a visionary, an exalted*
religieuse. *At the same instant a bird sings clearly
and purely in the garden and the old lady seems
to be almost young for a moment.*]

DOCTOR [*reading the title*]:
Poem of Summer?

MRS. VENABLE:
Poem of Summer, and the date of the summer, there
are twenty-five of them, he wrote one poem a year
which he printed himself on an eighteenth-century
hand-press at his—atelier in the—French—Quarter—so
no one but he could see it. . . .
[*She seems dizzy for a moment.*]

DOCTOR:
He wrote one poem a year?

MRS. VENABLE:
One for each summer that we traveled together. The
other nine months of the year were really only a
preparation.

DOCTOR:
Nine months?

MRS. VENABLE:
The length of a pregnancy, yes. . . .

DOCTOR:
The poem was hard to deliver?

MRS. VENABLE:
Yes, even with me. *Without* me, *impossible*, Doctor!
—he wrote no poem last summer.

DOCTOR:
He died last summer?

MRS. VENABLE:
Without me he died last summer, that was his last
summer's poem.

[*She staggers; he assists her toward a chair. She
catches her breath with difficulty.*]

One long-ago summer—now, why am I thinking of this?—my son, Sebastian, said, "Mother?—Listen to this!"—He read me Herman Melville's description of the Encantadas, the Galapagos Islands. Quote—take five and twenty heaps of cinders dumped here and there in an outside city lot. Imagine some of them magnified into mountains, and the vacant lot, the sea. And you'll have a fit idea of the general aspect of the Encantadas, the Enchanted Isles—extinct volcanos, looking much as the world at large might look—after a last conflagration—end quote. He read me that description and said that we had to go there. And so we did go there that summer on a chartered boat, a four-masted schooner, as close as possible to the sort of a boat that Melville must have sailed on. . . . We saw the Encantadas, but on the Encantadas we saw something Melville *hadn't* written about. We saw the great sea-turtles crawl up out of the sea for their annual egg-laying. . . . Once a year the female of the sea-turtle crawls up out of the equatorial sea onto the blazing sand-beach of a volcanic island to dig a pit in the sand and deposit her eggs there. It's a long and dreadful thing, the depositing of the eggs in the sand-pits, and when it's finished the exhausted female turtle crawls back to the sea half-dead. She never sees her offspring, but we did. Sebastian knew exactly when the sea-turtle eggs would be hatched out and we returned in time for it. . . .

DOCTOR:
You went back to the—?

MRS. VENABLE:
Terrible Encantadas, those heaps of extinct volcanos, in time to witness the hatching of the sea-turtles and their desperate flight to the sea!

[*There is a sound of harsh bird-cries in the air. She looks up.*]

—The narrow beach, the color of caviar, was all in motion! But the sky was in motion, too. . . .

DOCTOR:
The sky was in motion, too?

MRS. VENABLE:
—Full of flesh-eating birds and the noise of the birds, the horrible savage cries of the—

DOCTOR:
Carnivorous birds?

MRS. VENABLE:
Over the narrow black beach of the Encantadas as the just hatched sea-turtles scrambled out of the sand-pits and started their race to the sea. . . .

DOCTOR:
Race to the sea?

MRS. VENABLE:
To escape the flesh-eating birds that made the sky almost as black as the beach!
[*She gazes up again: we hear the wild, ravenous, harsh cries of the birds. The sound comes in rhyth-mic waves like a savage chant.*]

And the sand all alive, all alive, as the hatched sea-turtles made their dash for the sea, while the birds hovered and swooped to attack and hovered and— swooped to attack! They were diving down on the hatched sea-turtles, turning them over to expose their soft undersides, tearing the undersides open and rend-

ing and eating their flesh. Sebastian guessed that possibly only a hundredth of one per cent of their
number would escape to the sea. . . .

DOCTOR:
What was it about this that fascinated your son?

MRS. VENABLE:
My son was looking for—[*She stops short with a slight
gasp.*]—Let's just say he was interested in sea-turtles!

DOCTOR:
That isn't what you started to say.

MRS. VENABLE:
I stopped myself just in time.

DOCTOR:
Say what you started to say.

MRS. VENABLE:
I started to say that my son was looking for God
and I stopped myself because I thought you'd think
'Oh, a pretentious young crackpot!'—which Sebastian
was *not*!

DOCTOR:
Mrs. Venable, doctors look for God, too.

MRS. VENABLE:
Oh?

DOCTOR:
I think they have to look harder for him than priests
since they don't have the help of such well-known
guidebooks and well-organized expeditions as the
priests have with their scriptures and—churches. . . .

MRS. VENABLE:
You mean they go on a solitary safari like a poet?.

DOCTOR:
Yes. Some do. I do.

MRS. VENABLE:
I believe, I *believe* you! [*She laughs, startled.*]

DOCTOR:
Let me tell you something—the first operation I per-
formed at Lion's View.—You can imagine how anxious
and nervous I was about the outcome.

MRS. VENABLE:
Yes.

DOCTOR:
The patient was a young girl regarded as hopeless and
put in the Drum—

MRS. VENABLE:
Yes.

DOCTOR:
The name for the violent ward at Lion's View because
it looks like the inside of a drum with very bright
lights burning all day and all night.—So the attendants
can see any change of expression or movement among
the immates in time to grab them if they're about to
attack. After the operation I stayed with the girl, as
if I'd delivered a child that might stop breathing.—
When they finally wheeled her out of surgery, I still
stayed with her. I walked along by the rolling table
holding onto her hand—with my heart in my throat....
[*We hear faint music.*]

—It was a nice afternoon, as fair as this one. And the moment we wheeled her outside, she whispered something, she whispered: "Oh, how blue the sky is!"—And I felt proud, I felt proud and relieved, because up till then her speech, everything that she'd babbled, was a torrent of obscenities!

MRS. VENABLE:

Yes, well, now, I can tell you without any hesitation that my son *was* looking for God, I mean for a clear image of him. He spent that whole blazing equatorial day in the crow's-nest of the schooner watching this thing on the beach till it was too dark to see it, and when he came down the rigging he said "Well, now I've seen Him!," and he meant God.—And for several weeks after that he had a fever, he was delirious with it.—

[*The Encantadas music then fades in again, briefly, at a lower level, a whisper.*]

DOCTOR:

I can see how he *might* be, I think he *would* be disturbed if he thought he'd seen God's image, an equation of God, in that spectacle you watched in the Encantadas: creatures of the air hovering over and swooping down to devour creatures of the sea that had had the bad luck to be hatched on land and weren't able to scramble back into the sea fast enough to escape that massacre you witnessed, yes, I can see how such a spectacle could be equated with a good deal of—*experience, existence!*—but not with *God!* Can *you?*

MRS. VENABLE:

Dr. Sugar, I'm a reasonably loyal member of the Protestant Episcopal Church, but I understood what he meant.

DOCTOR:
Did he mean we must rise above God?

MRS. VENABLE:
He meant that God shows a savage face to people and
shouts some fierce things at them, it's all we see or
hear of Him. Isn't it all we ever really see and hear
of Him, now?—Nobody seems to know why. . . .
[*Music fades out again.*]

Shall I go on from there?

DOCTOR:
Yes, do.

MRS. VENABLE:
Well, next?—India—China—
[*Miss Foxhill appears with the medicine. Mrs.
Venable sees her.*]

MISS FOXHILL:
Mrs. Venable.

MRS. VENABLE:
Oh, God—elixir—of—. [*She takes the glass.*] Isn't it
kind of the drugstore to keep me alive. Where was I,
Doctor?

DOCTOR:
In the Himalayas.

MRS. VENABLE:
Oh yes, that long-ago summer. . . . In the Himalayas
he almost entered a Buddhist monastery, had gone so
far as to shave his head and eat just rice out of a wood
bowl on a grass mat. He'd promised those sly Buddhist
monks that he would give up the world and himself

and all his worldly possessions to their mendicant order.—Well, I cabled his father, "For God's sake notify bank to freeze Sebastian's accounts!"—I got back this cable from my late husband's lawyer: "Mr. Venable critically ill Stop Wants you Stop Needs you Stop Immediate return advised most strongly. Stop. Cable time of arrival. . . ."

DOCTOR:
Did you go back to your husband?

MRS. VENABLE:
I made the hardest decision of my life I stayed with my son. I got him through that crisis too. In less than a month he got up off the filthy grass mat and threw the rice bowl away—and booked us into Shepheard's Hotel in Cairo and the Ritz in Paris—. And from then on, oh, we—still lived in a—world of light and shadow. . . .
[*She turns vaguely with empty glass. He rises and takes it from her.*]

But the shadow was almost as luminous as the light.

DOCTOR:
Don't you want to sit down now?

MRS. VENABLE:
Yes, indeed I do, before I fall down.
[*He assists her into wheelchair.*]

—Are your hind-legs still on you?

DOCTOR [*still concerned over her agitation*]:
—My what? Oh—hind legs!—Yes . . .

MRS. VENEABLE:
Well, then you're not a donkey, you're certainly not

a donkey because I've been talking the hind-legs off a
donkey—several donkeys. . . . But I had to make it
clear to you that the world lost a great deal too when
I lost my son last summer. . . . You would have liked
my son, he would have been charmed by you. My
son, Sebastian, was not a family snob or a money
snob but he was a snob, all right. He was a snob
about personal charm in people, he insisted upon good
looks in people around him, and, oh, he had a perfect
little court of young and beautiful people around him
always, wherever he was, here in New Orleans or
New York or on the Riviera or in Paris and Venice,
he always had a little entourage of the beautiful and
the talented and the young!

DOCTOR:
Your son was young, Mrs. Venable?

MRS. VENABLE:
Both of us were young, and stayed young, Doctor.

DOCTOR:
Could I see a photograph of your son, Mrs. Venable?

MRS. VENABLE:
Yes, indeed you could, Doctor. I'm glad that you asked
to see one. I'm going to show you not one photograph
but two. Here. Here is my son, Sebastian, in a Renaissance pageboy's costume at a masked ball in Cannes.
Here is my son, Sebastian, in the same costume at a
masked ball in Venice. These two pictures were taken
twenty years apart. Now which is the older one,
Doctor?

DOCTOR:
This photograph looks older.

MRS. VENABLE:

The photograph looks older but not the subject. It takes character to refuse to grow old, Doctor—successfully to refuse to. It calls for discipline, abstention. One cocktail before dinner, not two, four, six—a single lean chop and lime juice on a salad in restaurants famed for rich dishes.
   [*Foxhill comes from the house.*]

MISS FOXHILL:

Mrs. Venable, Miss Holly's mother and brother are—
   [*Simultaneously Mrs. Holly and George appear in the window.*]

GEORGE:

Hi, Aunt Vi!

MRS. HOLLY:

Violet dear, we're here.

MISS FOXHILL:

They're here.

MRS. VENABLE:

Wait upstairs in my upstairs living room for me.
   [*To Miss Foxhill:*]

Get them upstairs. I don't want them at that window during this talk.
   [*To the Doctor:*]

Let's get away from the window.
   [*He wheels her to stage center.*]

DOCTOR:

Mrs. Venable? Did your son have a—well—what kind of a *personal*, well, *private* life did—

MRS. VENABLE:
That's a question I wanted you to ask me.

MISS FOXHILL:
Why?

MRS. VENABLE:
I haven't heard the girl's story except indirectly in a
watered-down version, being too ill to go to hear it
directly, but I've gathered enough to know that it's
a hideous attack on my son's moral character which,
being dead, he can't defend himself from. I have to
be the defender. Now. Sit down. Listen to me . . .
   [*The Doctor sits.*]

. . . before you hear whatever you're going to hear
from the girl when she gets here. My son, Sebastian,
was chaste. Not c-h-a-s-e-d! Oh, he was chased in
that way of spelling it, too, we had to be very fleet-
footed I can tell you, with his looks and his charm, to
keep ahead of pursuers, every kind of pursuer!—I
mean he was c-h-a-s-t-e!—Chaste. . . . .

DOCTOR:
I understood what you meant, Mrs. Venable.

MRS. VENABLE:
And you *believe* me, don't you?

DOCTOR:
Yes, but—

MRS. VENABLE:
But *what?*

DOCTOR:
Chastity at—what age was your son last summer?

MRS. VENABLE:

Forty, maybe. We really didn't count birthdays. . . .

DOCTOR:

He lived a celibate life?

MRS. VENABLE:

As strictly as if he'd *vowed* to! This sounds like
vanity, Doctor, but really I was actually the only
one in his life that satisfied the demands he made of
people. Time after time my son would let people
go, dismiss them!—because their, their, their!—*attitude*
toward him was—

DOCTOR:

Not pure as—

MRS. VENABLE:

My son, Sebastian, demanded! We were a famous
couple. People didn't speak of Sebastian and his mother
or Mrs. Venable and her son, they said "Sebastian and
Violet, Violet and Sebastian are staying at the Lido,
they're at the Ritz in Madrid. Sebastian and Violet,
Violet and Sebastian have taken a house at Biarritz for
the season," and every appearance, every time we
appeared, attention was centered on *us*!—*everyone
else*! *Eclipsed*! Vanity? Ohhhh, no, Doctor, you
can't call it that—

DOCTOR:

I didn't call it that.

MRS. VENABLE:

—It wasn't *folie de grandeur*, it was grandeur.

DOCTOR:

I see.

MRS. VENABLE:
An attitude toward life that's hardly been known in
the world since the great Renaissance princes were
crowded out of their palaces and gardens by successful shopkeepers!

DOCTOR:
I see.

MRS. VENABLE:
Most people's lives—what are they but trails of debris,
each day more debris, more debris, long, long trails
of debris with nothing to clean it all up but, finally,
death. . . .
   [*We hear lyric music.*]

My son, Sebastian, and I constructed our days, each
day, we would—carve out each day of our lives like
a piece of sculpture.—Yes, we left behind us a trail
of days like a gallery of sculpture! But, last summer—
   [*Pause: the music continues.*]

I can't forgive him for it, not even now that he's paid
for it with his life!—he let in this—*vandal*! This—

DOCTOR:
The girl that—?

MRS. VENABLE:
That you're going to meet here this afternoon! Yes.
He admitted this vandal and with her tongue for a
hatchet she's gone about smashing our legend, the
memory of—

DOCTOR:
Mrs. Venable, what do you think is her reason?

MRS. VENABLE:
Lunatics don't have reason!

DOCTOR:
I mean what do you think is her—motive?

MRS. VENABLE:
What a question!—We put the bread in her mouth
and the clothes on her back. People that like you for
that or even forgive you for it are, are—*hen's teeth*,
Doctor. The role of the benefactor is worse than
thankless, it's the role of a victim, Doctor, a sacrificial
victim, yes, they want your blood, Doctor, they
want your blood on the altar steps of their *outraged*,
outrageous egos!

DOCTOR:
Oh. You mean she resented the—

MRS. VENABLE:
Loathed!—They can't shut her up at St. Mary's.

DOCTOR:
I thought she'd been there for months.

MRS. VENABLE:
I mean keep her *still* there. She *babbles!* They couldn't
shut her up in Cabeza de Lobo or at the clinic in
Paris—she babbled, babbled!—smashing my son's reputation.—On the Berengaria bringing her back to the
States she broke out of the stateroom and babbled,
babbled; even at the airport when she was flown down
here, she babbled a bit of her story before they could
whisk her into an ambulance to St. Mary's. This is a
reticule, Doctor. [*She raises a cloth bag.*] A catch-all,
carry-all bag for an elderly lady which I turned into
last summer. . . . Will you open it for me, my hands

are stiff, and fish out some cigarettes and a cigarette
holder.
[*He does.*]

DOCTOR:
I don't have matches.

MRS. VENABLE:
I think there's a table-lighter on the table.

DOCTOR:
Yes, there is.
[*He lights it, it flames up high.*]

My Lord, what a torch!

MRS. VENABLE [*with a sudden, sweet smile*]:
"So shines a good deed in a naughty world," Doctor—
Sugar. . . .
[*Pause. A bird sings sweetly in the garden.*]

DOCTOR:
Mrs. Venable?

MRS. VENABLE:
Yes?

DOCTOR:
In your letter last week you made some reference to a,
to a—fund of some kind, an endowment fund of—

MRS. VENABLE:
I wrote you that my lawyers and bankers and certified
public accountants were setting up the Sebastian
Venable Memorial Foundation to subsidize the work
of young people like you that are pushing out the
frontiers of art and science but have a financial prob-

lem. You have a financial problem, don't you, Doctor?

DOCTOR:
Yes, we do have that problem. My work is such a *new* and *radical* thing that people in charge of state funds are naturally a little scared of it and keep us on a small budget, so small that—. We need a separate ward for my patients, I need trained assistants, I'd like to marry a girl I can't afford to marry!—But there's also the problem of getting right patients, not just—criminal psychopaths that the State turns over to us for my operation!—because it's—well—risky. . . . I don't want to turn you against my work at Lion's View but I have to be honest with you. There is a good deal of risk in my operation. Whenever you enter the brain with a foreign object . . .

MRS. VENABLE:
Yes.

DOCTOR:
—Even a needle-thin knife . . .

MRS. VENABLE:
Yes.

DOCTOR:
—In a skilled surgeon's fingers . . .

MRS. VENABLE:
Yes.

DOCTOR:
—There is a good deal of risk involved in—the operation. . . .

MRS. VENABLE:
You said that it pacifies them, it quiets them down, it suddenly makes them peaceful.

DOCTOR:
Yes. It does that, that much we already know, but—

MRS. VENABLE:
What?

DOCTOR:
Well, it will be ten years before we can tell if the immediate benefits of the operation will be lasting or —passing or even if there'd still be—and this is what haunts me about it!—any possibility, afterwards, of reconstructing a—totally sound person, it may be that the person will always be limited afterwards, relieved of acute disturbances but—*limited*, Mrs Venable....

MRS. VENABLE:
Oh, but what a blessing to them, Doctor, to be just peaceful, to be just suddenly—peaceful. . . .
[*A bird sings sweetly in the garden.*]

After all that horror, after those nightmares: just to be able to lift up their eyes and see—[*She looks up and raises a hand to indicate the sky*]—a sky not as black with savage, devouring birds as the sky that we saw in the Encantadas, Doctor.

DOCTOR:
—Mrs. Venable? I can't guarantee that a lobotomy would stop her—*babbling*!!

MRS. VENABLE:
That may be, maybe not, but after the operation, who would *believe* her, Doctor?

[*Pause: faint jungle music.*]

DOCTOR: [*quietly*]:
My God. [*Pause.*]—Mrs. Venable, suppose after meeting the girl and observing the girl and hearing this story she babbles—I still shouldn't feel that her condition's—intractable enough! to justify the risks of—suppose I shouldn't feel that non-surgical treatment such as insulin shock and electric shock and—

MRS. VENABLE:
SHE'S HAD ALL THAT AT SAINT MARY'S!!
Nothing else is left for her.

DOCTOR:
But if I disagreed with you? [*Pause.*]

MRS. VENABLE:
That's just part of a question: finish the question, Doctor.

DOCTOR:
Would you still be interested in my work at Lion's View? I mean would the Sebastian Venable Memorial Foundation still be interested in it?

MRS. VENABLE:
Aren't we always more interested in a thing that concerns us personally, Doctor?

DOCTOR:
Mrs. Venable!!
    [*Catharine Holly appears between the lace window curtains.*]

You're such an innocent person that it doesn't occur to you, it obviously hasn't even occurred to you that anybody less innocent than you are could possibly interpret this offer of a subsidy as—well, as sort of a *bribe*?

MRS. VENABLE [*laughs throwing her head back*]: Name it that—I don't care—. There's just two things to remember. She's a destroyer. My son was a *creator*! —Now if my honesty's shocked you—pick up your little black bag without the subsidy in it, and run away from this garden!—Nobody's heard our conversation but you and I, Doctor Sugar. . . .
[*Miss Foxhill comes out of the house and calls.*]

MISS FOXHILL:
Mrs. Venable?

MRS. VENABLE:
What is it, what do you want, Miss Foxhill?

MISS FOXHILL:
Mrs. Venable? Miss Holly is here, with—
[*Mrs. Venable sees Catharine at the window.*]

MRS. VENABLE:
Oh, my God. There she is, in the window!—I told you I didn't want her to enter my house again, I told you to meet them at the door and lead them around the side of the house to the garden and you didn't listen. I'm not ready to face her. I have to have my five o'clock cocktail first, to fortify me. Take my chair inside. Doctor? Are you still here? I thought you'd run out of the garden. I'm going back through the garden to the other entrance. Doctor? Sugar? You may stay in the garden if you wish to or run out of the garden if you wish to or go in this way if you wish to or do anything that you wish to but I'm

going to have my five o'clock daiquiri, *frozen!*—
before I face her. . . .
[*All during this she has been sailing very slowly
off through the garden like a stately vessel at sea
with a fair wind in her sails, a pirate's frigate or
a treasure-laden galleon. The young Doctor stares
at Catharine framed by the lace window curtains.
Sister Felicity appears beside her and draws her
away from the window. Music: an ominous fanfare.
Sister Felicity holds the door open for Catharine as
the Doctor starts quickly forward. He starts to
pick up his bag but doesn't. Catharine rushes out,
they almost collide with each other.*]

CATHARINE:
Excuse me.

DOCTOR:
I'm sorry. . . .
[*She looks after him as he goes into the house.*]

SISTER FELICITY:
Sit down and be still till your family come outside.

DIM OUT

Scene Two

Catharine removes a cigarette from a lacquered box on the table and lights it. The following quick, cadenced lines are accompanied by quick, dancelike movement, almost formal, as the Sister in her sweeping white habit, which should be starched to make a crackling sound, pursues the girl about the white wicker patio table and among the wicker chairs: this can be accompanied by quick music.

SISTER:
What did you take out of that box on the table?

CATHARINE:
Just a cigarette, Sister.

SISTER:
Put it back in the box.

CATHARINE:
Too late, it's already lighted.

SISTER:
Give it here.

CATHARINE:
Oh, please, let me smoke, Sister!

34

SISTER:
Give it here.

CATHARINE:
Please, Sister Felicity.

SISTER:
Catharine, give it here. You know that you're not allowed to smoke at Saint Mary's.

CATHARINE:
We're not at Saint Mary's, this is an afternoon out.

SISTER:
You're still in my charge. I can't permit you to smoke because the last time you smoked you dropped a lighted cigarette on your dress and started a fire.

CATHARINE:
Oh, I did not start a fire. I just burned a hole in my skirt because I was half unconscious under medication. [*She is now back of a white wicker chair.*]

SISTER [*overlapping her*]:
Catharine, give it here.

CATHARINE:
Don't be such a bully!

SISTER:
Disobedience has to be paid for later.

CATHARINE:
All right, I'll pay for it later.

SISTER [*overlapping*]:
Give me that cigarette or I'll make a report that'll

put you right back on the violent ward, if you don't.
[*She claps her hands twice and holds one hand out
across the table.*]

CATHARINE [*overlapping*]:
I'm not being violent, Sister.

SISTER [*overlapping*]:
Give me that cigarette, I'm holding my hand out
for it!

CATHARINE:
All right, take it, here, take it!
[*She thrusts the lighted end of the cigarette into the
palm of the Sister's hand. The Sister cries out and
sucks her burned hand.*]

SISTER:
You burned me with it!

CATHARINE:
I'm sorry, I didn't mean to.

SISTER [*shocked, hurt*]:
You deliberately burned me!

CATHARINE [*overlapping*]:
You said give it to you and so I gave it to you.

SISTER [*overlapping*]:
You stuck the lighted end of that cigarette in my
hand!

CATHARINE [*overlapping*]:
I'm *sick*, I'm *sick*—of being *bossed* and *bullied*!

SISTER [*commandingly*]:

Sit down!

[*Catherine sits down stiffly in a white wicker chair on forestage, facing the audience. The sister resumes sucking the burned palm of her hand. Ten beats. Then from inside the house the whirr of a mechanical mixer.*]

CATHARINE:

There goes the Waring Mixer, Aunt Violet's about to have her five o'clock frozen daiquiri, you could set a watch by it! [*She almost laughs. Then she draws a deep, shuddering breath and leans back in her chair, but her hands remain clenched on the white wicker arms.*]—We're in Sebastian's garden. *My God, I can still cry!*

SISTER:

Did you have any medication before you went out?

CATHARINE:

No. I didn't have any. Will you give me some, Sister?

SISTER [*almost gently*]:

I can't. I wasn't told to. However, I think the doctor will give you something.

CATHARINE:

The young blond man I bumped into?

SISTER:

Yes. The young doctor's a specialist from another hospital.

CATHARINE:

What hospital?

SISTER:
A word to the wise is sufficient. . . .
[*The Doctor has appeared in the window.*]

CATHARINE [*rising abruptly*]:
I knew I was being watched, he's in the window,
staring out at me!

SISTER:
Sit down and be still. Your family's coming outside.

CATHARINE [*overlapping*]:
LION'S VIEW, IS IT! DOCTOR?
[*She has advanced toward the bay window. The
Doctor draws back, letting the misty white gauze
curtains down to obscure him.*]

SISTER [*rising with a restraining gesture which is
almost pitying*]:
Sit down, dear.

CATHARINE:
IS IT LION'S VIEW? DOCTOR?!

SISTER:
Be still. . . .

CATHARINE:
WHEN CAN I STOP RUNNING DOWN THAT
STEEP WHITE STREET IN CABEZA DE
LOBO?

SISTER:
Catharine, dear, sit down.

CATHARINE:
I loved him, Sister! Why wouldn't he let me save

him? I tried to hold onto his hand but he struck me away and ran, ran, ran in the wrong direction, Sister!

SISTER:
Catharine, dear—be still.
[*The Sister sneezes.*]

CATHARINE:
Bless you, Sister. [*She says this absently, still watching the window.*]

SISTER:
Thank you.

CATHARINE:
The Doctor's still at the window but he's too blond to hide behind window curtains, he catches the light, he shines through them. [*She turns from the window.*] —We were *going* to blonds, blonds were next on the menu.

SISTER:
Be still now. Quiet, dear.

CATHARINE:
Cousin Sebastian said he was famished for blonds, he was fed up with the dark ones and was famished for blonds. All the travel brochures he picked up were advertisements of the blond northern countries. I think he'd already booked us to—Copenhagen or— Stockholm.—Fed up with dark ones, famished for light ones: that's how he talked about people, as if they were—items on a menu.—"That one's delicious-looking, that one is appetizing," or "that one is *not* appetizing"—I think because he was really nearly half-starved from living on pills and salads. . . .

SISTER:
Stop it!—Catharine, be still.

CATHARINE:
He liked me and so I loved him. . . . [*She cries a little again.*] If he'd kept hold of my hand I could have saved him!—Sebastian suddenly said to me last summer: "Let's fly north, little bird—I want to walk under those radiant, cold northern lights—I've never *seen* the aurora borealis!"—Somebody said once or wrote, once: "We're all of us children in a vast kindergarten trying to spell God's name with the wrong alphabet blocks!"

MRS. HOLLY [*offstage*]:
Sister?

[*The Sister rises.*]

CATHERINE [*rising*]:
I think it's *me* they're calling, they call *me* "Sister," Sister!

Scene Three

The Sister resumes her seat impassively as the girl's mother and younger brother appear from the garden. The mother, Mrs. Holly, is a fatuous Southern lady who requires no other description. The brother, George, is typically good-looking, he has the best "looks" of the family, tall and elegant of figure. They enter.

MRS. HOLLY:
Catharine, dear! Catharine—
    [*They embrace tentatively.*]

Well, well! Doesn't she look fine, George?

GEORGE:
Uh huh.

CATHARINE:
They send you to the beauty parlor whenever you're going to have a family visit. Other times you look awful, you can't have a compact or lipstick or anything made out of metal because they're afraid you'll swallow it.

MRS. HOLLY [*giving a tinkly little laugh*]:
I think she looks just splendid, don't you, George?

41

GEORGE:
Can't we talk to her without the nun for a minute?

MRS. HOLLY:
Yes, I'm sure it's all right to. Sister?

CATHARINE:
Excuse me, Sister Felicity, this is my mother, Mrs. Holly, and my brother, George.

SISTER:
How do you do.

GEORGE:
How d'ya do.

CATHARINE:
This is Sister Felicity. . . .

MRS. HOLLY:
We're so happy that Catharine's at Saint Mary's! So very grateful for all you're doing for her.

SISTER [sadly, mechanically]:
We do the best we can for her, Mrs. Holly.

MRS. HOLLY:
I'm sure you do. Yes, well—I wonder if you would mind if we had a little private chat with our Cathie?

SISTER:
I'm not supposed to let her out of my sight.

MRS. HOLLY:
It's just for a minute. You can sit in the hall or the garden and we'll call you right back here the minute the private part of the little talk is over.

[*Sister Felicity withdraws with an uncertain nod and a swish of starched fabric.*]

GEORGE [*to Catherine*]:
Jesus! What are you up to? Huh? Sister? Are you trying to RUIN us?!

MRS. HOLLY:
GAWGE! WILL YOU BE QUIET. You're upsetting your sister!
[*He jumps up and stalks off a little, rapping his knee with his zipper-covered tennis racket.*]

CATHARINE:
How elegant George looks.

MRS. HOLLY:
George inherited Cousin Sebastian's wardrobe but everything else is in probate! Did you know that? That everything else is in probate and Violet can keep it in probate just as long as she wants to?

CATHARINE:
Where is Aunt Violet?

MRS. HOLLY:
George, come back here!
[*He does, sulkily.*]

Violet's on her way down.

GEORGE:
Yeah. Aunt Violet has an elevator now.

MRS. HOLLY:
Yais, she has, she's had an elevator installed where the back stairs were, and, Sister, it's the cutest little

thing you ever did see! It's paneled in Chinese lacquer,
black an' gold Chinese lacquer, with lovely bird-pic-
tures on it. But there's only room for two people
at a time in it. Gorge and I came down on foot.—I
think she's havin' her frozen daiquiri now, she still
has a frozen daiquiri promptly at five o'clock ev'ry
afternoon in the world . . . in warm weather. . . .
Sister, the horrible death of Sebastian just about *killed*
her!—She's now slightly better . . . but it's a question
of time.—Dear, you know, I'm sure that you understand, why we haven't been out to see you at Saint
Mary's. They said you were too disturbed, and a
family visit might disturb you more. But I want you
to know that nobody, absolutely nobody in the city,
knows a thing about what you've been through. Have
they, George? Not a thing. Not a soul even knows
that you've come back from Europe. When people
enquire, when they question us about you, we just
say that you've stayed abroad to study something
or other. [*She catches her breath.*] Now. Sister?—I
want you to please be *very* careful what you say to
your Aunt Violet about what happened to Sebastian
in Cabeza de Lobo.

CATHARINE:
What do you want me to say about what—?.

MRS. HOLLY:
Just don't repeat that same fantastic story! For my
sake and George's sake, the sake of your brother and
mother, don't repeat that horrible story again! Not to
Violet! Will you?.

CATHARINE:
Then I am going to have to tell Aunt Violet what
happened to her son in Cabeza de Lobo?.

MRS. HOLLY:
Honey, that's why you're here. She has *INSISTED* on hearing it straight from YOU!

GEORGE:
You were the only witness to it, Cathie.

CATHARINE:
No, there were others. That *ran*.

MRS. HOLLY:
Oh, Sister, you've just had a little sort of a—*nightmare* about it! Now, listen to me, will you, Sister? Sebastian has left, has BEQUEATHED!—to you an' Gawge in his *will*—

GEORGE: [*religiously*]:
To each of us, fifty grand, each!—AFTER! TAXES! —GET IT?

CATHARINE:
Oh, yes, but if they give me an injection—I won't have any choice but to tell exactly what happened in Cabeza de Lobo last summer. Don't you see? I won't have any choice but to tell the truth. It makes you tell the truth because it shuts something off that might make you able not to and *everything* comes out, decent or *not* decent, you have no control, but always, always the truth!

MRS. HOLLY:
Catharine, darling. I don't know the full story, but surely you're not too sick in your *head* to know in your *heart* that the story you've been telling is just —too—

GEORGE: [*cutting in*]:
Cathie, Cathie, you got to forget that story! Can'tcha?
For *your* fifty grand?

MRS. HOLLY:
Because if Aunt Vi contests the will, and we know
she'll contest it, she'll keep it in the courts forever!—
We'll be—

GEORGE:
It's in PROBATE NOW! And'll never get out of
probate until you drop that story—we can't afford
to hire lawyers good enough to contest it! So if you
don't stop telling that crazy story, we won't have a
pot to—cook *greens* in!

[*He turns away with a fierce grimace and a sharp,
abrupt wave of his hand, as if slapping down something. Catharine stares at his tall back for a moment
and laughs wildly.*]

MRS. HOLLY:
Catharine, don't laugh like that, it scares me, Catharine.
[*Jungle birds scream in the garden.*]

GEORGE [*turning his back on his sister*]:
Cathie, the money is all tied up.
[*He stoops over sofa, hands on flannel knees, speaking directly into Catharine's face as if she were hard
of hearing. She raises a hand to touch his cheek
affectionately; he seizes the hand and removes it
but holds it tight.*]

If Aunt Vi decided to contest Sebastian's will that
leaves us all of this cash?!—Am I coming through to
you?

CATHARINE:
Yes, little brother, you are.

GEORGE:
You see, Mama, she's crazy like a coyote!
[*He gives her a quick cold kiss*]

We won't get a single damn penny, honest t' God
we won't! So you've just GOT to stop tellin' that
story about what you say happened to Cousin Sebastian in Cabeza de Lobo, even if it's what it *couldn't*
be, TRUE!—You got to drop it, Sister, you can't tell
such a story to civilized people in a civilized up-to-
date country!

MRS. HOLLY:
Cathie, why, why, why!—did you invent such a tale?

CATHARINE:
But, Mother, I DIDN'T invent it. I know it's a hideous story but it's a true story of our time and the
world we live in and what did truly happen to Cousin
Sebastian in Cabeza de Lobo. . . .

GEORGE:
Oh, then you are going to tell it. Mama, she IS going
to tell it! Right to Aunt Vi, and lose us a hundred
thousand!—Cathie? You are a BITCH!

MRS. HOLLY:
GAWGE!

GEORGE:
I repeat it, a bitch! She isn't crazy, Mama, she's no
more crazy than I am, she's just, just—PERVERSE!
Was ALWAYS!—perverse. . . .

[*Catharine turns away and breaks into quiet sobbing.*]

MRS. HOLLY:
Gawge, Gawge, apologize to Sister, this is no way for you to talk to your sister. You come right back over here and tell your sweet little sister you're sorry you spoke like that to her!

GEORGE [*turning back to Catharine*]:
I'm sorry, Cathie, but you know we NEED that money! Mama and me, we—Cathie? I got *ambitions!* And, Cathie, I'm YOUNG!—I *want* things, I *need* them, Cathie! So will you please think about ME? Us?

MISS FOXHILL [*offstage*]:
Mrs. Holly? Mrs. Holly?

MRS. HOLLY:
Somebody's callin' fo' me. Catharine, Gawge put it very badly but you know that it's TRUE! WE DO HAVE TO GET WHAT SEBASTIAN HAS LEFT US IN HIS WILL, DEAREST! AND YOU WON'T LET US DOWN? PROMISE? YOU WON'T? LET US DOWN?

GEORGE [*fiercely shouting*]: HERE COMES AUNT VI! Mama, Cathie, Aunt Violet's—here is Aunt Vi!

Scene Four

Mrs. Venable enters downstage area. Entrance music.

MRS. HOLLY:
Cathie! Here's Aunt Vi!

MRS. VENABLE:
She sees me and I see her. That's all that's necessary. Miss Foxhill, put my chair in this corner. Crank the back up a little.
[*Miss Foxhill does this business.*]

More. More. Not that much!—Let it back down a little. All right. Now, then. I'll have my frozen daiquiri, now. . . . Do any of you want coffee?

GEORGE:
I'd like a chocolate malt.

MRS. HOLLY:
Gawge!

MRS. VENABLE:
This isn't a drugstore.

MRS. HOLLY:
Oh, Gawge is just being Gawge.

49

MRS. VENABLE:

That's what I *thought* he was being!

[*An uncomfortable silence falls. Miss Foxhill creeps out like a burglar. She speaks in a breathless whisper, presenting a cardboard folder toward Mrs. Venable.*]

MISS FOXHILL:

Here's the portfolio marked Cabeza de Lobo. It has all your correspondence with the police there and the American consul.

MRS. VENABLE:

I asked for the *English transcript!* It's in a separate—

MISS FOXHILL:

Separate, yes, here it is!

MRS. VENABLE:

Oh . . .

MISS FOXHILL:

And here's the report of the private investigators and here's the report of—

MRS. VENABLE:

Yes, yes, yes! Where's the doctor?

MISS FOXHILL:

On the phone in the library!

MRS. VENABLE:

Why does he choose such a moment to make a phone-call?

MISS FOXHILL:

He didn't make a phone-call, he received a phone-call from—

MRS. VENABLE:
Miss Foxhill, why are you talking to me like a burglar!?
[*Miss Foxhill giggles a little desperately.*]

CATHARINE:
Aunt Violet, she's frightened.—Can I move? Can I get up and move around till it starts?

MRS. HOLLY:
Cathie, Cathie, dear, did Gawge tell you that he received bids from every good fraternity on the Tulane campus and went Phi Delt because Paul Junior did?

MRS. VENABLE:
I see that he had the natural tact and good taste to come here this afternoon outfitted from head to foot in clothes that belonged to my son!

GEORGE:
You gave 'em to me, Aunt Vi.

MRS. VENABLE:
I didn't know you'd parade them in front of me, George.

MRS. HOLLY [*quickly*]:
Gawge, tell Aunt Violet how grateful you are for—

GEORGE:
I found a little Jew tailor on Britannia Street that makes alterations so good you'd never guess that they weren't cut *out* for me to *begin* with!

MRS. HOLLY:
AND so reasonable!—Luckily, since it seems that

Sebastian's wonderful, wonderful bequest to Gawge
an' Cathie is going to be tied up a while!?

GEORGE:
Aunt Vi? About the will?
[*Mrs. Holly coughs.*]

I was just wondering if we can't figure out some way
to, to—

MRS. HOLLY:
Gawge means to EXPEDITE it! To get through the
red tape quicker?

MRS. VENABLE:
I understand his meaning. Foxhill, get the Doctor.
[*She has risen with her cane and hobbled to the
door.*]

MISS FOXHILL [*exits calling*]:
Doctor!

MRS. HOLLY:
Gawge, no more about money.

GEORGE:
How do we know we'll ever see her again?
[*Catharine gasps and rises; she moves downstage,
followed quickly by Sister Felicity.*]

SISTER [*mechanically*]:
What's wrong, dear?

CATHARINE:
I think I'm just dreaming this, it doesn't seem real!
[*Miss Foxhill comes back out, saying:*]

MISS FOXHILL:
He had to answer an urgent call from Lion's View.
[*Slight, tense pause.*]

MRS. HOLLY:
Violet! *Not* Lion's View!
[*Sister Felicity had started conducting Catharine
back to the patio; she stops her, now.*]

SISTER:
Wait, dear.

CATHARINE:
What for? I know what's coming.

MRS. VENABLE [*at same time*]:
Why? are you all prepared to put out a thousand a
month plus extra charge for treatments to keep the
girl at St. Mary's?

MRS. HOLLY:
Cathie? Cathie, dear?
[*Catharine has returned with the Sister.*]

Tell Aunt Violet how grateful you are for her makin'
it possible for you to rest an' recuperate at such a
sweet, sweet place as St. Mary's!

CATHARINE:
No place for lunatics is a sweet, sweet place.

MRS. HOLLY:
But the food's good there. Isn't the food good there?

CATHARINE:
Just give me written permission not to eat fried grits.
I had yard privileges till I refused to eat fried grits.

SISTER:

She lost yard privileges because she couldn't be trusted in the yard without constant supervision or even with it because she'd run to the fence and make signs to cars on the highway.

CATHARINE:

Yes, I did, I did that because I've been trying for weeks to get a message out of that "sweet, sweet place."

MRS. HOLLY:

What message, dear?

CATHARINE:

I got panicky, Mother.

MRS. HOLLY:

Sister, I don't understand.

GEORGE:

What're you scared of, Sister?

CATHARINE:

What they might do to me now, after they've done all the rest!—That man in the window's a specialist from Lion's View! We get newspapers. I know what they're . . .

[*The Doctor comes out.*]

MRS. VENABLE:

Why, doctor, I thought you'd left us with just that little black bag to remember you by!

DOCTOR:

Oh, no: Don't you remember our talk? I had to answer a call about a patient that—

MRS. VENABLE:
This is Dr. Cukrowicz. He says it means "sugar" and we can call him "Sugar"—
[*George laughs.*]

He's a specialist from Lion's View.

CATHARINE [*cutting in*]:
WHAT DOES HE SPECIALIZE IN?

MRS. VENABLE:
Something new. When other treatments have failed.
[*Pause. The jungle clamor comes up and subsides again.*]

CATHARINE:
Do you want to bore a hole in my skull and turn a knife in my brain? Everything else was done to me!
[*Mrs. Holly sobs. George raps his knee with the tennis racket.*]

You'd have to have my mother's permission for that.

MRS. VENABLE:
I'm paying to keep you in a private asylum.

CATHARINE:
You're not my legal guardian.

MRS. VENABLE:
Your mother's dependent on me. All of you are!—
Financially. . . .

CATHARINE:
I think the situation is—clear to me, now. . . .

MRS. VENABLE:
Good! In that case. . . .

DOCTOR:
I think a quiet atmosphere will get us the best results.

MRS. VENABLE:
I don't know what you mean by a quiet atmosphere.
She shouted, I didn't.

DOCTOR:
Mrs. Venable, let's try to keep things on a quiet level,
now. Your niece seems to be disturbed.

MRS. VENABLE:
She has every reason to be. She took my son from
me, and then she—

CATHARINE:
Aunt Violet, you're not being fair.

MRS. VENABLE:
Oh, aren't I?

CATHARINE [to the others]:
She's not being fair.
    [Then back to Mrs. Venable:]

Aunt Violet, you know why Sebastian asked me to
travel with him.

MRS. VENABLE:
Yes, I do know why!

CATHARINE:
You weren't able to travel. You'd had a—[She stops
short.]

MRS. VENABLE:

Go on! *What* had I had? Are you afraid to say it in front of the Doctor? She meant that I had a stroke. —I DID NOT HAVE A STROKE!—I had a slight aneurism. You know what that is, Doctor? A little vascular convulsion! Not a hemorrhage, just a little convulsion of a blood-vessel. I had it when I discovered that she was trying to take my son away from me. Then I had it. It gave a little temporary— muscular—contraction.—To one side of my face. . . . [*She crosses back into main acting area.*] These people are not blood-relatives of mine, they're my dead husband's relations. I always detested these people, my dead husband's sister and—her two worthless children. But I did more than my duty to keep their heads above water. To please my son, whose weakness was being excessively softhearted, I went to the expense and humiliation, yes, public humiliation, of giving this girl a debut which was a fiasco. Nobody liked her when I brought her out. Oh, she had some kind of—notoriety! She had a sharp tongue that some people mistook for wit. A habit of laughing in the faces of decent people which would infuriate them, and also reflected adversely on me and Sebastian, too. But, he, Sebastian, was amused by this girl. While I was disgusted, sickened. And halfway through the season, she was dropped off the party lists, yes, dropped off the lists in spite of my position. Why? Because she'd lost her head over a young married man, made a scandalous scene at a Mardi Gras ball, in the middle of the ballroom. Then everybody dropped her like a hot—rock, but—[*She loses her breath.*] My son, Sebastian, still felt sorry for her and took her with him last summer instead of me. . . .

CATHARINE [*springing up with a cry*]:
I can't change truth, I'm not God! I'm not even sure

that He could, I don't think God can change truth!
How can I change the story of what happened to her
son in Cabeza de Lobo?

MRS. VENABLE [*at the same time*]:
She was in love with my son!

CATHARINE [*overlapping*]:
Let me go back to Saint Mary's. Sister Felicity, let's
go back to Saint—

MRS. VENABLE [*overlapping*]:
Oh, no! That's not where you'll go!

CATHARINE [*overlapping*]:
All right, *Lion's View* but don't ask me to—

MRS. VENABLE [*overlapping*]:
You *know* that you were!

CATHARINE [*overlapping*]:
That I was *what*, Aunt Violet?

MRS. VENABLE [*overlapping*]:
Don't call me "Aunt," you're the niece of my dead
husband, not me!

MRS. HOLLY [*overlapping*]:
Catharine, Catharine, don't upset your—Doctor? Oh,
Doctor!
   [*But the Doctor is calmly observing the scene, with
   detachment. The jungle garden is loud with the
   sounds of its feathered and scaled inhabitants.*]

CATHARINE:
I don't want to, I didn't want to come here! I know

what she thinks, she thinks I murdered her son, she
thinks that I was responsible for his death.

MRS. VENABLE:
That's right. I told him when he told me that he was
going with you in my place last summer that I'd
never see him again and I never did. And only you
know why!

CATHARINE:
Oh, my God, I—
[*She rushes out toward garden, followed immedi-
ately by the Sister.*]

SISTER:
Miss Catharine, Miss Catharine—

DOCTOR [*overlapping*]:
Mrs. Venable?

SISTER [*overlapping*]:
Miss Catharine?

DOCTOR [*overlapping*]:
Mrs. Venable?

MRS. VENABLE:
What?

DOCTOR:
I'd like to be left alone with Miss Catharine for a
few minutes.

MRS. HOLLY:
George, talk to her, George.
[*George crouches appealingly before the old lady's*

chair, peering close into her face, a hand on her knee.]

GEORGE:
Aunt Vi? Cathie can't go to Lion's View. Everyone in the Garden District would know you'd put your niece in a state-asylum, Aunt Vi.

MRS. VENABLE:
Foxhill!

GEORGE:
What do you want, Aunt Vi?

MRS. VENABLE:
Let go of my chair. Foxhill? Get me away from these people!

GEORGE:
Aunt Vi, listen, think of the talk it—

MRS. VENABLE:
I can't get up! Push me, push me away!

GEORGE [*rising but holding chair*]:
I'll push her, Miss Foxhill.

MRS. VENABLE:
Let go of my chair or—

MISS FOXHILL:
Mr. Holly, I—

GEORGE:
I got to talk to her.
[*He pushes her chair downstage.*]

MRS. VENABLE:
Foxhill!

MISS FOXHILL:
Mr. Holly, she doesn't want you to push her.

GEORGE:
I know what I'm doing, leave me alone with Aunt Vi!

MRS. VENABLE:
Let go me or I'll *strike* you!

GEORGE:
Oh, Aunt Vi!

MRS. VENABLE:
Foxhill!

MRS. HOLLY:
George—

GEORGE:
Aunt Vi?

[*She strikes at him with her cane. He releases the chair and Miss Foxhill pushes her off. He trots after her a few steps, then he returns to Mrs. Holly, who is sobbing into a handkerchief. He sighs, and sits down beside her, taking her hand. The scene fades as light is brought up on Catharine and the Sister in the garden. The Doctor comes up to them. Mrs. Holly stretches her arms out to George, sobbing, and he crouches before her chair and rests his head in her lap. She strokes his head. During this: the Sister has stood beside Catharine, holding onto her arm.*]

CATHARINE:
You don't have to hold onto me. I can't run away.

DOCTOR:
Miss Catharine?

CATHARINE:
What?

DOCTOR:
Your aunt is a very sick woman. She had a stroke last spring?

CATHARINE:
Yes, she did, but she'll never admit it. . . .

DOCTOR:
You have to understand why.

CATHARINE:
I do, I understand why. I didn't want to come here.

DOCTOR:
Miss Catharine, do you hate her?

CATHARINE:
I don't understand what hate is. How can you hate anybody and still be sane? You see, I still think I'm sane!

DOCTOR:
You think she did have a stroke?

CATHARINE:
She had a slight stroke in April. It just affected one side, the left side, of her face . . . but it was disfiguring, and after that, Sebastian couldn't use her.

DOCTOR:
Use her? Did you say use her?
[*The sounds of the jungle garden are not loud but
ominous.*]

CATHARINE:
Yes, we all use each other and that's what we think
of as love, and not being able to use each other is
what's—*hate*. . . .

DOCTOR:
Do you hate her, Miss Catharine?

CATHARINE:
Didn't you ask me that, once? And didn't I say that
I didn't understand hate. A ship struck an iceberg at
sea—everyone sinking—

DOCTOR:
Go on, Miss Catharine!

CATHARINE:
But that's no reason for everyone drowning for hating
everyone drowning! Is it, Doctor?

DOCTOR:
Tell me: what was your feeling for your cousin
Sebastian?

CATHARINE:
He liked me and so I loved him.

DOCTOR:
In what way did you love him?

CATHARINE:
The only way he'd accept:—a sort of motherly way.
I tried to save him, Doctor.

DOCTOR:
From what? Save him from what?

CATHARINE:
Completing—a sort of!—*image!*—he had of himself as
a sort of!—*sacrifice* to a!—*terrible* sort of a—

DOCTOR:
—God?

CATHARINE:
Yes, a—*cruel* one, Doctor!

DOCTOR:
How did you feel about that?

CATHARINE:
Doctor, my feelings are the sort of feelings that you
have in a dream. . . .

DOCTOR:
Your life doesn't seem real to you?

CATHARINE:
Suddenly last winter I began to write my journal in
the third person.
[*He grasps her elbow and leads her out upon forestage. At the same time Miss Foxhill wheels Mrs.
Venable off, Mrs. Holly weeps into a handkerchief
and George rises and shrugs and turns his back to
the audience.*]

DOCTOR:
Something happened last winter?

CATHARINE:
At a Mardi Gras ball some—some boy that took me

to it got too drunk to stand up! [*A short, mirthless note of laughter.*] I wanted to go home. My coat was in the cloakroom, they couldn't find the check for it in his pockets. I said, "Oh, hell, let it go!"—I started out for a taxi. Somebody took my arm and said, "I'll drive you home." He took off his coat as we left the hotel and put it over my shoulders, and then I looked at him and—I don't think I'd ever seen him before then, really!—He took me home in his car but took me another place first. We stopped near the Duelling Oaks at the end of Esplanade Street. . . . Stopped!—I said, "What for?"—He didn't answer, just struck a match in the car to light a cigarette in the car and I looked at him in the car and I knew "what for"!—I think I got out of the car before he got out of the car, and we walked through the wet grass to the great misty oaks as if somebody was calling us for help there!

[*Pause. The subdued, toneless bird-cries in the garden turn to a single bird-song.*]

DOCTOR:
After that?

CATHARINE:
I lost him.—He took me home and said an awful thing to me. "We'd better forget it," he said, "my wife's expecting a child and—." —I just entered the house and sat there thinking a little and then I suddenly called a taxi and went right back to the Roosevelt Hotel ballroom. The ball was still going on. I thought I'd gone back to pick up my borrowed coat but that wasn't what I'd gone back for. I'd gone back to make a scene on the floor of the ballroom, yes, I didn't stop at the cloakroom to pick up Aunt Violet's old mink stole, no, I rushed right into the ballroom and spotted him on the floor and ran up to him and beat him as

hard as I could in the face and chest with my fists till
—Cousin Sebastian took me away.—After that, the next
morning, I started writing my diary in the third
person, singular, such as "She's still living this morning," meaning that *I* was. . . .—"WHAT'S NEXT
FOR HER? GOD KNOWS!"—I couldn't go out any
more.—However one morning my Cousin Sebastian
came in my bedroom and said: "Get up!"—Well . . .
if you're still alive after dying, well then, you're
obedient, Doctor.—I got up. He took me downtown
to a place for passport photos. Said: "Mother can't
go abroad with me this summer. You're going to go
with me this summer instead of Mother."—If you
don't believe me, read my journal of Paris!—"She
woke up at daybreak this morning, had her coffee and
dressed and took a brief walk—"

DOCTOR:
Who did?

CATHARINE:
She did. *I* did—from the Hotel Plaza Athénée to the
Place de l'Étoile as if pursued by a pack of Siberian
wolves! [*She laughs her tired, helpless laugh.*]—Went
right through all stop signs—couldn't wait for green
signals.—"Where did she think she was going? Back
to the Duelling Oaks?"—Everything chilly and dim
but his hot, ravenous mouth! on—

DOCTOR:
Miss Catharine, let me give you something.
    [*The others go out, leaving Catharine and the
    Doctor onstage.*]

CATHARINE:
Do I have to have the injection again, this time? What
am I going to be stuck with this time, Doctor? I

don't care. I've been stuck so often that if you con-
nected me with a garden hose I'd make a good
sprinkler.

DOCTOR [*preparing needle*]:
Please take off your jacket.
  [*She does. The Doctor gives her an injection.*]

CATHARINE:
I didn't feel it.

DOCTOR:
That's good. Now sit down.
  [*She sits down.*]

CATHARINE:
Shall I start counting backwards from a hundred?

DOCTOR:
Do you like counting backwards?.

CATHARINE:
Love it! Just love it! One hundred! Ninety-nine!
Ninety-eight! Ninety-seven. Ninety-six. Ninety—
five.— Oh!—I already feel it! How funny!

DOCTOR:
That's right. Close your eyes for a minute.
  [*He moves his chair closer to hers. Half a minute
  passes.*]

Miss Catharine? I want you to give me something.

CATHARINE:
Name it and it's yours, Doctor Sugar.

DOCTOR:
Give me all your resistance.

CATHARINE:
Resistance to what?

DOCTOR:
The truth. Which you're going to tell me.

CATHARINE:
The truth's the one thing I have never resisted!

DOCTOR:
Sometimes people just think they don't resist it, but
still do.

CATHARINE:
They say it's at the bottom of a bottomless well, you
know.

DOCTOR:
Relax.

CATHARINE:
Truth.

DOCTOR:
Don't talk.

CATHARINE:
Where was I, now? At ninety?

DOCTOR:
You don't have to count backwards.

CATHARINE:
At ninety something?

DOCTOR:
You can open your eyes.

CATHARINE:
Oh, I do feel funny!
[*Silence, pause.*]

You know what I think you're doing? I think you're
trying to hypnotize me. Aren't you? You're looking
so straight at me and doing something to me with your
eyes and your—eyes. . . . Is that what you're doing
to me?

DOCTOR:
Is that what you *feel* I'm doing?

CATHARINE:
Yes! I feel so peculiar. And it's not just the drug.

DOCTOR:
Give me all your resistance. See. I'm holding my hand
out. I want you to put yours in mine and give me
all your resistance. Pass all of your resistance out of
your hand to mine.

CATHARINE:
Here's my hand. But there's no resistance in it.

DOCTOR:
You are totally passive.

CATHARINE:
Yes, I am.

DOCTOR:
You will do what I ask.

CATHARINE:
Yes, I will try.

DOCTOR:
You will tell the true story.

CATHARINE:
Yes, I will.

DOCTOR:
The absolutely true story. No lies, nothing not spoken.
Everything told, exactly.

CATHARINE:
Everything. Exactly. Because I'll have to. Can I—can
I stand up?

DOCTOR:
Yes, but be careful. You might feel a little bit dizzy.
[*She struggles to rise, then falls back.*]

CATHARINE:
I can't get up! Tell me to. Then I think I could do it.

DOCTOR:
Stand up.
[*She rises unsteadily.*]

CATHARINE:
How funny! Now I can! Oh, I do feel dizzy! Help
me, I'm—
[*He rushes to support her.*]

—about to fall over. . . .
[*He holds her. She looks out vaguely toward the
brilliant, steaming garden. Looks back at him. Suddenly sways toward him, against him.*]

DOCTOR:
You see, you lost your balance.

CATHARINE:
No, I didn't. I did what I wanted to do without you
telling me to.
[*She holds him tight against her.*]

Let me! Let! Let! Let me! Let me, let me, oh, let
me. . . .
[*She crushes her mouth to his violently. He tries to
disengage himself. She presses her lips to his fiercely,
clutching his body against her. Her brother George
enters.*]

Please hold me! I've been so lonely. It's lonelier
than death, if I've gone mad, it's lonelier than death!

GEORGE [*shocked, disgusted*]:
Cathie!—you've got a hell of a nerve.
[*She falls back, panting, covers her face, runs a few
paces and grabs the back of a chair. Mrs. Holly
enters.*]

MRS. HOLLY:
What's the matter, George? Is Catharine ill?

GEORGE:
No.

DOCTOR:
Miss Catharine had an injection that made her a little
unsteady.

MRS.HOLLY:
What did he say about Catharine?
[*Catharine has gone out into the dazzling jungle of
the garden.*]

SISTER [*returning*]:
She's gone into the garden.

DOCTOR:
That's all right, she'll come back when I call her.

SISTER:
It may be all right for you. You're not responsible
for her.
[*Mrs. Venable has re-entered.*]

MRS. VENABLE:
Call her now!

DOCTOR:
Miss Catharine! Come back.
[*To the Sister:*]

Bring her back, please, Sister!
[*Catharine enters quietly, a little unsteady.*]

Now, Miss Catharine, you're going to tell the true
story.

CATHARINE:
Where do I start the story?

DOCTOR:
Wherever you think it started.

CATHARINE:
I think it started the day he was born in this house.

MRS. VENABLE:
Ha! You see!

GEORGE:
Cathie.

DOCTOR:
Let's start later than that. [*Pause.*] Shall we begin with last summer?

CATHARINE:
Oh. Last summer.

DOCTOR:
Yes. Last summer.
[*There is a long pause. The raucous sounds in the garden fade into a bird-song which is clear and sweet. Mrs. Holly coughs. Mrs. Venable stirs impatiently. George crosses downstage to catch Catharine's eye as he lights a cigarette.*]

CATHARINE:
Could I—?

MRS. VENABLE:
Keep that boy away from her!

GEORGE:
She wants to smoke, Aunt Vi.

CATHARINE:
Something helps in the—hands. . . .

SISTER:
Unh unh!

DOCTOR:
It's all right, Sister. [*He lights her cigarette.*] About last summer: how did it begin?

CATHARINE:
It began with his kindness and the six days at sea that took me so far away from the—Duelling Oaks that I

forgot them, nearly. He was affectionate with me, so sweet and attentive to me, that some people took us for a honeymoon couple until they noticed that we had—separate staterooms, and—then in Paris, he took me to Patou and Schiaparelli's—*this* is from Schiaparelli's! [*Like a child, she indicates her suit.*]—bought me so many new clothes that I gave away my old ones to make room for my new ones in my new luggage to—travel. . . . I turned into a peacock! Of course, so was *he* one, too. . . .

GEORGE:
Ha Ha!

MRS. VENABLE:
Shh!

CATHARINE:
But then I made the mistake of responding too much to his kindness, of taking hold of his hand before he'd take hold of mine, of holding onto his arm and leaning on his shoulder, of appreciating his kindness more than he wanted me to, and, suddenly, last summer, he began to be restless, and—oh!

DOCTOR:
Go on.

CATHARINE:
The Blue Jay notebook!

DOCTOR:
Did you say notebook?

MRS. VENABLE:
I know what she means by that, she's talking about the school composition book with a Blue Jay trade-

mark that Sebastian used for making notes and re-
visions on his "*Poem of Summer*." It went with him
everywhere that he went, in his jacket pocket, even
his dinner jacket. I have the one that he had with
him last summer. *Foxhill! The Blue Jay notebook!*

[*Miss Foxhill rushes in with a gasp.*]

It came with his personal effects shipped back from
Cabeza de Lobo.

DOCTOR:

I don't quite get the connection between new clothes
and so forth and the Blue Jay notebook.

MRS. VENABLE:

I HAVE IT!—Doctor, tell her I've found it.

[*Miss Foxhill hears this as she comes back out of
house: gasps with relief, retires.*]

DOCTOR:

With all these interruptions it's going to be awfully
hard to—

MRS. VENABLE:

This is important. I don't know why she mentioned
the Blue Jay notebook but I want you to see it. Here
it is, here! [*She holds up a notebook and leafs swiftly
through the pages.*] Title? "*Poem of Summer*," and
the date of the summer—1935. After that: *what?
Blank pages, blank pages,* nothing but *nothing!*—last
summer. . . .

DOCTOR:

What's that got to do with—?

MRS. VENABLE:

His destruction? I'll tell you. A poet's vocation is

something that rests on something as thin and fine as the web of a spider, Doctor. That's all that holds him *over*!—out of destruction. . . . Few, very few are able to do it alone! Great help is needed! I *did* give it! She *didn't*.

CATHARINE:
She's right about that. I failed him. I wasn't able to keep the web from—breaking. . . . I saw it breaking but couldn't save or—repair it!

MRS. VENABLE:
There now, the truth's coming out. We had an agreement between us, a sort of contract or covenant between us which he broke last summer when he broke away from me and took her with him, not me! When he was frightened and I knew when and what of, because his hands would shake and his eyes looked in, not out, I'd reach across a table and touch his hands and say not a word, just look, and touch his hands with my hand until his hands stopped shaking and his eyes looked out, not in, and in the morning, the poem would be continued. *Continued until it was finished!*
   [*The following ten speeches are said very rapidly, overlapping.*]

CATHARINE:
I—couldn't!

MRS. VENABLE:
Naturally not! He was *mine*! I *knew* how to help him, I *could*! You didn't, you couldn't!

DOCTOR:
These interruptions—

MRS. VENABLE:
I would say "You *will*" and he *would*, I—!

CATHARINE:
Yes, you see, I failed him! And so, last summer, we
went to Cabeza de Lobo, we flew down there from
where he gave up writing his poem last summer. . . .

MRS. VENABLE:
Because he'd broken our—

CATHARINE:
Yes! Yes, something had broken, that string of pearls
that old mothers hold their sons by like a—sort of a—
sort of—*umbilical* cord, *long—after* . . .

MRS. VENABLE:
She means that I held him back from—

DOCTOR:
Please!

MRS. VENABLE:
Destruction!

CATHARINE:
All I know is that suddenly, last summer, he wasn't
young any more, and we went to Cabeza de Lobo,
and he suddenly switched from the evenings to the
beach. . . .

DOCTOR:
From evenings? To beach?

CATHARINE:
I mean from the evenings to the afternoons and from
the fa—fash—

[*Silence: Mrs. Holly draws a long, long painful breath. George stirs impatiently.*]

DOCTOR:
Fashionable! Is that the word you—?

CATHARINE:
Yes. Suddenly, last summer Cousin Sebastian changed to the afternoons and the beach.

DOCTOR:
What beach?

CATHARINE:
In Cabeza de Lobo there is a beach that's named for Sebastian's name saint, it's known as La Playa San Sebastian, and that's where we started spending all afternoon, every day.

DOCTOR:
What kind of beach was it?

CATHARINE:
It was a big city beach near the harbor.

DOCTOR:
It was a big public beach?

CATHARINE:
Yes, public.

MRS. VENABLE:
It's little statements like that that give her away.
[*The Doctor rises and crosses to Mrs. Venable without breaking his concentration on Catharine.*]

After all I've told you about his fastidiousness, can you accept such a statement?

DOCTOR:
You mustn't interrupt her.

MRS. VENABLE [*overlapping him*]:
That Sebastian would go every day to some dirty free public beach near a harbor? A man that had to go out a mile in a boat to find water to swim in?

DOCTOR:
Mrs. Venable, no matter what she says you have to let her say it without any more interruptions or this interview will be useless.

MRS. VENABLE:
I won't speak again. I'll keep still, if it kills me.

CATHARINE:
I don't want to go on. . . .

DOCTOR:
Go on with the story. Every afternoon last summer your Cousin Sebastian and you want out to this free public beach?

CATHARINE:
No, it wasn't the free one, the free one was right next to it, there was a fence between the free beach and the one that we went to that charged a small charge of admission.

DOCTOR:
Yes, and what did you do there?
[*He still stands beside Mrs. Venable and the light gradually changes as the girl gets deeper into her*

*story: the light concentrates on Catharine, the other
figures sink into shadow.*]

Did anything happen there that disturbed you about
it?

CATHARINE:
Yes!

DOCTOR:
What?

CATHARINE:
He bought me a swim-suit I didn't want to wear. I
laughed. I said, "I can't wear that, it's a scandal to the
jay-birds!"

DOCTOR:
What did you mean by that? That the suit was im-
modest?

CATHARINE:
My God, yes! It was a one-piece suit made of white
lisle, the water made it transparent! [*She laughs sadly
at the memory of it.*] —I didn't want to swim in it,
but he'd grab my hand and drag me into the water,
all the way in, and I'd come out looking naked!

DOCTOR:
Why did he do that? Did you understand why?

CATHARINE:
—Yes! To attract!—Attention.

DOCTOR:
He wanted you to attract attention, did he, because

he felt you were moody? Lonely? He wanted to
shock you out of your depression last summer?

CATHARINE:
Don't you understand? I was PROCURING for him!
[*Mrs. Venable's gasp is like the sound that a great
hooked fish might make.*]

She used to do it, too.
[*Mrs. Venable cries out.*]

Not consciously! She didn't *know* that she was procuring for him in the smart, the fashionable places
they used to go to before last summer! Sebastian was
shy with people. She wasn't. Neither was I. We both
did the same thing for him, made contacts for him,
but she did it in nice places and in decent ways and
I had to do it the way that I just told you!—Sebastian
was lonely, Doctor, and the empty Blue Jay notebook
got bigger and bigger, so big it was big and empty as
that big empty blue sea and sky. . . . I knew what I
was doing. I came out in the French Quarter years
before I came out in the Garden District. . . .

MRS. HOLLY:
Oh, Cathie! Sister . . .

DOCTOR:
Hush!

CATHARINE:
And before long, when the weather got warmer and
the beach so crowded, he didn't need me any more
for that purpose. The ones on the free beach began
to climb over the fence or swim around it, bands of
homeless young people that lived on the free beach
like scavenger dogs, hungry children. . . . So now he

let me wear a decent dark suit. I'd go to a faraway empty end of the beach, write postcards and letters and keep up my—third-person journal till it was—five o'clock and time to meet him outside the bathhouses, on the street. . . . He would come out, *followed*.

DOCTOR:
Who would follow him out?

CATHARINE:
The homeless, hungry young people that had climbed over the fence from the free beach that they lived on. He'd pass out tips among them as if they'd all—shined his shoes or called taxis for him. . . . Each day the crowd was bigger, noisier, greedier!—Sebastian began to be frightened.—At last we stopped going out there. . . .

DOCTOR:
And then? After that? After you quit going out to the public beach?

CATHARINE:
Then one day, a few days after we stopped going out to the beach—it was one of those white blazing days in Cabeza de Lobo, not a blazing hot *blue* one but a blazing hot *white* one.

DOCTOR:
Yes?

CATHARINE:
We had a late lunch at one of those open-air restaurants on the sea there.—Sebastian was white as the weather. He had on a spotless white silk Shantung suit and a white silk tie and a white panama and white shoes, white—white lizard skin—pumps! He—[*She*

*throws back her head in a startled laugh at the recol-
lection*]—kept touching his face and his throat here
and there with a white silk handkerchief and popping
little white pills in his mouth, and I knew he was having a bad time with his heart and was frightened
about it and that was the reason we hadn't gone out
to the beach. . . .

[*During the monologue the lights have changed,
the surrounding area has dimmed out and a hot
white spot is focused on Catharine.*]

"I think we ought to go north," he kept saying, "I
think we've done Cabeza de Lobo, I think we've done
it, don't you?" *I* thought we'd done it!—but I had
learned it was better not to seem to have an opinion
because if I did, well, Sebastian, well, you know
Sebastian, he always preferred to do what no one else
wanted to do, and I always tried to give the impression that I was agreeing reluctantly to his wishes . . .
it was a—game. . . .

SISTER:
She's dropped her cigarette.

DOCTOR:
I've got it, Sister.
[*There are whispers, various movements in the
penumbra. The Doctor fills a glass for her from
the cocktail shaker.*]

CATHARINE:
Where was I? Oh, yes, that five o'clock lunch at one
of those fish-places along the harbor of Cabeza de
Lobo, it was between the city and the sea, and there
were naked children along the beach which was
fenced off with barbed wire from the restaurant and

we had our tables less than a yard from the barbed
wire fence that held the beggars at bay. . . . There
were naked children along the beach, a band of fright-
fully thin and dark naked children that looked like
a flock of plucked birds, and they would come darting up to the barbed wire fence as if blown there
by the wind, the hot white wind from the sea, all
crying out, *"Pan, pan, pan!"*

DOCTOR [*quietly*]:
What's *pan?*

CATHARINE:
The word for bread, and they made gobbling noises
with their little black mouths, stuffing their little black
fists to their mouths and making those gobbling noises,
with frightful grins!—Of course we were sorry that
we had come to this place but it was too late to go. . . .

DOCTOR [*quietly*]:
Why was it "too late to go"?

CATHARINE:
I told you Cousin Sebastian wasn't well. He was popping those little white pills in his mouth. I think he
had popped in so many of them that they had made
him feel weak. . . . His, his!—eyes looked—dazed, but
he said: "Don't look at those little monsters. Beggars
are a social disease in this country. If you look at
them, you get sick of the country, it spoils the whole
country for you. . . ."

DOCTOR:
Go on.

CATHARINE:
I'm going on. I have to wait now and then till it gets

clearer. Under the drug it has to be a vision, or nothing comes. . . .

DOCTOR:
All right?

CATHARINE:
Always when I was with him I did what he told me.
I didn't look at the band of naked children, not even
when the waiters drove them away from the barbed
wire fence with sticks!—Rushing out through a wicket
gate like an assault party in war!—and beating them
screaming away from the barbed wire fence with the
sticks. . . . Then! [*Pause.*]

DOCTOR:
Go on, Miss Catherine, what comes next in the vision?

CATHARINE:
The, the the!—band of children began to—serenade
us. . . .

DOCTOR:
Do what?

CATHARINE:
Play for us! On instruments! Make music!—if you
could call it music. . . .

DOCTOR:
Oh?

CATHARINE:
Their, their—instruments were—instruments of percussion!—Do you know what I mean?

DOCTOR [*making a note*]:
Yes. Instruments of percussion such as—*drums?*

CATHARINE:
I stole glances at them when Cousin Sebastian wasn't
looking, and as well as I could make out in the white
blaze of the sand-beach, the instruments were tin cans
strung together.

DOCTOR [*slowly, writing*]:
Tin—cans—strung—together.

CATHARINE:
And, and, and, and—and!—*bits of metal, other* bits of
metal that had been flattened out, made into—

DOCTOR:
What?

CATHARINE:
Cymbals! You know? *Cymbals?*

DOCTOR:
Yes. Brass plates hit together.

CATHARINE:
That's right, Doctor.—Tin cans flattened out and
clashed together!—Cymbals. . . .

DOCTOR:
Yes. I understand. What's after that, in the vision?

CATHARINE [*rapidly, panting a little*]:
And others had paper bags, bags made out of—coarse
paper!—with something on a string inside the bags
which they pulled up and down, back and forth, to
make a sort of a—

DOCTOR:
Sort of a—?

CATHARINE:
Noise like—

DOCTOR:
Noise like?

CATHARINE [*rising stiffly from chair*]:
Ooompa! Oompa! Oooooompa!

DOCTOR:
Ahhh ... a sound like a *tuba*?

CATHARINE:
That's right!—they made a sound like a tuba. . . .

DOCTOR:
Oompa, oompa, oompa, like a tuba.
[*He is making a note of the description.*]

CATHARINE:
Oompa, oompa, oompa, like a—
[*Short pause.*]

DOCTOR:
—Tuba. . . .

CATHARINE:
All during lunch they stayed at a—a fairly *close*—
distance. . . .

DOCTOR:
Go on with the vision, Miss Catharine.

CATHARINE [*striding about the table*]:
Oh, I'm going on, nothing could stop it now!!

DOCTOR:
Your Cousin Sebastian was *entertained* by this—*concert?*

CATHARINE:
I think he was *terrified* of it!

DOCTOR:
Why was he terrified of it?

CATHARINE:
I think he recognized some of the musicians, some of the boys, between childhood and—older. . . .

DOCTOR:
What did he do? Did he do anything about it, Miss Catharine?—Did he complain to the manager about it?

CATHARINE:
What manager? *God?* Oh, *no!*—The manager of the fishplace on the beach? Haha!—No!—You don't understand my cousin!

DOCTOR:
What do you mean?

CATHARINE:
He! — accepted! — all! — as — how! — things! — are! — And thought nobody had any right to complain or interfere in any way whatsoever, and even though he knew that what was awful was awful, that what was wrong was wrong, and my Cousin Sebastian was certainly never sure that anything was wrong!—He thought it unfitting to ever take any action about

anything whatsoever!—except to go on doing as something in him directed. ...

DOCTOR:
What did something in him direct him to do?—I mean on this occasion in Cabeza de Lobo.

CATHARINE:
After the salad, before they brought the coffee, he suddenly pushed himself away from the table, and said, "They've got to stop that! Waiter, make them stop that. I'm not a well man, I have a heart condition, it's making me sick!"—This was the first time that Cousin Sebastian had ever attempted to correct a human situation!—I think perhaps that *that* was his fatal error. . . . It was then that the waiters, all eight or ten of them, charged out of the barbed wire wicket gate and beat the little musicians away with clubs and skillets and anything hard that they could snatch from the kitchen!—Cousin Sebastian left the table. He stalked out of the restaurant after throwing a handful of paper money on the table and he fled from the place. I followed. It was all white outside. White hot, a blazing white hot, hot blazing white, at five o'clock in the afternoon in the city of—Cabeza de Lobo. It looked as if—

DOCTOR:
It looked as if?

CATHARINE:
As if a huge white bone had caught on fire in the sky and blazed so bright it was white and turned the sky and everything under the sky white with it!

DOCTOR:
—White ...

CATHARINE:
Yes—white ...

DOCTOR:
You followed your Cousin Sebastian out of the restaurant onto the hot white street?

CATHARINE:
Running up and down hill....

DOCTOR:
You ran up and down hill?

CATHARINE:
No, no! *Didn't!*—move either *way!*—at first, we were—
[*During this recitation there are various sound effects. The percussive sounds described are very softly employed.*]
I rarely made any suggestion but *this* time I *did*. ...

DOCTOR:
What did you suggest?

CATHARINE:
Cousin Sebastian seemed to be paralyzed near the entrance of the café, so I said, "Let's go." I remember that it was a very wide and steep white street, and I said, "Cousin Sebastian, down that way is the waterfront and we are more likely to find a taxi near there. ... Or why don't we go back in?—and have them *call* us a taxi! Oh, let's do! Let's do *that*, that's better!" And he said, "*Mad*, are you *mad*? Go back in that filthy place? Never! That gang of kids shouted vile things about me to the waiters!" "Oh," I said, "then let's go down toward the docks, down there at the bottom of the hill, let's not try to climb the hill in this dreadful heat." And Cousin Sebastian

shouted, "Please shut up, let me handle this situation, will you? I want to handle this thing." And he started up the steep street with a hand stuck in his jacket where I knew he was having a pain in his chest from his palpitations. . . . But he walked faster and faster, in panic, but the faster he walked the louder and closer it got!

DOCTOR:
What got louder?

CATHARINE:
The music.

DOCTOR:
The music again.

CATHARINE:
The oompa-oompa of the—following band.—They'd somehow gotten through the barbed wire and out on the street, and they were following, following!—up the blazing white street. The band of naked children pursued us up the steep white street in the sun that was like a great white bone of a giant beast that had caught on fire in the sky!—Sebastian started to run and they all screamed at once and seemed to fly in the air, they outran him so quickly. I screamed. I heard Sebastian scream, he screamed just once before this flock of black plucked little birds that pursued him and overtook him halfway up the white hill.

DOCTOR:
And you, Miss Catharine, what did *you* do, then?

CATHARINE:
Ran!

DOCTOR:
Ran where?

CATHARINE:
Down! Oh, I ran down, the easier direction to run was down, down, down, down!—The hot, white, blazing street, screaming out "Help" all the way, till—

DOCTOR:
What?

CATHARINE:
—Waiters, police, and others—ran out of buildings and rushed back up the hill with me. When we got back to where my Cousin Sebastian had disappeared in the flock of featherless little black sparrows, he—he was lying naked as they had been naked against a white wall, and this you won't believe, nobody *has* believed it, nobody *could* believe it, nobody, nobody on earth could possibly believe it, and I don't *blame* them!—They had *devoured* parts of him.

[*Mrs. Venable cries out softly.*]

Torn or cut parts of him away with their hands or knives or maybe those jagged tin cans they made music with, they had torn bits of him away and stuffed them into those gobbling fierce little empty black mouths of theirs. There wasn't a sound any more, there was nothing to see but Sebastian, what was left of him, that looked like a big white-paper-wrapped bunch of red roses had been *torn, thrown, crushed!*—against that blazing white wall. . . .

[*Mrs. Venable springs with amazing power from her wheelchair, stumbles erratically but swiftly toward the girl and tries to strike her with her cane. The Doctor snatches it from her and catches her as she is about to fall. She gasps hoarsely several times as he leads her toward the exit.*]

MRS. VENABLE [*offstage*]:
Lion's View! State asylum, cut this hideous story out of her brain!
[*Mrs. Holly sobs and crosses to George, who turns away from her, saying:*]

GEORGE:
Mom, I'll quit school, I'll get a job, I'll—

MRS. HOLLY:
Hush son! Doctor, can't you say something?
[*Pause. The Doctor comes downstage. Catharine wanders out into the garden followed by the Sister.*]

DOCTOR [*after a while, reflectively, into space*]:
I think we ought at least to consider the possibility that the girl's story could be true. . . .

PERIOD OF ADJUSTMENT

High Point over a Cavern

A SERIOUS COMEDY

To the director and the cast

Period of Adjustment was presented at the Helen Hayes Theatre in New York on November 10, 1960, by Cheryl Crawford. It was directed by George Roy Hill; the stage settings and lighting were by Jo Mielziner and the costumes by Patricia Zipprodt; production stage manager, William Chambers. The cast, in order of appearance, was as follows:

RALPH BATES	JAMES DALY
ISABEL HAVERSTICK	BARBARA BAXLEY
GEORGE HAVERSTICK	ROBERT WEBBER
SUSIE	HELEN MARTIN
LADY CAROLER	ESTHER BENSON
MRS. McGILLICUDDY	NANCY R. POLLOCK
MR. McGILLICUDDY	LESTER MACK
THE POLICE OFFICER	CHARLES MC DANIEL
DOROTHY BATES	ROSEMARY MURPHY

The Scene

The action of the play takes place in Ralph Bates' home in a suburb of a mid-southern city. The time is Christmas Eve.

ACT ONE

The set is the interior and entrance of a "cute" little Spanish-type suburban bungalow. Two rooms are visible onstage, the living room with its small dining alcove and the bedroom. There are doors to the kitchen and bath. A bit of the stucco exterior surrounds the entrance, downstage right or left. A Christmas wreath is on the door, while above the door is an ornamental porch light, or coach lantern, with amber glass or possibly glass in several colors. The fireplace in the fourth wall of the set is represented by a flickering red light. Of course the living room contains a TV set with its back to the audience, its face to a big sofa that opens into a bed. The dog is a cocker spaniel. There's a rather large Christmas tree, decorated with a child's toys under it and a woman's fur coat in an open box, but no child and no woman. RALPH BATES, a boyish-looking man in his middle thirties, is approaching the TV set, facing upstage, with a can of beer and opener.

TV COMMERCIAL: Millions of Americans each day are discovering the difference between this new miracle product and the old horse-and-buggy type of cleanser which made washday a torture to Mom and left her too tired at sundown to light up the house with the sunshine of her smile.

RALPH: *No snow!*

(*He hoists himself onto a very high bar stool facing the TV.*)

TV COMMERCIAL: So don't let unnecessary fatigue cast a shadow over your household, especially not at this—

(*He leaps off the stool and crouches to change the channel. He gets snatches of several dramatic and musical*

*offerings, settles for a chorus of "White Christmas,"
sighs, picks up a poker and stabs at the flickering ruddy
light in the fourth wall. It comes up brighter. He crouches
to fan the fire with an antique bellows: the fire brightens.
He sighs again, hoists himself back onto the brass-
studded red-leather-topped stool, which has evidently been
removed from the "cute" little bar, which is upstage.
For theatrical purpose, this stool is about half a foot
higher than any other sitting-surface on the stage. Whenever* RALPH *assumes a seat on this stool he is like a
judge mounting his judicial bench, except he's not pompous or bewigged about it. He is detached, considering,
thinking, and over his face comes that characteristic look
of a gentle gravity which is the heart of* RALPH. *Perhaps
his pose should suggest Rodin's "Thinker."* RALPH *is one
of those rare people that have the capacity of heart to
truly care, and care deeply, about other people.
A car horn, urgent, is heard out front, offstage.* RALPH
*slides off the stool and rushes out the front door; he
stands under the amber coach lantern. It's snowing, the
snowflakes are projected on his figure, tiny, obliquely
falling particles of shadow. There's a muffled shout from
the car that's stopped below the terrace of the bungalow.)*

RALPH (*shouting back*): Hey, there, drive her up under th'
carport!

GEORGE (*Texas voice*): Whacha say, boy?

RALPH: PUT 'ER UNDER THE CARPORT!

GEORGE: Wheels won't catch, too steep!

RALPH: Back her all the way out and then shoot 'er up in
first!

ISABEL'S VOICE (*high-pitched with strain*): Will you please
let me out first, George!

(*There is the sound of a car door.* RALPH *ducks back in,
grinning, and seizes a carton of rice.*)

RALPH: Yeah, come on in, little lady.

(ISABEL *appears before the house, small and white-faced with fatigue, eyes dark-circled, manner dazed and uncertain. She wears a cheap navy-blue cloth coat, carries a shiny new patent-leather purse, has on red wool mittens.* RALPH *pelts her with rice. She ducks the bombardment with a laugh that's more like a sob.*)

ISABEL: Oh, no, please! I never want to see rice again in my life, not uncooked anyhow. . . . That fire looks wonderful to me. I'm Isabel Crane, Mr. Bates.

(*She removes a red mitten and extends her hand.*)

RALPH: I thought you'd married that boy.

(*Both speak in deep Southern voices; hers is distinctly Texan.*)

ISABEL: I mean Mrs. George Haverstick.

(*She says her new name with a hint of grimness.*)

RALPH (*still in the door*): Wait'll I put m'shoes on, I'll come out!

(*This shout is unheard.*)

ISABEL: You have a sweet little house.

RALPH (*with a touch of amiable grimness*): Yeah, we sure do. Wheels cain't git any traction, 'stoo damn steep.

(*He shouts down.*)

LOCK IT UP, LEAVE IT OUT FRONT!—I guess he's gonna do that, yep, that's what he's doin', uh-huh, that's what he's doin'. . . .

ISABEL: Does it snow often in Dixon?

RALPH: No, no, rarely, rarely.

(*He gives her a glance.* RALPH *has a sometimes discon-*

*certing way of seeming either oblivious to a person he's
with or regarding the person with a sudden intense concentration, as if he'd just noticed something startling or
puzzling about them. But this is a mannerism that the
actor should use with restraint.)*

ISABEL: It was snowing all the way down here; it's my
first acquaintance with snow except for one little flurry of
snow in Saint Louis the day befo' Thanksgivin' day, this is
my first real acquaintance with, with—with a real *snow*. . . .
What *is* he doing down there?

RALPH: He's unloadin' th' car.

ISABEL: I just want my small zipper bag. Will you please
call down to him that's all I want of my things?

RALPH *(shouting)*: Leave all that stuff till later. Ha ha. I
didn't know you could get all that in a car.

ISABEL: Surely he isn't removing our wedding presents! Is
he *insane*, Mr. Bates?

(She goes to the door.)

*George! Just my small zipper bag, not everything in the
car! Oh, Lord.*

(She retreats into the room.)

He must think we're going to *live* here for the rest of our
lives! He didn' even warn you all we were coming.

RALPH: He called me up from West Dixon.

ISABEL: Yes, just across the river.

RALPH: What is that car, a Caddy?

ISABEL: It's a fifty-two Cadillac with a mileage close to a
hundred and twenty thousand. It ought to be retired with an
old-age pension, Mr. Bates.

RALPH (*at the door*): It looks like one of them funeral limousines.

ISABEL (*wryly*): Mr. Bates, you have hit the nail on the head with the head of the hammer. That is just what it was. It's piled up a hundred and twenty thousand miles between Burkemeyer's Mortuary and various graveyards serving Greater Saint Louis. JAWGE, CAN YOU HEAR ME, JAWGE? Excuse me, Mr. Bates.

(*She slips past him onto the terrace again.*)

JAWGE, JUST MY SMALL ZIPPER BAG.

(*Indistinct shout from below. She turns back in.*)

I give up, Mr. Bates.

(*She ducks under his arm to enter the house again and stands behind* RALPH *in the doorway.*)

RALPH (*still chuckling at the door*): What's he want with a funeral limousine? On a honeymoon trip?

ISABEL: I asked him that same question and got a very odd answer. He said there's no better credit card in the world than driving up at a bank door in a Cadillac limousine.

(*She tries to laugh.*)

Oh, I don't know, I—love Spanish-type architecture, Spanish mission-type houses, I—don't think you ought to stand in that door with just that light shirt on you, this is a—such a —*sweet* house. . . .

(*She seems close to tears. Something in her tone catches his attention and he comes in, closing the door.*)

RALPH: Ha, ha, well, how's it going? Is the marriage in orbit?

ISABEL (*tries to laugh at this, too*): Oh! Will you please do me a favor? Don't encourage him, please don't invite him to spend the night here, Mr. Bates! I'm thinking of your wife, because last night—in Cape Girardeau, Missouri?—he thought it would be very nice to look up an old war buddy he had there, too. He sincerely thought so, and possibly the war buddy thought so, too, but NOT the wife! Oh, no, not *that* lady, no! They'd hardly got through their first beer cans with—remembrances of Korea, when that bright little woman began to direct us to a highway motel which she said was only a hop, skip and jump from their house but turned out to be almost across the state line into—Arkansas? Yaias, Arkansas. I think I can take this off, now!

(*She removes a red woolen muffler. He takes it from her and she murmurs "Thanks."*)

What is holding him up? Why is he—? Mr. Bates, I did tell him that this is one night of the year when you just don't intrude on another young married couple.

RALPH: Aw, come off that, little lady! Why, I been beggin' that boy ever since we got out of the service to come to Dixon. He had to git married to make it. Why, every time I'd git drunk, I'd call that boy on the phone to say "Git to hell down here, you old Texas jack rabbit!" And I'd just about given up hope he'd ever show!

ISABEL: Is he still fooling with luggage?

(*There is a noise outside. RALPH goes to the open door.*)

RALPH: *Hey!*

ISABEL: *What?*

RALPH: Ha ha ha! He put these bags at the door and run back down to the car.

ISABEL: *What* did he—?

RALPH: Gone back down for more luggage. I'll take these in.

ISABEL (*as the bags are brought in*): Those are *my* pieces of luggage! All but the small zipper bag which is all that I wanted!

RALPH (*calling out the open door*): *Hey!*

ISABEL: *What?*

RALPH: *Hey, boy!* He's gotten back in the car an' driven *off*, ha ha!

ISABEL (*rushing to the door*): *Driven? Off?* Did you say? My heavens. You're right, he's *gone!* Mr. Bates, he's *deposited me on your hands and driven away.*

(*She is stunned.*)

Oh, *how funny!* Isn't this *funny!*

(*Laughs wildly, close to sobbing.*)

It's no *surprise* to me, though! All the way down here from Cape Girardeau, where we stopped for our wedding night, Mr. Bates, I had a feeling that the first chance he got to, he would abandon me somewhere!

RALPH: Aw, now, take it easy!

ISABEL: That's what he's done! Put me and my bags in your hands and run away.

RALPH: Aw, now, no! The old boy wouldn't do that, ha ha, for Chrissakes. He just remembered something he had to, had to—go and get at a—drugstore.

ISABEL: If that was the case wouldn't he mention it to me?

RALPH: Aw now, I known that boy a long time and he's always been sort of way out, but never way out that far!

ISABEL: Where is your wife? Where's Mrs. Bates, Mr. Bates?

RALPH: Oh, she's not here, right now.

ISABEL: I'm SUCH A FOOL!

(*She giggles a little hysterically.*)

Oh, I'm such a *fool!* . . . Why didn't I know better, can you answer me that? . . . I hope the news of our approach didn't drive your wife away on Christmas eve, Mr. Bates. . . .

RALPH: No, honey.

ISABEL: He brought up everything but the little blue zipper bag which is all I asked faw! . . . It had my, all my, it had my—*night* things in it. . . .

RALPH: Just let me get you a drink. I'm sorry I don't have any egg nog. But I can make a wonderful hot buttered rum. How about a little hot buttered rum?

ISABEL: Thank you, no, I don't drink. . . .

RALPH: It's never too late to begin to.

ISABEL: No, I don't want liquor.

RALPH: Coffee? Want some hot coffee?

ISABEL: Where is your wife, Mr. Bates?

RALPH: Oh, she's—not here now, I'll tell you about that later.

ISABEL: She will be outraged. This is one night of the year when you don't want outside disturbances—on your hands. . . .

RALPH: I think I know what to give you.

ISABEL: I did expect it but yet I didn't expect it!—I mean it occurred to me, the possibility of it, but I thought I was just being morbid.

RALPH: Aw, now, I know that boy. We been through two

wars together, took basic training together and officer's training together. He wouldn't ditch you like that unless he's gone crazy.

ISABEL: George Haverstick is a very sick man, Mr. Bates. He was a patient in neurological at Barnes Hospital in Saint Louis, that's how I met him. I was a student nurse there.

(*She is talking quickly, shrilly. She has a prim, severe manner that disguises her prettiness.*)

RALPH: Yeah? What was wrong with him in the hospital, honey?

ISABEL: If we see him again, if he ever comes back to this house, you will *see* what's wrong. *He shakes!* Sometimes it's just barely noticeable, just a constant, slight tremor, you know, a sort of—vibration, like a—like an electric vibration in his muscles or nerves?

RALPH: Aw. That old tremor has come back on him, huh? He had that thing in Korea.

ISABEL: How bad did he have it in Korea, Mr. Bates?

RALPH: You know—like a heavy drinker—except he didn't drink heavy.

ISABEL: It's like he had Parkinson's disease but he doesn't have it.

(*She speaks like an outraged spinster, which is quite incongruous to her pretty, childlike appearance.*)

RALPH: What in hell is it then?

ISABEL: THAT is a MYSTERY! He shakes, that's all. He just shakes. Sometimes you'd think that he was shaking to pieces. . . . Was that a car out front?

(*She goes to the window.*)

No! I've caught a head cold, darn it.

(*Blows her nose.*)

When I met Mr. George Haverstick—Excuse me, you're watching TV!

RALPH (*turning off set*): Naw, I'm not watchin' TV.

ISABEL. I'm so wound up, sitting in silence all day beside my—silent bridegroom, I can't seem to stop talking now, although I—hardly know you. Yes. I met him at Barnes Hospital, the biggest one in Saint Louis, where I was taking my training as a nurse, he had gone in Barnes instead of the Veterans Hospital because in the Veterans Hospital they couldn't discover any physical cause of this tremor and he thought they just said there wasn't any physical cause in order to avoid having to pay him a physical disability—compensation! I had him as a patient at Barnes Hospital, on the night shift. My, did he keep me running! The little buzzer was never out of his hand. Couldn't sleep under any kind of sedation less than enough to knock an elephant out! —Well, that's where I met George, I was very touched by him, honestly, very, very touched by the boy! I thought he sincerely loved me. . . . Yes, I *have* caught a head cold, or am I crying? I guess it's fatigue—exhaustion.

RALPH: You're just going through a period of adjustment.

ISABEL: Of course at Barnes he got the same diagnosis, or lack of diagnosis, that he'd gotten at the Vets Hospital in Korea and Texas and elsewhere, no physical basis for the tremor, perfect physical health, suggested—psychiatry to him! He blew the roof off! You'd think they'd accused him of beating up his grandmother, at least, if not worse! I swear! Mr. Bates, I still have sympathy for him, but it wasn't fair of him not to let me know he'd quit his job at the airfield till after our marriage. He gave me that information after the wedding, right after the wedding he told me, right on the bridge, Eads Bridge between Saint Louis and East Saint Louis, he said, "Little Bit? Take a good look at Saint Louie because it may be your last one!" I'm quoting him exactly, those were his words. I don't know why I didn't say drive me right back. . . . Isn't it strange that I didn't say turn around on the other side of this bridge and drive me right back? I gave up student nursing at a great hospital to marry a man not honest enough to let me know he'd given up his job till an hour after the wedding!

RALPH: George is a high-strung boy. But they don't make them any better.

ISABEL: A man's opinion of a man! If they don't make them any better than George Haverstick they ought to stop production!

(RALPH *throws back his head, laughing heartily.*)

No, I mean it, if they don't make them better than a man that would abandon his bride in less than—how many hours?—on the doorstep of a war buddy and drive on without her or any apology to her, if that's the best they make them, I say *don't make them!*

(*There is a pause. She has crouched before the fire again, holding her hands out to the flickering glow.*)

Did George tell you on the phone that he's quit his job?

RALPH (*pouring brandy*): What job did he quit, honey?

ISABEL: He was a ground mechanic at Lambert's airfield in Saint Louis. I had lost my job too, I hadn't quit, no, I was politely dismissed. My first day in surgery?—I *fainted!*—when the doctor made the incision and I saw the blood, I keeled over. . . .

RALPH: That's understandable, honey.

ISABEL: Not in a nurse, not in a girl that had set her heart on nursing, that—how long has he been gone?

RALPH: Just a few minutes, honey. Xmas Eve traffic is heavy and George being George, he may have stopped at a bar on his way back here. . . . You'd been going steady how long?

ISABEL: Ever since his discharge from Barnes Hospital. Isn't this suburb called High Point?

RALPH: Yes. High Point over a cavern.

ISABEL: His place was in High Point, too. Another suburb called High Point, spelled Hi dash Point—hyphenated.

RALPH: I guess all fair-sized American cities have got a suburb called High Point, hyphenated or not, but this is the only one I know of that's built on a cavern.

ISABEL (*without really listening to him*): Cavern?

(*She laughs faintly as if it were a weak joke.*)

Well, I said, George, on the bridge, we're not driving down to Florida in that case. We're going to find you a job; we're going from city to city until you find a new job and I don't care if we cross the Rio Grande, we're not going to stop until you find one! Did I or didn't I make the right decision? In your opinion, Mr. Bates.

RALPH: Well. How did he react to it?

ISABEL: Stopped talking and started shaking! So violently I was scared he would drive that funeral car off the road! Ever since then it's been hell! And I am—

(*She springs up from the fireplace chair.*)

—not exactly the spirit of Christmas, am I?

(*She goes to the window to look out; sees nothing but windy snow. There is a low rumble. A picture falls off the wall.*)

What was that?

RALPH: Oh, nothing. The ground just settled a little. We get that all the time here because this suburb, High Point, is built over a great big underground cavern and is sinking into it gradually, an inch or two inches a year. It would cost three thousand dollars to stabilize the foundation of this house even temporarily! But it's not publicly known and we homeowners and the promoters of the project have got together to keep it a secret till we have sold out, in alphabetical order, at a loss but not a complete sacrifice. Collusion, connivance. Disgusting but necessary.

(*She doesn't hear this, murmurs "What?" as she crosses back to the window at the sound of a car going by.*)

ISABEL: It's funny, I had a hunch he was going to leave me somewhere.

(*She laughs sadly, forlornly, and lets the white window curtains fall together.*)

RALPH: Why don't you take off your coat and sit back down by the fire? That coat keeps the heat off you, honey. That boy's comin' back.

ISABEL: Thank you.

(*She removes her coat.*)

RALPH (*observing with solemn appreciation the perfect neatness of her small body*): I'm *sure* that boy's coming back. I am now *positive* of it! That's a cute little suit you're wearing. Were you married in that?

ISABEL: Yes, I was married in this traveling suit. Appropriately.

RALPH: You couldn't have looked any prettier in white satin.

(*RALPH is at the bar preparing a snifter of brandy for her. Now he puts a match to it and as it flares up blue, she cries out a little.*)

ISABEL: What is, what are you—?

RALPH: Something to warm up your insides, little lady.

ISABEL: Well, isn't that sweet of you? Will it burn if I touch it?

RALPH: Naw, naw, naw, take it, take it.

ISABEL: Beautiful. Let me hold it to warm my hands first, before I—

(*He puts the snifter glass of blue-flaming brandy in her hands and they return to the fireplace.*)

I'm not a drinker, I don't think doctors or nurses have any right to be, but I guess *now*—I'm *out* of the nursing profession! *So* . . . What a sweet little bar. What a sweet little house. And such a sweet Christmas tree.

RALPH: Yeah. Everything's sweet here. I married a homely girl, honey, but I tried to love her.

(ISABEL *doesn't really hear this remark.*)

ISABEL: I hope your wife didn't take your little boy out because we were coming.

RALPH: I sure did make an effort to love that woman. I almost stopped realizing that she was homely.

ISABEL: So he didn't actually tell you he was going to a drugstore, Mr. Bates?

RALPH (*uncomfortably*): He didn't say so. I just figured he was.

ISABEL: I—well, he's abandoned me here.

RALPH: How long've you known George?

ISABEL: I'm afraid I married a stranger.

RALPH: Everybody does that.

ISABEL: Where did you say your wife was?

RALPH: My wife has quit me.

ISABEL: No! You're joking, aren't you?

RALPH: She walked out on me this evening when I let her know I'd quit my job.

ISABEL (*beginning to listen to him*): Surely it's just temporary, Mr. Bates.

RALPH: Nope. Don't think so. I quit my job and so my wife quit me.

ISABEL: I don't think a woman leaves a man as nice as you, Mr. Bates, for such a reason as that.

RALPH: Marriage is an economic arrangement in many ways, let's face it, honey. Also, the situation between us was complicated by the fact that I worked for her father. But that's another story. That's a long other story and you got your mind on George.

ISABEL: I think my pride has been hurt.

RALPH: I told you he's coming back and I'm just as sure of it as I'm sure Dorothea isn't. Or if she does, that she'll find me waiting for her. Ohhhhh, nooooo! I'm cutting out of this High Point over a Cavern on the first military transport I can catch out of Dixon.

ISABEL (*vaguely*): You don't mean that, Mr. Bates, you're talking through your hat, out of hurt feelings, hurt pride.

(*She opens the front door and stands looking out as forlornly as a lost child. She really does have a remarkably cute little figure and* RALPH *takes slow, continual and rather wistful stock of it with his eyes.*)

RALPH: I got what I had comin' to me, that I admit, for marryin' a girl that didn't attract me.

(*He comes up behind her at the door.*)

ISABEL: Did you say didn't attract you?

RALPH: Naw, she didn't attract me in the beginning. She's one year older'n me and I'm no chicken. But I guess I'm not the only man that would marry the only daughter of an old millionaire with diabetes and gallstones and one kidney. Am I?

ISABEL: It's nice out here.

RALPH: But I'm telling you I'm convinced there is no greater assurance of longevity in this world than one kidney, gallstones an' diabetes! That old man has been cheating the undertaker for yea many years. Seems to thrive on one kidney and . . .

(*He tosses the beer can down the terrace.*)

Oh, they live on anything—nothing!

ISABEL: Do you always throw beer cans on your front lawn, Mr. Bates?

RALPH: Never before in my life. I sure enjoyed it. George is gonna be shocked when he sees me. I sacrificed my youth to—

ISABEL: What?

RALPH: Yep, it's nice out here. I mean, nicer than in there.

ISABEL: You sacrificed your youth?

RALPH: Oh, that. Yeah! I'll tell you more about that unless it bores you.

ISABEL: No.

RALPH: She had fallen into the hands of a psychiatrist when I married this girl. This psychiatrist was charging her father fifty dollars a session to treat her for a condition that he diagnosed as "psychological frigidity." She would shiver violently every time she came within touching distance of a possible boy friend. Well—I think the psychiatrist misunderstood her shivers.

ISABEL: She might have shivered because of—

RALPH: That's what I *mean!* Why, the night I met her, I heard a noise like castanets at a distance. I thought some Spanish dancers were about to come on! Ha ha! Then I noticed her teeth—she had buck teeth at that time which were later extracted!—were chattering together and her whole body was uncontrollably shaking!

ISABEL: We both married into the shakes! But Mr. Bates, I don't think it's very nice of you to ridicule the appearance of your wife.

RALPH: Oh, I'm not!

ISABEL: You WERE!

RALPH: At my suggestion she had the buck teeth extracted. It was like kissing a rock pile before the extractions! I swear!

ISABEL: Now, Mr. Bates.

RALPH: This snow almost feels warm as white ashes out of a—chimney.

ISABEL: Excuse me. I'll get my—sweater.

(*She goes in. He remains on the little paved terrace. When she comes out again in her cardigan, he goes on talking as if there'd been no interruption.*)

RALPH: Yep, her old man was payin' this head-shrinker fifty dollars per session for this condition he diagnosed as "psychological frigidity." I cured her of that completely almost overnight. But at thirty-seven, my age, you ain't middle-aged but you're in the shadow of it and it's a spooky shadow. I mean, when you look at *late* middle-aged couples like the McGillicuddys, my absent wife's parents . . .

ISABEL: Mr. Bates, don't you think I should go downtown and take a hotel room? Even if George comes back, he ought not to find me here like a checked package waiting for him to return with the claim check. Because if you give up your pride, what are you left with, really?

(*She turns and goes back inside. He follows her in. Immediately after they enter, a* NEGRO GIRL *appears on the terrace.*)

Don't you agree, Mr. Bates?

(*The* GIRL *rings the doorbell.*)

RALPH: *Here he is now. You see?*

(ISABEL, *who had sunk onto a hassock before the fireplace, now rises tensely as* RALPH *calls out:*)

COME ON IN, LOVER BOY! THAT DOOR AIN'T LOCKED!

(RALPH *opens the door.*)

Oh . . . What can I do fo' you, Susie?

(SUSIE *comes into the room with a sheepish grin.*)

SUSIE: 'Scuse me for comin' to the front door, Mr. Bates, but that snow's wet and I got a hole in muh shoe!

RALPH: You alone?

SUSIE: Yes, suh.

RALPH: They sent you for somethin'?

SUSIE: Yes, suh, they sent me faw th' chile's Santie Claus.

RALPH: Aw, they did, huh? Well, you go right back an' tell the McGillicuddys that "the chile's Santie Claus" is stayin' right here till the chile comes over for it, because I bought it, not them, and I am at least *half* responsible for the "chile's" existence, *also.* Tell them the chile did not come into the world without a father and it's about time for the chile to acknowledge that fact and for them to acknowledge that fact and— How did you git here, Susie?

SUSIE: Charlie brought me.

RALPH: Who's Charlie?

SUSIE: Charlie's they new *showfer*, Mr. Bates.

RALPH: Aw. Well, tell my wife and her folks, the McGillicuddys, that I won't be here tomorrow but "the chile's Santie Claus" will be here under the tree and say that I said Merry Christmas. Can you remember all that?

SUSIE: Yes, suh.

(*She turns and shouts through the door:*) Charlie! Don't come up, I'm comin' right down, Charlie!

(*The sound of a Cadillac motor starting is heard below the terrace as* SUSIE *leaves.* RALPH *looks out of the open door till the car is gone, then slams it shut.*)

RALPH: Dig that, will yuh! Sent a colored girl over to collect the kid's Christmas! This is typical of the Stuart McGillicuddys. I'd like to have seen Mr. Stuart McGillicuddy, the look on his face, when that Western Union messenger give him my message of resignation this afternoon and he was at last exposed to my true opinions of him!

ISABEL: You should have let her take the child's Christmas to it.

RALPH: They'll be over. Don't worry. And—I will be waiting for them with both barrels, man—will I blast 'em! Think of the psychiatrist fees that I saved her fat-head father! I even made her think that she was attractive, and over a five-year period got one pay raise when she give birth to my son which she has turned to a sissy.

(ISABEL *hasn't listened to his speech.*)

ISABEL: I thought that was George at the door. . . .

RALPH: That's life for you.

ISABEL: What?

RALPH: I said isn't that life for you!

ISABEL: *What* is life for us *all*?

(*She sighs.*)

My philosophy professor at the Baptist college I went to, he said one day, "We are all of us born, live and die in the shadow of a giant question mark that refers to three questions: Where do we *come* from? *Why? And where, oh where, are we going!*"

RALPH: When did you say you got married?

ISABEL: Yesterday. Yesterday morning.

RALPH: That lately? Well, he'll be back before you can say—Joe Blow.

(*He appreciates her neat figure again.*)

ISABEL: What?

RALPH: Nothing.

ISABEL: Well!

RALPH: D'you like Christmas music?

ISABEL: Everything but "White Christmas."

(*As she extends her palms to the imaginary fireplace, RALPH is standing a little behind her, still looking her up and down with solemn appreciation.*)

RALPH: Aw, y' don't like "White Christmas"?

ISABEL: The radio in that car is practically the only thing in it that *works*! We had it on all the time.

(She gives a little tired laugh.)

Conversation was impossible, even if there had been a desire to talk! It kept playing "White Christmas" because it was snowing I guess all the way down here, yesterday and —today....

RALPH: A radio in a funeral limousine?

ISABEL: I guess they just played it on the way back from the graveyard. Anyway, once I reached over and turned the volume down. He didn't say anything, he just reached over and turned the volume back up. Isn't it funny how a little thing like that can be so insulting to you? Then I started crying and still haven't stopped! I pretended to be looking out the car window till it got dark.

RALPH: You're just going through a little period of adjustment to each other.

ISABEL: What do you do with a bride left on your doorstep, Mr. Bates?

RALPH: Well, I, *ha ha!*—never *had* that experience!

ISABEL: Before? Well, now you're faced with it, I hope you know how to handle it. You know why I know he's left me? He only took in my bags, he left his own in the car, he brought in all of mine except my little blue zipper overnight bag, *that* he kept for some reason. Perhaps he intends to pick up another female companion who could use its contents.

RALPH: Little lady, you're in a bad state of nerves.

ISABEL: Have you ever been so tired that you don't know what you're doing or saying?

RALPH: Yes. Often.

ISABEL: That's my condition, so make allowances for it. Yes, indeed, that *sure* is a mighty *far* drugstore. . . .

(*She wanders back to the window, and parts the curtain to peer out.*)

RALPH: He seems gone twice as long because you're thinking about it.

ISABEL: I don't know why I should care except for my overnight bag with my toilet articles in it.

RALPH (*obliquely investigating*): Where did you spend last night?

ISABEL (*vaguely*): Where did we spend last night?

RALPH: Yeah. Where did you stop for the night?

ISABEL (*rubbing her forehead and sighing with perplexity*): In a, in a—oh, a tourist camp called the—Old Man River Motel? Yes, the Old Man River Motel.

RALPH: That's a mistake. The first night ought to be spent in a real fine place regardless of what it cost you. It's so important to get off on the right foot.

(*He has freshened his drink and come around to the front of the bar. She has gone back to the window at the sound of a car.*)

If you get off on the wrong foot, it can take a long time to correct it.

(*She nods in slow confirmation of this opinion.*)

Um-hmmm. Walls are built up between people a hell of a damn sight faster than—broken down. . . . Y'want me to give you my word that he's coming back? I will, I'll give you my word. Hey.

(*He snaps his fingers.*)

Had he brought me a Christmas present? If not, *that's* what he's doing. *That* explains where he went to.

(*There is a pause. She sits sadly by the fireplace.*)

What went wrong last night?

ISABEL: Let's not talk about that.

RALPH: I don't mean to pry into such a private, intimate thing, but—

ISABEL: No, let's don't! I'll just put it this way and perhaps you will understand me. In spite of my being a student nurse, till discharged—my experience has been limited, Mr. Bates. Perhaps it's because I grew up in a small town, an only child, too protected. I wasn't allowed to date till my last year at High and then my father insisted on meeting the boys I went out with and laid down pretty strict rules, such as when to bring me home from parties and so forth. If he smelled liquor on the breath of a boy? At the door? That boy would not enter the door! And that little rule ruled out a goodly number.

RALPH: I bet it did. They should've ate peanuts befo' they called for you, honey.

(*He chuckles, reflectively poking at the fire.*)

That's what we done at the Sisters of Mercy Orphans' Home in Mobile.

ISABEL (*touched*): Oh. Were you an *orphan*, Mr. Bates?

RALPH: Yes, I had that advantage.

(*He slides off the high stool again to poke at the fire. She picks up the antique bellows and fans the flames, crouching beside him.*)

ISABEL: So you were an orphan! People that grow up orphans, don't they value love more?

RALPH: Well, let's put it this way. They get it less easy. To get it, they have to give it: so, yeah, they do value it more.

(*He slides back onto the bar stool. She crouches at the fireplace to fan the fire with the bellows; the flickering light brightens their shy, tender faces.*)

ISABEL: But it's also an advantage to have a parent like my daddy.

(*She's again close to tears.*)

Very strict but devoted. Opposed me going into the nursing profession but I had my heart set on it, I thought I had a vocation, I saw myself as a Florence Nightingale nurse. A lamp in her hand? Establishin' clinics in the—upper Amazon country. . . .

(*She laughs a little ruefully.*)

Yais, I had heroic daydreams about myself as a dedicated young nurse working side by side with a—

(*She pauses shyly.*)

RALPH: With a dedicated young doctor?

ISABEL: No, the doctor would be older, well, not too old, but—older. I saw myself passing among the pallets, you know, the straw mats, administering to the plague victims in the jungle, exposing myself to contagion. . . .

(*She exhibits a bit of humor here.*)

RALPH: *Catchin'* it?

ISABEL: Yais, contractin' it eventually *m'self.* . . .

RALPH: What were the symptoms of it?

ISABEL: A slight blemish appearing on the—hands?

(*She gives him a darting smile.*)

RALPH (*joining in the fantasy with her*): Which you'd wear gloves to conceal?

ISABEL: Yais, rubber gloves all the time.

RALPH: A crusty-lookin' blemish or more like a fungus?

(*They laugh together.*)

ISABEL: I don't think I—yais, I did, I imagined it being like *scaa-ales!* Like silver fish scales appearing on my hainds and then progressing gradually to the wrists and *fo'*-arms. . . .

RALPH: And the young doctor discovering you were concealing this condition?

ISABEL: The *youngish middle-aged* doctor, Mr. Bates! Yais, discovering I had contracted the plague myself and then a big scene in which she says, Oh, no, you musn't touch me but he seizes her passionately in his arms, of course, and— exposes himself to contagion.

(RALPH *chuckles heartily getting off stool to poke at the fire again. She joins him on the floor to fan the flames with the bellows.*)

ISABEL: And love is stronger than death. You get the picture?

RALPH: Yep, I've seen the picture.

ISABEL: We've had a good laugh together. You're a magician, Ralph, to make me laugh tonight in my present situation. George and I never laugh, we never laugh together. Oh, he makes JOKES, YAIS! But we never have a really genuine laugh together and that's a bad sign, I think, because I don't think a married couple can go through life without laughs together any more than they can without tears.

RALPH: Nope.

(*He removes his shoes.*)

Take your slippers off, honey.

ISABEL: I have the funniest sensation in the back of my head, like—

RALPH: Like a tight rope was coming unknotted?

ISABEL: Exactly! Like a tight rope was being unknotted!

(*He removes her slippers and puts them on the hearth, crosses into the bedroom and comes out with a pair of fluffy pink bedroom slippers. He crouches beside her and feels the sole of her stocking.*)

RALPH: Yep, damp. Take those damp stockings off.

ISABEL (*unconsciously following the suggestion*): Does George have a sense of humor? In your opinion? Has he got the ability to laugh at himself and at life and at—human situations? Outside of off-color jokes? In your opinion, Mr. Bates?

RALPH (*taking the damp stockings from her and hanging them over the footlights*): Yes. We had some good laughs together, me an'—"Gawge," ha ha. . . .

ISABEL: We never had any together.

RALPH: That's the solemnity of romantic love, little lady, I mean like Romeo and Juliet was not exactly a joke book, ha ha ha.

ISABEL: "The solemnity of romantic love"!—I wouldn't expect an old war buddy of George's to use an expression like that.

RALPH: Lemme put these on your feet, little lady.

(*She sighs and extends her feet and he slips the soft fleecy pink slippers on them.*)

But you know something? I'm gonna tell you something which isn't out of the joke books either. You got a wonderful boy in your hands, on your hands, they don't make them any better than him and I mean it.

(*He does.*)

ISABEL: I appreciate your loyalty to an old war buddy.

RALPH: Naw, naw, it's not just tha†

ISABEL: But if they don't make them any better than George Haverstick, they ought to stop making them, they ought to *cease producing!*

(*She utters a sort of wild, sad laugh which stops as abruptly as it started. Suddenly she observes the bedroom slippers on her feet.*)

What's these, where did they come from?

RALPH: Honey, I just put them on you. Didn't you know?

ISABEL: No!—How strange!—I didn't, I wasn't at all aware of it. . . .

(*They are both a little embarrassed.*)

Where is your wife, Mr. Bates?

RALPH: Honey, I told you she quit me and went home to her folks.

ISABEL: Oh, excuse me, I remember. You told me. . . .

(*Suddenly the blazing logs make a sharp cracking noise; a spark apparently has spit out of the grate onto* ISABEL'S *skirt. She gasps and springs up, retreating from the fireplace, and* RALPH *jumps off the bar stool to brush at her skirt. Under the material of the Angora wool skirt is the equal and warmer softness of her young body.* RALPH *is abruptly embarrassed, coughs, turns back to the fireplace and picks up copper tongs to shift the position of crackling logs.*)

(*This is a moment between them that must be done just right to avoid misinterpretation.* RALPH *would never make a play for the bride of a buddy. What should come out of the moment is not a suggestion that he will or might but that Dotty's body never felt that way. He remembers bodies that did. What comes out of ISABEL's reaction is a warm understanding of his warm understanding; just that, nothing more, at all.)*

ISABEL: Thank you. This Angora wool is, is—highly inflammable stuff, at least I would—think it—might be. . . .

RALPH: Yeah, and I don't want "Gawge" to come back here and find a toasted marshmallow bride . . . by my fireplace.

(They sit down rather self-consciously, RALPH on the high stool, ISABEL on the low hassock.)

ISABEL: Yais . . .

RALPH: Huh?

ISABEL: Daddy opposed me going into nursing so much that he didn't speak to me, wouldn't even look at me for a whole week before I took off for Saint Louie.

RALPH: Aw? Tch!

ISABEL: However, at the last moment, just before the train pulled out of the depot, he came stalking up the platform to the coach window with a gift package and an envelope. The package contained flannel nighties and the envelope had in it a list of moral instructions in the form of prayers such as: "O Heavenly Father, give thy weak daughter strength to—

(She giggles.)

—resist the—

(She covers her mouth with a hand to suppress a spasm of laughter.)

Oh, my Lord. Well, you would have to know Daddy to appreciate the—

RALPH: Honey, I reckon I know your daddy. That's what I meant about the orphan's advantage, honey.

(*They laugh together.*)

ISABEL: We sure do have some good laughs together, Mr. Bates. Now where did I get *these*?

(*She means the bedroom slippers.*)

These aren't mine, where did, how did—? *Oh—yes, you—*

(*They resume their grave contemplation of the fire.*)

"Heavenly Father, give thy weak daughter the strength of will to resist the lusts of men. Amen."

(RALPH *chuckles sadly.*)

And I was never tempted to, *not* to, resist them, till— George. . . .

RALPH: Did George arouse a—?

ISABEL: I don't suppose another man could see George the way I see him: SAW him. So *handsome?* And so *afflicted?* So afflicted and—*handsome?* With that mysterious *tremor?* With those SHAKES?

RALPH: How did "Gawge" come on?

ISABEL: Huh? Oh. No. I don't mean he came on like a—

RALPH: Bull? Exactly?

ISABEL: No, no, no, no. It was very strange, very— strange. . . .

RALPH: What?

ISABEL: He always wanted us to go out on double dates or with a whole bunch of—others. And when we were alone?

Together? There was a—funny, oh, a very *odd*—sort of—*timidity!*—between us. . . . And that, of course, is what touched me; oh, that—*touched* me. . . .

(*There is a pause in the talk.* RALPH *descends from his high perch and passes behind her low hassock with a smile behind her back which is a recognition of the truth of her romantic commitment to George. This is also in the slight, tender pat that he gives to the honey-colored crown of her head.*)

And so although I had many strong opportunities to give in to my "weakness" on, on—weekend dates with young interns and doctors at Barnes?—I was never tempted to do so. But with George—

RALPH: You did? Give in?

ISABEL: Mr. Bates, George Haverstick married a virgin, and I can't say for sure that it was my strength of will and not *his* that—deserves the credit. . . .

(RALPH *returns to the fireplace with beer.*)

RALPH: Yeah, well. Now I'm going to tell you something about that boy that might surprise you after your experience last night at the Old Man River Motel.

(*He opens a beer can.*)

He always bluffs about his ferocious treatment of women, believe me! To hear him talk you'd think he spared them no pity! However, I happen to know he didn't come on as strong with those dolls in Tokyo and Hong Kong and Korea as he liked to pretend to. Because I heard from those dolls. . . . He'd just sit up there on a pillow and drink that rice wine with them and teach them *English!* Then come downstairs from there, hitching his belt and shouting, *"Oh, man! Oh, brother!"*—like he' laid 'em to waste.

ISABEL: That was not his behavior in the Old Man River Motel. Last night.

RALPH: What went wrong in the Old Man River Motel?

ISABEL: Too many men think that girls in the nursing profession must be—*shock*proof. I'm not, I wasn't—last night. . . .

RALPH: Oh. Was he drunk?

ISABEL: He'd been drinking all day in that heaterless retired funeral hack in a snowstorm to keep himself warm. Since I don't drink, I just had to endure it. Then. We stopped at the Old Man River Motel, as dreary a place as you could find on this earth! The electric heater in our cabin lit up but gave off no heat! Oh, *George* was comfortable there! Threw off his clothes and sat down in front of the heater as if I were not even present.

RALPH: Aw.

ISABEL: Continuing drinking!

RALPH: Aw.

ISABEL: Then began the courtship, and, oh, what a courtship it was, such tenderness, romance! I finally screamed. I locked myself in the bathroom and didn't come out till he had gotten to bed and then I—slept in a chair. . . .

RALPH: You wouldn't—

ISABEL: Mr. Bates, I just couldn't! The atmosphere just wasn't right. And he—

(*She covers her face.*)

—I can't tell you more about it just now except that it was a nightmare, him in the bed, pretending to be asleep, and me in the chair pretending to be asleep too and both of us knowing the other one *wasn't* asleep and, and, and—I can't tell you more about it right now, I just can't tell more than I've told you about it, I—

(*Her sobs become violent and there is a pause.*)

RALPH: Hey! Let me kiss the bride! Huh? Can I kiss the bride?

ISABEL: You're very kind, Mister Bates. I'm sure you were more understanding with your wife when you were going through this—

RALPH: —period of adjustment? Yeah. That's all it is, it's just a little—period of adjustment.

(*He bestows a kiss on her tear-stained cheek and a pat on her head. She squeezes his hand and sinks down again before the fireplace.*)

ISABEL: It isn't as if I'd given him to believe that I was *experienced*! I made it clear that I *wasn't*. He knows my background and we'd talked at great *length* about my—inhibitions which I know are—*inhibitions*, but—which an understanding husband wouldn't expect his bride to overcome at *once*, in a tourist cabin, after a *long—silent—ride!*—in a *funeral hack* in a *snowstorm* with the *heater not working* in a *shocked! condition!*—having just been told that—we were *both* unemployed, and—

RALPH: Little Bit, Little Bit—you had a sleepless night in that motel—why don't you put in a little sack time now. You need it, honey. Take Dotty's bed in there and think about nothing till morning.

ISABEL: You mean you know, now, that George is not coming back?

RALPH: No. I mean that Dotty's not coming back.

ISABEL: I don't think you ever thought that he would come back for me any more than I did.

RALPH: Take Dotty's bed, get some sleep on that foam-rubber mattress while I sit here and watch the Late Late Show on TV.

ISABEL: But, Mister Bates, if your wife does come back here I wouldn't want her to find a stranger in your bedroom.

RALPH: Honey, finding a stranger in a bedroom is far from being the biggest surprise of a lifetime. So you go on in there and lock the door.

ISABEL: Thank you, Mister Bates.

(*She enters bedroom.*)

I'm only locking the door because of the slight possibility that Mister George Haverstick the fourth might come back drunk and try to repeat the comedy and tragedy of last night. I hope you realize that.

RALPH: Oh, sure. Good night, sleep tight, honey.

(*She locks the bedroom door as* RALPH *returns to the fireplace.*)

RALPH (*to himself and the audience*): What a bitch of a Christmas.

CURTAIN

ACT TWO

No time lapse.

ISABEL *jumps up as a car is heard stopping out front. She looks wildly at* RALPH, *who gives her a nod and a smile as he crosses to the front door. Snow blows into the living room as he goes out and shouts:*

RALPH: HEY!

(ISABEL *catches her breath, waiting.*)

Ha ha!

(ISABEL *expels her breath and sits down.* RALPH, *shouting through snow:*)

Your wife thought she was deserted!

GEORGE (*from a distance*): *Hey!*

(ISABEL *springs up and rushes to a mirror to wipe away tears.*

(*A car door is heard slamming in front of the house.* ISABEL *sits down. She immediately rises, rubbing her hands together, and then sits down again. Then she springs up and starts toward the bedroom. Stops short as*

(GEORGE *enters.*)

I'm the son of a camel, ha ha! My mother was a camel with two humps, a double hump—dromedary! Ha ha ha!

(GEORGE *and* RALPH *catch each other in a big, rocking hug.* ISABEL *stares, ignored, as the male greetings continue.*)

RALPH: *You ole son of a tail gun!*

GEORGE: *How'sa young squirrel? Ha ha!*

RALPH: *How'sa Texas jack rabbit?*

(*There is a sudden, incongruous stillness. They stare, all three of them,* ISABEL *at* GEORGE, GEORGE *and* RALPH *at each other.* GEORGE *is suddenly embarrassed and says:*)

GEORGE: Well, I see yuh still got yuh dawg.

RALPH: Yeah, m' wife's folks are cat lovers.

GEORGE: You'll get your wife back tomorrow.

RALPH: Hell, I don't want her back.

GEORGE: Y'don't want 'er back?

RALPH: That's right.

GEORGE: Hell, in that case, you won't be able to beat 'er off with a stick, ha ha!

(*His laugh expires as he catches* ISABEL's *outraged look.*)

Won't be able to beat her away from the door with a stick t'morrow. . . .

(*They stare at each other brightly, with little chuckles, a constant series of little chuckles.* ISABEL *feels ignored.*)

ISABEL: I doubt that Mr. Bates means it.

GEORGE: Didn't you all have a kid of some kind? I don't remember if it was a boy or a girl.

ISABEL: The toys under the tree might give you a clue as to that.

RALPH: Yeah, it's a boy, I guess. Drink?

GEORGE: You bet.

(GEORGE *goes to the bar and starts mixing drinks.*)

ISABEL: How old is your little boy?

RALPH: Three years old and she's awready made him a sissy.

GEORGE: They'll do it ev'ry time, man.

(*He keeps chuckling, as does* RALPH.)

RALPH: I didn't want this kind of a dawg, either. I wanted a Doberman pinscher, a dawg with some guts, not a whiner! But she wanted a poodle and this flop-eared sad sack of a spaniel was a compromise which turned out to be worse'n a poodle, ha, ha. . . .

GEORGE: I'll bet yuh dollars to doughnuts your wife and kid'll be back here tomorrow.

RALPH (*in his slow drawl*): They won't find me here if they do. I'm all packed to go. I would of been gone when you called but I'm waitin' t' git a call from a boy about t' git married. I want him to come over here an' make a cash offer on all this household stuff since I spent too much on Christmas and won't be around to collect my unemployment.

GEORGE: Come along with us. We got a big car out there an' we're as free as a breeze. Ain't that right, Little Bit?

ISABEL: Don't ask me what's right. I don't know! I *do* know, though, that couples with children don't separate at Christmas, and, George, let your friend work out his problems himself. You don't know the situation and don't have any right to interfere in it. And now will you please go get my little blue zipper bag for me? *Please?*

RALPH (*to* GEORGE, *as if she hadn't spoken*): Naw, I'm just going out to the army airfield a couple miles down the highway and catch the first plane going west.

GEORGE: We'll talk about that.

ISABEL: *George!*

GEORGE: Aw, HERE! I forgot to give you your present! After drivin' almost back into Dixon to find a liquor store open.

(*He extends a gift-wrapped magnum of champagne.*)

RALPH: Lover Jesus, champagne?

GEORGE: Imported and already cold.

RALPH (*glancing briefly at* ISABEL): Didn't I tell you that he was buyin' me something? She thought you'd deserted her, boy.

ISABEL: *All right, I'll get it myself! I'll go out and get it out of the car myself!*

(*She rushes out into snow, leaving the door open.*

(GEORGE *closes the door without apparently noticing her exit.*)

GEORGE: Boy, you an' me have got a lot to talk over.

RALPH: We sure got lots of territory to cover.

GEORGE: So your goddam marriage has cracked up on yuh, has it?

RALPH: How's yours goin'? So far?

GEORGE: We'll talk about it *later*. Discuss it *thoroughly! Later!*

RALPH: Y'got married yestiddy mawnin'?

GEORGE: Yeah.

RALPH: How was last night?

GEORGE: We'll talk about *that* later, too.

(ISABEL *rushes into the room in outrage, panting.*)

ISABEL: *I* can't break the lock on that *car!*

GEORGE: Little Bit, I didn't know that you wuh bawn in a barn.

(*He means she left the door open again.*)

ISABEL: I didn't know a lot about you, either!

(GEORGE *closes door.*)

Mr. Bates! Mr. Bates!

(*He turns toward her with a vague smile.*)

The gentleman I married refuses to get my zipper bag out of the car or unlock the car so I can get it myself.

(*The phone rings.* RALPH *picks it up.*)

RALPH (*in a slow, hoarse drawl, at the phone*): Aw, hi, Smokey. I'm glad you got my message. Look. I quit Regal Dairy Products and I'm flyin' out of here late tonight or early tomorrow morning and I thought maybe you might like to look over some of my stuff here, the household equipment, and make me a cash offer for it. I'll take less in cash than a check since I'm not gonna stop at the Coast, I'm flying straight through to Hong Kong so it would be difficult for me to cash yuh check an' of course I expect to make a sacrifice on the stuff here. Hey! Would you like a beaver-skin coat, sheared beaver-skin coat for Gertrude? Aw. I'd let you have it for a, for a—third off! Aw. Well, anyhow, come over right away, Smokey, and make me an offer in cash on as much of this household stuff as you figure that you could use when you git married. O.K.?

(*He hangs up.*)

GEORGE: Hong Kong?

RALPH: Yeah.

GEORGE: Well, how about that! Back to Miss Lotus Blossom in the Pavilion of Joys?

RALPH: I never had it so good. At least not *since*.

ISABEL (*acidly*): Mr. Bates, your character has changed since my gypsy husband appeared! He seems to have had an immediate influence on you, and not a good one. May I wash up in your bathroom?

(*They both look at her with slight, enigmatic smiles.*)

RALPH: What's that, honey?

ISABEL: Will you let me use your bathroom?

RALPH: Aw, sure, honey. I'm sorry you—

GEORGE: Now what's the matter with her?

(*He turns to* ISABEL.)

Now what's the matter with you?

ISABEL: May I talk to you alone? In another room?

RALPH: You all go in the bedroom and straighten things out.

(RALPH *goes out into the snow flurry.* GEORGE *leads* ISABEL *into next room.*)

GEORGE: Now what's the matter with you?

ISABEL: Is this a sample of how I'm going to be treated?

GEORGE: What do you mean? How have I treated you, huh?

ISABEL: I might as well not be present! For all the attention I have been paid since you and your buddy had this tender reunion!

GEORGE: Aren't you being a little unreasonable, honey?

ISABEL: I don't think so. George? If you are unhappy, our marriage can still be annulled. Y'know that, don't you?

GEORGE: You want to get *out* of it, do you?

(RALPH *comes back in with her traveling case. He sets it down and goes to the kitchenette.*)

ISABEL: I don't think it's really very unreasonable of me to want to be treated as if I LIVED! EXISTED!

GEORGE: Will you quit actin' like a spoiled little bitch? I want to tell you something. You're the first woman that ever put me down! Sleepin' las' night in a chair? What kind of basis is that for a happy marriage?

ISABEL: You had to get drunk on a highway! In a heaterless funeral car, after informing me you had just quit your job! Blasting my eardrums, afterward, with a car radio you wouldn't let me turn down. How was I supposed to react to such kindness? Women are human beings and I am not an exception to that rule, I assure you! I HATED YOU LAST NIGHT AFTER YOU HAD BEEN HATING ME AND TORTURING ME ALL DAY LONG!

(RALPH *comes back into the front room.*)

GEORGE: Torturing you, did you say? WHY DON'T YOU SIMMER DOWN! We ain't ALONE here, y'know!

RALPH (*quietly, from the living room*): You all are just goin' through a perfectly usual little period of adjustment. That's all it is, I told her—

GEORGE: Aw! You all have been talking?

ISABEL: What did you think we'd been doing while you were gone in that instrument of torture you have for a car?

GEORGE: You've got to simmer down to a lower boiling point, baby.

RALPH (*entering the bedroom*): Just goin' through a period of adjustment. . . .

ISABEL: Adjustment to what, Mr. Bates? Humiliation? For the rest of my life? Well, I won't have it! I don't want such an "adjustment." I want to— May I—

(*She sobs.*)

—freshen up a little bit in your bathroom before we drive downtown? To check in at a hotel?

RALPH: Sure you can.

GEORGE: I ain't goin' downtown—or checkin' in no hotel.

(*He goes back into the living room.*)

ISABEL: YOU may do as you *please! I'm* checking in a hotel.

RALPH (*offering her a glass*): You never finished your drink.

ISABEL: I don't care to, thanks. Too many people think that liquor solves problems, all problems. I think all it does is *confuse* them!

RALPH: I would say that it—*obfuscates* them a little, but—

ISABEL: Does *what* to them, Mr. Bates?

RALPH: I work crossword puzzles. I—ha ha!—pick up a lot of long words. Obfuscates means obscures. And problems need obfuscation now and then, honey. I don't mean total or permanent obfuscation, I just mean *temporary* obfuscation, that's all.

(*He is touched by the girl and he is standing close to her, still holding the glass out toward her. He has a fine, simple sweetness and gentleness when he's not "bugged" by people.)*

D'ya always say *Mister* to men?

ISABEL: Yes, I do till I know them. I had an old-fashioned upbringing and I can't say I regret it. Yes.

(She is still peering out the door at her new husband.)

RALPH: I wish you would say Ralph to me like you *know* me, honey. You got a tension between you, and tensions obfuscate love. Why don't you get that cross look off your face and give him a loving expression? Obfuscate his problems with a sweet smile on your face and—

ISABEL: You do that! I'm not in a mood to "obfuscate" his problems. Mr. Bates, I think he'd do better to face them like I'm facing mine, such as the problem of having married a man that seems to dislike me after one day of marriage.

RALPH: Finish this drink and obfuscate that problem because it doesn't exist.

(He closes the bedroom door. As he comes back to ISABEL with the glass, GEORGE reopens the door between the two rooms, glares in for a moment and switches the overhead light on, then goes back into the parlor. RALPH smiles tolerantly at this show of distrust which is not justified.)

ISABEL: You have a sweet little bedroom, Mr. Bates.

RALPH: I married a *sweet, homely* woman. Almost started to *like* her. I can like *anybody,* but—

ISABEL: Mr. Bates? Ralph? This house has a *sweetness* about it!

RALPH: You don't think it's "tacky"?

ISABEL: No. I think it's—sweet!

RALPH: We got it cheap because this section of town is built right over a cavern.

ISABEL (*without listening*): What?

RALPH: This High Point suburb is built over an underground cavern and is gradually sinking down in it. You see those cracks in the walls?

ISABEL: Oh. . . .

(*She hasn't listened to him or looked.*)

Oh! My little blue bag. May I have it?

RALPH (*through the door*): She wants a little blue bag.

GEORGE: *Here, give it to her, goddam it!*

(*He tosses the bag into the bedroom.* ISABEL *screams.* RALPH *catches the bag.*)

Now whatcha screamin' faw?

ISABEL: Thank heaven Mr. Bates is such a good catch. All my colognes and perfumes are in that bag, including a twenty-five-dollar bottle of Vol-de-nuit. Mr. Bates, will it be necessary for me to phone the hotel?

GEORGE: Didn't you hear what I said?

ISABEL: Mr. Bates! Would you mind phoning some clean, inexpensive hotel to hold a room for us tonight?

GEORGE: I said I'm not gonna check in a hotel tonight!

ISABEL: Reserve a *single* room, please!

RALPH: Sure, sure, honey, I'll do that. Now you just rest an' fresh up an'— Come on, George, let her alone here now, so she can rest an' calm down.

(*He leads* GEORGE *back into the parlor.*)

GEORGE: Look at my hands! Willya look at my hands?

RALPH: What about your hands?

GEORGE: Remember that tremor? Which I had in Korea? Those shakes? Which started in Korea?

RALPH: Aw, is it come back on yuh?

GEORGE: Are you blind, man?

RALPH: Yeah. How's your drink?

GEORGE: She in the bathroom yet?

RALPH: Naw, she's still in the bedroom.

GEORGE: Wait'll she gits in the bathroom so we can talk.

RALPH: What's your drink, ole son?

GEORGE: Beer's fine. Jesus!

RALPH (*at the bar*): Rough?

GEORGE: Just wait'll she gits in the bathroom so I can tell you about last night.

RALPH: Here.

(*He hands him a beer.*)

GEORGE (*at the bedroom door*): She's still sittin' there bawling on that bed. Step outside a minute.

(*He goes to the front door and out onto the tiny paved porch. The interior dims as* RALPH *follows him out. For a while they just stand drinking beer with the snow shadows swarming about them.*)

RALPH: Chilly.

GEORGE: I don't feel chilly.

RALPH: *I* do.

(*He pauses.*)

You're not for that little lady in that damn silly little sissy mess of a bedroom!

GEORGE: What's wrong with the bedroom, it looked like a nice little bedroom.

RALPH: A bedroom is just as nice as whoever sleeps in it with you.

GEORGE: I missed that. What was that, now?

(*He rests an arm on Ralph's shoulders.*)

RALPH: How would you like ev'ry time you wint t'bed with your wife, you had to imagine on the bed in the dark that it wasn't her on it with you, in the dark with you, but any one of a list of a thousand or so lovely lays? I done a despicable thing. I married a girl that had no attraction for me excepting I felt sorry for her and her old man's money! I got what I should have gotten: nothing! Just a goddam desk job at Regal Dairy Products, one of her daddy's business operations in Memphis, at eighty-five lousy rutten dollars a week! With my background? In the Air Force?

GEORGE: Man an air record will cut you no ice on the ground. All it leaves you is a—mysterious tremor. Come on back in. I'm freezing to death out here. I'll git her into that bathroom so we can talk.

(*He tosses the beer cans into yard.*)

RALPH: Don't y'know better'n to throw beer cans in a man's front yard?

(*He says this vaguely, glumly, as he follows GEORGE back into the cottage and shuts the door behind them. GEORGE goes to bedroom.*)

GEORGE (*entering*): Little Bit, you told me you couldn't

wait to get under a good hot shower. There's a good shower in that bathroom. Why don't you go and get under that good hot shower?

ISABEL: I have a lot to think over, George.

GEORGE: Think it over under a good shower in that bathroom, will you? I want to take a bath, too.

ISABEL (*suddenly turning to face him from the bed*): George, I feel so lonely!

GEORGE: Yeah, and whose fault is that?

ISABEL: I don't know why I suddenly felt so lonely!

(*She sobs again. He regards her coolly from the door.*)

GEORGE: Little Bit, go in the bathroom and take your shower, so I can go take mine, or do you want us to go in and take one together?

(*She rises with a sigh and goes to bathroom door.*)

Naw, I didn't think so.

(*She enters the bathroom. He waits till the shower starts, then returns to the front room.*)

There now, she's in!

(*He shakes both fists in the air with a grimace of torment.*)

Look! I got to get rid of that girl. I got to get rid of her quick. Jesus, you got to help me. I can't stay with that girl.

RALPH: Man, you're married to her.

GEORGE: You're married to one! Where's yours? You son of a tail gun! Don't tell me I'm married to her when we ain't exchanged five remarks with each other since we drove out of Cape Girardeau where she refused to— Has she come out of the bathroom? No!—Even *undress!* But huddled up in a chair all night in a blanket, crying? Because she had the misfortune to be my wife?

RALPH: I wouldn't count on it.

GEORGE: On what?

RALPH: Her thinking it's such a misfortune.

GEORGE: I described to you how we passed the night, last night!

RALPH: Is this girl a virgin?

GEORGE: She is a *cast-iron* virgin! And's going to stay one! Determined!

RALPH: I wouldn't count on that.

GEORGE: I would. I count on it. First thing I do tomorrow is pack her onto a plane back to Saint Louie.

RALPH: You must have done something to shock her.

GEORGE: That's the truth, I tried to sleep with her.

RALPH: Maybe you handled the little lady too rough.

GEORGE: Now don't talk to me like a wise old man of the mountain about how to deal with a woman. Who was it had to make dates for who at Big Springs and who was it even had to make arrangements for you with those Tokyo dolls?

RALPH: That's not women, that's gash.

GEORGE: Gash are women.

RALPH: They are used women. You've got an unused woman and got to approach her as one.

GEORGE: She's gonna stay unused as far as I am concerned.

(*He stoops by the Christmas tree.*)

Now what the hell is this thing?

(*He has crouched among the toys under the tree.*)

RALPH: Rocket launcher. Miniature of the rocket-launchin' pad at Cape Canaveral.

GEORGE: No snow! How's it work?

RALPH: Gimme the countdown. I'll show you.

GEORGE: Ten. Nine. Eight. Seven. Six. Five. Four. Three. Two. Oww!

(*The rocket has fired in his face.*)

RALPH: Ain't you got sense enough to stand clear of a rocket launcher? Ha ha! Last week, just last week, I caught the little bugger playin' with a rag doll. Well. I snatched that doll away from him an' pitched it into the fireplace. He tried to pull it out an' burned his hand! Dotty called me a monster! The child screamed "I hate you!" an' kicked my shins black an' blue! But I'll be damned if any son of Ralph Bates will grow up playin' with dolls. Why, I'll bet you he rides this hawss side-saddle! Naw, a sissy tendency in a boy's got to be nipped in the bud, otherwise the bud will blossom.

GEORGE: I would prefer to have a little girl.

(*He says this wistfully, still rubbing his bruised forehead.*)

Little girls prefer Daddy. Female instinct comes out early in them.

RALPH: I wanted a boy but I'm not sure I got one. However, I got him a real red-blooded boy's Christmas, at no small expense for a man in my income bracket!

(ISABEL *comes out of the bathroom.*)

I like the kid, I mean I—sure would suffer worse than he would if the neighborhood gang called him "Sissy!" I'm tolerant. By nature. But if I git partial custody of the kid, even one month in summer, I will correct the sissy tendency in him. Because in this world you got to be what your physical sex is or correct it in Denmark. I mean we got a *man's* world coming up, man! Technical! Terriffic! And it's gotta be *fearless! Terrific!*

ISABEL: Mr. Bates.

GEORGE (*on his way to the door*): Whadaya want?

ISABEL: I called for Mistuh Bates.

GEORGE: Mistuh Bates, Mrs. Haverstick is anxious to talk to you, suh.

ISABEL: I just want to know if you have called the hotel.

RALPH (*entering*): Sure, sure, honey. Don't worry about a thing. Everything's gonna be fine.

ISABEL (*she is in a silk robe*): Thanks, Ralph. You've been awf'ly kind to me. Oh! I helped myself to a little Pepto-Bismol I found in your sweet little bathroom.

RALPH: Aw, that pink stuff? Take it all. I never touch it. It's Dorothea's. She used to get acid stomach.

ISABEL: It's very soothing.

(GEORGE *crosses to the bedroom door, head cocked, somewhat suspicious.*)

RALPH: Well, I cured her of that. I doubt that she's hit that Pepto-Bismol bottle once in the last five years.

ISABEL: I rarely suffer from an upset stomach. Rarely as snow in Memphis!

(*She laughs lightly.*)

But the human stomach is an emotional barometer with some people. Some get headaches, others get upset stomachs.

RALPH: Some even git diarrhea.

ISABEL: The combination of nervous strain and— Oh! What's this?

(*She picks up a gorgeously robed statue of the infant Jesus.*)

RALPH: Aw, that.

(*He moves farther into the bedroom.* GEORGE *moves closer to the door.*)

That's the Infant of Prague. Prague, Czechoslovakia?

ISABEL: Oh?

RALPH: It was discovered there in the ruins of an old monastery. It has miraculous properties.

ISABEL: Does it?

RALPH: They say that it does. Whoever gives you the Infant of Prague gives you a piece of money to put underneath it for luck. Her father presented this infant to Dorothea so the piece of money was *naturally one penny*. It's s'posed to give you prosperity if you're not prosperous and a child if you're childless. It give us a child but the money is yet to come in, the money's just been goin' out. However, I don't blame the Infant of Prague for that, because—

ISABEL: Mr. Bates? Ralph? You know, very often people can be absolutely blind, stupid, and helpless about their own problems and still have a keen intuition about the problems of others?

RALPH: Yeah?

ISABEL: There is such a tender atmosphere in this sweet little house, especially this little bedroom, you can almost—

touch it, feel it! I mean you can *breathe* the tender atmosphere in it!

RALPH (*in a slow, sad drawl*): The color scheme in this bedroom is battleship gray. And will you notice the cute inscriptions on the twin beds? "His" on this one, "Hers" on that one? The linen's marked his and hers, too. Well. The space between the two beds was no-man's land for a while. Her psychological frigidity was like a, like a—artillery barrage!—between his and hers. I didn't try to break through it the first few nights. Nope. I said to myself, "Let *her* make the first move."

ISABEL: *Did* she?

RALPH: What do *you* think?

ISABEL: I think she *did*.

RALPH: *Right you are!*

(*He gives her a little congratulatory pat on the shoulder.*)

GEORGE: What's this heart-to-heart talk goin' on in here?

RALPH (*chuckling*): Come on out of here, boy. I got something to tell you.

(*He leads GEORGE out.*)

GEORGE: What were you up to in there?

RALPH (*whispering loudly*): Go in there, quick, before she gets dressed, you fool!

GEORGE: I'll be damned if I will!

RALPH: I'll turn the TV on loud.

ISABEL (*calling out*): I'll be dressed in a jiffy!

RALPH: Go ON! You just got a jiffy!

GEORGE: Yeah, and I've got some pride, too. She put me down last night, first woman ever to put me down in—

RALPH: I know, you told me. GO IN! Lock the door and—

GEORGE: YOU go in! That's what you WANT to do! I never had a girl yet that you didn't want to take over. This time you're welcome. GO IN! GO BACK IN AND BREATHE THE TENDER ATMOSPHERE OF THAT—

RALPH: Gawge? Hey—You're *shakin'*, man, you're shakin' to pieces! What kind of a son of a bitch d'you take me faw?

GEORGE: The kind which you are, which you always have been!

RALPH: She is right about you. You are not well, son. . . .

GEORGE: Where d'ya git this "son" stuff! Don't call me "son."

RALPH: Then grow up, will yuh! What's your drink? Same?

GEORGE: Same . . .

RALPH: You're shakin' because you want to go in that bedroom. Go IN! Take the bottle in with you! I'll sit here and watch TV till—

(ISABEL *has put on her traveling suit. She comes into the living room.*)

—Too late *now*!

ISABEL (*in a sweet Texas drawl*): Mr. Bates? Ralph? It breaks my heart to see all those lovely child's toys under the tree and the little boy not here to have his Christmas.

RALPH: He's with his mother.

ISABEL: I know, but his Christmas is here.

RALPH: He's a Mama's boy. He's better off with his Mama.

ISABEL: How are *you* feeling, now, George?

(GEORGE *grunts and turns to the bar.*

(ISABEL *makes a despairing gesture to Ralph.*

(GEORGE *wheels about abruptly, suspecting some dumb-play.*

(ISABEL *laughs lightly and then sighs deeply.)* ..

GEORGE: I thought you'd set your heart on a single hotel room tonight.

ISABEL: George, you're shaking worse than I've ever seen you.

GEORGE: That's, that's not your problem, that's—*my* problem, not *yours!*

RALPH (*to* ISABEL): *Honey? Come here a minute.*

(*He whispers something to her.*)

ISABEL: Oh, no. No! Mr. Bates, you are confusing the function of a wife with that of a— I feel sorry, I feel very sorry for you not-so-young young men who've depended for love, for tenderness in your lives, on the sort of women available near army camps, in occupied territories! Mr. Bates? Ralph?

RALPH: Just take his hand and lead him into the—

ISABEL: RALPH! No! BELIEVE ME!

RALPH: All right. . . .

(*There is a pause.*)

ISABEL: Ralph, why did you quit YOUR job? Did you get the shakes, too?

GEORGE: Don't get bitchy with him.

ISABEL: I WASN'T BEING BITCHY!

RALPH: She wasn't being bitchy. She asked a logical question.

ISABEL: Just a question!

GEORGE: Can't you mind your own business for a change? You got fired too, don't forget! All three of us here is jobless!

ISABEL: I am not forgetting.

(*Primly, with dignity.*)

I am not forgetting a thing, and I have a lot to remember.

GEORGE: Good. I hope you remember it. *Memorize* it!

(*He is getting tight.*)

ISABEL (*sniffling a little*): I think I caught cold in that car.

GEORGE: Hell, you were born with a cold—

ISABEL: *Stop that!*

GEORGE: In your damn little—   (Overlapping, barely intelligible)

ISABEL: MR. BATES, MAKE HIM STOP!

RALPH: Let him blow off some steam.

GEORGE: Incurable cold! You didn't catch it from me.

ISABEL: I wish you had shown this side of your nature before, just a hint, just a clue, so I'd have known what I was in for.

GEORGE: What hint did you give *me*? What clue did *I* have to *your* nature?

ISABEL: Did I disguise my nature?

GEORGE: You sure in hell did.

ISABEL: In what *way*, tell me, please!

GEORGE: You didn't put the freeze on me at Barnes Hospital!

(*To* RALPH.)

She was nurse at Barnes when I went there for those tests? To find out the cause of my shakes? She was my night nurse at Barnes.

ISABEL: Oh, stop! Don't be so crude! How can you be so crude?

GEORGE: She was my night nurse at Barnes and gave me alcohol rubdowns at bedtime.

ISABEL: That was my job. I had to.

GEORGE: Hell, she stroked and petted me with her hands like she had on a pair of silk gloves.

ISABEL: This is insufferable. I am going downtown.

(*She covers her face, sobbing.*)

Just give me carfare downtown.

GEORGE: You remember those dolls with silk gloves on their hands in Tokyo, Ralph? Hell, she could of given them Jap dolls lessons!

ISABEL: I DID NOT TOUCH YOUR BODY EXCEPT AS A NURSE HIRED TO DO IT! YOU KNOW I DIDN'T! I DID NOT TOUCH YOUR BIG OLD LECHEROUS BODY.

GEORGE: How'd you give me a rubdown without touching my body? Huh? How could you give me rubdowns without touching my body? Huh?

ISABEL: Please, please, make him be still. Mr. Bates? You

believe me? He's making out I seduced him while I was his nurse.

GEORGE: I didn't say that. Don't say I said that. I didn't say that. I said you had soft little fingers and you knew what you were doing. She'd say, "Turn over." I couldn't turn over. I had to stay on my stomach. I was embarrassed not to.

ISABEL: Ah—I feel nauseated. What filth you have in your mind!

RALPH: Honey? Little lady? Come over and sit here with me. All this will all straighten out. It's going to be all straightened out.

(GEORGE *pours himself a drink. The glass slips out of his shaking fingers.*)

GEORGE: *Worse than ever, worse than ever before!* How could I have kept that job? A ground mechanic with hands that can't hold tools?

ISABEL: Go take your tranquillizers. They're in my zipper bag.

GEORGE: Oh, Jesus.

RALPH (*picking up the dropped glass*): See, honey? That boy isn't well. Make some allowances for him. You're both nice kids, both of you, wonderful people. And very good-looking people. I'm afraid you're doomed to be happy for a long time together, soon as this little period of adjustment that you're going through right now passes over.

(GEORGE *holds his violently shaking hands in front of him, staring at them fiercely.*

(*He goes to the bedroom.*)

ISABEL: May I call my father, collect?

RALPH: Don't call home, now. Why upset the old people on Christmas Eve?

ISABEL: I'll just say I miss them and want to come home for Christmas.

RALPH: They'll know something's wrong if you go home without your brand-new husband.

ISABEL: Husband! What husband? That man who describes me as a Tokyo whore? Implies that I seduced him in a hospital because I was required to give him alcohol rubdowns at night?

RALPH: All he meant was you excited him, honey.

ISABEL: I assure you that was *not* my intention! I am naturally gentle, I am gentle bv nature, and if my touch on his big lecherous body created—*sexual fantasies* in his *mind*! —that's hardly *my* fault, is it?

GEORGE (*returning*): I am sorry that I upset you.

ISABEL: Will you tell him the truth?

GEORGE: Sure I will. What about?

ISABEL: Did I deliberately excite you in Barnes Hospital?

GEORGE: No. I never said that.

ISABEL: Anybody that heard you would get that impression.

GEORGE: You didn't deliberately do it, you just did it because I was horny for you, that's all, that's all, that's—all. . . .

(*He slumps in a chair with a long, despairing sigh.*

(*There is a silent pause.*)

ISABEL: I don't blame you alone, George. I blame myself, too. Not for deliberate sexual provocation, but for not realizing before our marriage yesterday that we were—opposite types.

GEORGE (*sadly*): Yes, opposite types. . . .

ISABEL: *I want to talk to my father!*

GEORGE: Talk to him. Call him. I'll pay Ralph the charges.

ISABEL: May I?

RALPH: Sure, honey, call your folks and wish 'em a Merry Christmas.

ISABEL: Thank you. I will if I can stop crying.

RALPH: George? This little girl needs you. Go on, be nice to her, boy.

GEORGE: I need somebody, too. She hasn't got the incurable shakes, *I* have, *I* got 'em! Was *she* nice to *me?* *Last night?*

ISABEL (*tearfully*): Operator? I want to call long distance, Sweetwater, Texas. Oh-seven-oh-three. No, anybody that answers. It will be Daddy. Mama can't get out of—

(*She sobs.*)

—bed!

(RALPH *makes a sign to* GEORGE *to go over and sit by her.* GEORGE *disregards the suggestion.*)

RALPH: You better hang up and let them call you back. Long distance is very busy on Christmas Eve. Everyone callin' the home folks.

ISABEL: I just hope I stop crying! I don't want Daddy to hear me.

(*She pauses.*)

Poor ole thing. So sweet and faithful to Mama, bedridden with arthritis for seven years, now . . . Hello? What? Oh.

You'll call me back when you complete the connection, will you, because it's very important, it's really very urgent. . . .

(*She hangs up. There is silence.*)

RALPH (*finally*): One bad night in a rutten highway motel and you all are acting like born enemies toward each other!

GEORGE: Don't upset her, she's going to talk to her daddy. And tell him she's married to a stinker.

ISABEL: No, I'm not. I'm going to tell him that I am blissfully happy, married to the kindest man in the world, the second kindest, the kindest man next to my daddy!

GEORGE: Thanks.

ISABEL: Waits hand and foot on Mama, bedridden with arthritis.

GEORGE: You told Ralph about that.

ISABEL: And has held down a job in a pharmacy all these years. . . .

GEORGE: Wonderful. I didn't expect to marry a girl in love with her father.

ISABEL: George Haverstick, you are truly a monster!

(*The phone rings.*

(*She snatches it up.*)

What?—DAD! OH, PRECIOUS DADDY!

(*She bursts into violent tears.*)

Can't talk, can't talk, can't talk, can't talk, *can't—talk*!

RALPH: Honey, gi' me the phone!

(*She surrenders it to him.*)

Hello? Hi, Pop, Merry Christmas. No, this isn't George, this is a buddy of his. Isabel wants to talk to you to tell you how happy she is, but she just broke up with emotion. You know how it is, don't you. Pop? Newlyweds? They're naturally full of emotion. They got to go through a little period of adjustment between them.——Fine, yes, she's fine. She'll talk to you soon as she blows her nose. Hey, honey? Your daddy wants to talk to you.

(*She takes the phone, then bursts into violent sobbing again, covering her mouth and handing the phone back to* RALPH.)

Pop? I'll have to talk for her. She's all shook up.

(*He forces the phone back into* ISABEL's *hand*.)

ISABEL (*choked*): Dad?

(*She bawls again, covering the mouthpiece.* RALPH *takes the phone back from her.*)

RALPH: Pop? Just talk to her, Pop. She's too shook up to talk back.

(*He forces the phone into her hands again.*)

ISABEL: Dad? How are you, Daddy? Are you? That's wonderful, Daddy. Oh, I'm fine, too. I got married yesterday. Yesterday . . . How is Mom? Just the same? Daddy? I may be seeing you soon. Yes. You know I gave up my nursing job at Barnes when I married and so I have lots of free time and I might just suddenly pop in on you—*tomorrow!*—— I love you and miss you so much! Good-by, Merry Christmas, Daddy!

(*She hangs up blindly and goes over to the Christmas tree.*)

I think it's awful your little boy's missing his Christmas. Such a wonderful Christmas. A choo-choo train with depot and tunnel, cowboy outfit, chemical set and a set of alphabet blocks. . . .

GEORGE: He knows what he got for his kid, you don't have to tell him.

(*There is a pause.*)

ISABEL: Well, now, I feel better, after talking to Daddy.

GEORGE: Does it make you feel uplifted, spiritually?

ISABEL: I feel less lonely. That's all.

GEORGE: I wonder if it would have that effect on me if I called my daddy or mama in Amarillo? That's in Texas, too. Maybe I'd feel less lonely. Huh, Little Bit?

(*She starts out.*)

Just wait a minute. I want to tell you something. In my thirty-four years I've been with a fair share of women and you are the first, you are the first of the lot, that has found me repulsive.

ISABEL: I don't find you "repulsive," not even your vanity, George, silly but not repulsive.

RALPH: Hey, now, you all quit this.

GEORGE: Can you stand there and tell me you find me attractive?

ISABEL: I'm afraid I can't, at this moment.

GEORGE: Well, goddam it, what in hell did you marry me faw?

ISABEL: Mr. Bates, your animal is standing by the door as as if it wants out. Shall I let it out for you?

RALPH: You two are just goin' through this adjustment period that all young couples go through.

ISABEL: Such a sweet animal! What is this animal's name?

GEORGE: The animal is a dog.

ISABEL: I know it's a dog.

GEORGE: Then why don't you call it a dog!

RALPH: Better put 'er lead on 'er. Her name is Bess.

ISABEL: Shall we take a walk, Bessie? Huh? A nice little run in the snow. See! She does want out. Oh! My coat. . . .

RALPH: Here, put on this one, honey.

(*He takes the beaver coat out of the Christmas box under the tree.*)

ISABEL: Oh, what beautiful sheared beaver! It's your wife's Christmas present?

RALPH: It was but it ain't no more.

ISABEL: How soft! Now I know that you love her. You couldn't feel the softness of this fur and not know it was bought as a present for someone you love.

RALPH: Put it on. It's yours. A wedding present to you.

ISABEL: Oh, no I—

RALPH: WILL YOU PLEASE PUT IT ON YUH?

ISABEL: I guess the snow won't hurt it. Come on, Bessie, that's a good lady, come on. . . .

(*She goes out.*)

GEORGE: I know of *two* animals that want out and one of them ain't no dawg!

ISABEL (*returning*): I heard you say that!

GEORGE: Well, good.

ISABEL: If you want out of our marriage, a divorce isn't necessary. We can just get an annulment! So maybe last night was fortunate after all!

(*She stares at him a moment and then goes back out with the dog. As they leave, the dog is barking at something outside.*

(GEORGE *comes up beside* RALPH *and rests an affectionate arm on his shoulders.*

(*The tempo now becomes very fast.*)

RALPH: You old Texas jack rabbit!

GEORGE: You tail-gunner son of a—How you feel?

RALPH: I feel fine!

(*They chuckle shyly together. Then:*

(*They catch each other in an affectionate bear hug.*)

GEORGE: How much money you got?

RALPH: Why?

GEORGE: Remember how we talked about going into something together when we got out of the service? Well, we're out of the service. How much money do you think you can raise?

RALPH: What are *your* assets, Buddy?

GEORGE: I've saved five hundred dollars and can get a thousand for that '52 Caddy.

RALPH: You can't go into no business on as little as that.

GEORGE: You're selling out this house and everything in it, ain't you?

RALPH: I'd have to split it with Dorothea, I reckon.

GEORGE: Look. Let's cut out tomorrow. Let's go to Texas together. We can swing the financing to pick up a piece of ranchland near San Antone and raise us a herd of fine cattle.

RALPH: Why San Antone?

GEORGE: I said near it. It's a beautiful town. A winding river goes through it.

RALPH: Uh-huh. You mentioned "swing the financing." How did you—visualize—that?

GEORGE: Noticed my car out there?

RALPH: That funeral limousine?

GEORGE: We cut out of here tomorrow bright and early and drive straight through to West Texas. In West Texas we git us a colored boy, put a showfer's cap on him an' set him back of the wheel. He drives us up in front of the biggest San Antone bank and there we demand an immediate interview with the president of it. My folks staked out West Texas. The name of the first George Haverstick in West Texas is engraved on the memorial tablet to the Alamo heroes in San Antone! I'm not snowin' you, man! An' they's no better credit card in West Texas than an ancestor's name on that memorial tablet. We will arrive at lunch time an'—invite this bank executive to lunch at the San Antone country club to which I can git us a guest card an' befo' we're in sight of the golf links the financing deal will be swung!

RALPH: Man, a bank president has rode in a awful lot of funeral processions. It's almost one of his main professional duties. He's rode in too many funeral limousines not to know when he's in one. And ain't you afraid that he might, well— notice your shakes?

GEORGE: This little tremor would disappear completely the moment I crossed into Texas!

RALPH: I hope so, man, permanently and completely, but—

GEORGE: Go on. Tear down the project!

RALPH: There's no Ralph Bates, first, second, third, fourth or fifth on that memorial tablet to those—Alamo heroes.

GEORGE: Haven't you blazoned your name in the memory of two wars?

RALPH: Who remembers two wars? Or even one, after some years. There's a great public amnesia about a former war hero.

(*He goes reflectively to the front door.*)

GEORGE: Where you goin'?

RALPH: I'm goin' out to think in this cool night air.

(*He exits onto the paved terrace, switching off the interior lights.* GEORGE *follows gravely.* RALPH *stoops to light up a string of colored bulbs that cover the arched entrance to carport.*

(*It casts a dim rainbow glow on the terrace. Shadowy flakes of snow drift through it.*)

Why San Antone? Why cattle? Why not electric equipment?

GEORGE: I know San Antone and cattle!

RALPH: And I know electric equipment.

GEORGE: Yes, you can turn on a set of little Christmas tree lights.

RALPH: I don't want to be your ranch hand!

GEORGE: We'd buy in *equal.*

RALPH: How? One minute you say you'll liquidate all your assets that only appear to be an old funeral car, the next you say we'll drive a bank president out in this funeral car, and you want me to put up all that I realize on the sale of this property here? Your sense of equity is very unequal, and shit-fire anyhow, even if I sell this property, by remote control, from Hong Kong, and Dotty's folks would sure in hell block the transaction—well, look at the cracks in this stucco, y'know how they got there? This Goddam High Point suburb—*listen!*—happens to be built over a great big underground cavern into which it is *sinking!*

GEORGE: *Sinking?*

RALPH: I'm not snowing you, man, this whole community here is gradually sinking, inch by inch by year, into this subterranean cavern and the property owners and the real-estate promoters are in collusion to keep this secret about it: so we can sell out to the next bunch of suckers: DIS-GUSTING!

GEORGE: Built over a—

RALPH: *Cavern: yes!*—a *big subterranean cavern,* but so is *your* project, not to mention your *marriage. Cattle!—Cattle?*

GEORGE: The Texas Longhorn isn't just cattle, it's a—dig-nified beast.

RALPH: Did you say Texas Longhorn? Son, the Texas Longhorn is not only dignified, it is *obsolete.*

GEORGE: Historical, yeah, like the Haversticks of West Texas.

RALPH: The Haversticks of West Texas are not yet ob-solete, are they?

GEORGE: I am the last one of 'em an' the prospects of an-other don't look bright at this moment. But the Texas Long-horn—

(*He exhales.*)

—compared to modern beef cattle such as your Hereford or your Black Angus—it has no carcass value.

RALPH: Well, in that case, why don't you *breed* the Black Angus or the—

GEORGE: I anticipated that question.

RALPH: I hope you're prepared with some answer. . . .

GEORGE (*draws on cigarette and flips it away*): Le' me put it this way. How would you like to breed a herd of noble cattle, a herd that stood for the frontier days of this country!—an' ride to the depot one mawnin' in your station wagon, the name of your ranch stamped on it, to watch these great, dignified beasts being herded onto a string of flatcars, penned in and hauled off to K City packin' houses, Chicago slaughterhouses, the shockin' atrocities which cannot even be thought about without a shudder!—an' wave 'em good-by as if they was off for a mother-lovin' church picnic?

RALPH: It's—it's a—heart-breakin' pitcher!

(*He chuckles.*)

But I do love a good steak, ha ha! A prime-cut sirloin, however— What would you want to breed this noble herd for? For *kicks*, for—?

GEORGE: *You* got TV in there, ain't you? Turn on your TV any late afternoon or early evenin' and what do you get—beside the commercials, I mean? A goddam Western, on film. Y'know what I see, outside the camera range? A big painted sign that says: "Haverstick-Bates Ranch"—or "Bates-Haverstick," you can have top billing!—"The Last Stand of the Texas Longhorn, a Dignified Beast! We breed cattle for TV Westerns." We breed us some buffalo, too. The buffalo is also a dignified beast, almost extinct, only thirty thousand head of the buffalo left in this land. We'll increase that number by a sizable fraction. Hell, we could double that number befo' we—

RALPH: Hang up our boots an' saddles under the—dignified sky of West Texas?

GEORGE (*with feeling*): There *is* dignity in that sky! There's dignity in the agrarian, the pastoral—way of—existence! A dignity too long lost out of the—American dream—

(*He is shaking a good deal with emotion.*)

—as it used to be in the West Texas-Haverstick days. . . .

RALPH: But I want to be dignified, too.

GEORGE: Human dignity's what I'm—

RALPH: I don't want to be caught short by a Texas Longhorn while crossing a pasture one mawnin' in West Texas! Ha ha ha. Naw, I don't want to catch me an ass full of Texas Longhorns before I can jump a fence rail out of that West Texas pasture. I—

GEORGE: SHUT UP! WILL YUH? YOU TV WATCHIN', CANNED-BEER DRINKIN', SPANISH-SUBURBAN-STUCCO-TYPE SON OF—Y'KNOW I THINK BEER IS DOPED? DOPED? I THINK THEY DOPE IT TO CREATE A NATIONAL TOLERANCE OF THE TV COMMERCIAL! No—No—I'm sorry I come through Dixon. . . .

(*He moves away, sadly.*)

I cherished a memory of you—

(CAROLERS *are heard from a distance.*)

—idolized an old picture of which I was suddenly faced with a, with a—*goddam travesty* of it!—When you opened the door and I was confronted with a —DEFEATED! MIDDLE-AGED! NEGATIVE! LOST!—poor bastard . . .

RALPH: What do you think I saw when I opened that door? A ghostly apparition!

GEORGE: ME?

RALPH: A young man I used to know with an old man's affliction: the palsy!

GEORGE: Thanks!—I appreciate that.

(*Next door the* CAROLERS *sing:* "*God Rest Ye Merry, Gentlemen, May Nothing Ye Dismay!*")

Oh, man, oh, brother, I sure do appreciate that!

(*He sits down quickly, shaking fiercely, in a metal porch chair, turning it away from* RALPH *to face the audience.* RALPH *is immediately and truly contrite.*)

Yeah. In addition to those other changes I mentioned in you, you've now exposed another which is the worst of the bunch. You've turned *vicious!*

RALPH: Aw, now—

GEORGE: Yeah, yeah, bitter and vicious! To ridicule an affliction like *mine*, like *this*, is vicious, *vicious!*

(*He holds up his shaky hand.* RALPH *reaches his hand out to take it but doesn't. Instead he drops his hand on* GEORGE's *shoulder.*)

Take that mother-grabbin' hand off my shoulder or I'll break it off you!

RALPH: You ridiculed *my* afflictions.

GEORGE: What afflictions?

RALPH: My life has been an affliction.

(*He says this without self-pity, simply as a matter of fact.*)

GEORGE: Now don't make me cry into this can of Budweiser with that sad, sad story of your childhood in that home for illegitimate orphans.

RALPH: *Foundlings!* Home. I was not illegitimate.

GEORGE: Foundlings are illegitimate.

RALPH: Not—*necessarily—always* . . .

(He says this with a humility that might be touching to anyone less absorbed in his own problems than GEORGE. RALPH *looks up at the drift of snow from the dark.)*

No, I meant to live a life in a Spanish-type stucco cottage in a—high point over a cavern, that is an affliction for someone. that wanted and dreamed of—*oh, I wish I could be the first man in a moon rocket!* No, not the moon, but Mars, Venus! Hell, I'd like to be transported and transplanted to colonize and fertilize, to be the Adam on a—star in a different *galaxy*, yeah, that far away even!—it's wonderful knowing that such a thing is no longer inconceivable, huh?

GEORGE: You're talking out of character. You're a dedicated conformist, the most earthbound earth man on earth.

RALPH: If you think that about me, you never known me.

GEORGE *(starts off the terrace)*: I'm going walking, alone!

(He stops abruptly.)

Naw, if she sees me walking, she'll think I'm out looking for her.

RALPH: Goddam it, why don't you? Intercept her and don't say a word, just stick your hand inside that beaver-skin coat I give her and apply a little soft pressure to her—solar plexus—putting your other arm around her waist, and bring her back here, gently. . . .

GEORGE: That's what *you* want to do. Go on, *you* intercept her! And bring her back here gently!

RALPH: O.K., I *would* like to do it. But do you think I'd *do* it?

GEORGE: Can you honestly say you wouldn't put the make on her if you thought she'd give in?

RALPH: Nope! I wouldn't do it. And if you don't believe me, git back in that funeral hack and drive to West Texas in it, you—*legitimate* bastard.

GEORGE: Nope, I don't think you would. You're too much of a square.

RALPH: *There's her! There she is!*

GEORGE: Where?

RALPH: Corner. Why's she turning around? She must be lost, go get her. Look. She's joining the carolers!

GEORGE: Good, let her stay with them, and sing! Carols!

RALPH: Naw, I better go get her.

GEORGE: Go and get your *own* wife: leave mine alone!

(RALPH *puts his arm around* GEORGE'S *shoulder.*)

And I told you to keep your rutten hand off my shoulder.

RALPH: Break it off me.

GEORGE: What I mean is, the point is—you *chose* your afflictions! Married into them. Mine I didn't choose! It just come on me, mysteriously: my shakes. You wouldn't even be interested in the awful implications of an affliction like mine.

(*He holds up his shaking hand.*)

RALPH: Sure, I'm interested in it, but—

GEORGE: S'pose it never lets up? This thing they can't treat or even find the cause of! S'pose I shake all my life like, like —dice in a crap shooter's fist?—Huh?—I mean at all moments of tension, all times of crisis, I shake! . . . Huh? And there's other aspects to it beside the career side. It could affect my love life. Huh? I could start shaking so hard when I started to make out with a girl that I couldn't do it. You know? Couldn't make the scene with her. . . .

(*There is a slight pause.*)

RALPH: Aw. Was that it?

GEORGE: Was what what?

RALPH: Was that the trouble at the Old Man River Motel, last night, you were scared of impotence with her? Was that the problem?

GEORGE: I don't have that problem. I *never* had that problem.

RALPH: No?

GEORGE: *No!*

(*Tense pause.*)

WHY? Do *you* have that problem?

RALPH: Sometimes. I wasn't excited enough by Dotty to satisfy her, sometimes. . . .

GEORGE: The thought of her old man's money couldn't always excite you?

RALPH: Nope, it couldn't always, that's the truth.

(*He switches off the lights, senselessly, and switches them back on again.*)

Poor ole Dotty. She's got so she always wants it and when I can't give it to her I feel guilty, guilty. . . .

(*He turns the Christmas lights off again, turns them back on again.*)

GEORGE: Well, you know me. An Everready battery, built-in in me.

RALPH (*turning to him with a slow, gentle smile*): Yeah, I understand, son.

GEORGE: *Don't be so damned understanding!*

RALPH: Well, there she goes—Mrs. George Haverstick the Fifth. Look. She's going up to the wrong Spanish-type stucco cottage, there's five almost identical ones in this block.

GEORGE: Don't your dawg know where it lives?

RALPH: Aw, it's a dignified beast. A constant Frigidaire pointer. Points at the Westinghouse Frij an' whines for a handout whenever you enter the kitchen. Knows everyone on the block an' pays calls like a new preacher wherever he thinks—

(*Whistles at dog*)

—he might be offered a—

(*Whistles*)

—handout.

(VOICES *down the block, hearty, drunken.*)

You better go git your wife. That Spanish-type stucco cottage is occupied by a bachelor decorator and you know how they destroy wimmen. . . . He is running a sort of a unofficial USO at his house. Service men congregate there.

GEORGE: HAH!

(*He is amused by the picture.*)

RALPH: I got to climb back in a back window because you shut this door and I had put the catch on it.

(*He crosses out the door to the carport as* GEORGE *gazes gravely off.*
The CAROLERS *are closer. They go into "God Rest Ye Merry, Gentlemen" again.*
GEORGE *is not inclined to be merry. He glares into the starless air.*
In the bedroom, a windowpane is smashed and RALPH's *arm reaches through, his fingers groping for the window*

*latch. He finds it, gets the window up and clambers
through with some muttered invectives against the hostility of the inanimate objects of the world. As soon as he
enters the interior, light and sound inside are brought
up. Oddly enough, a TV Western is in progress, approaching the climax of an Indian attack or a cattle
stampede. It catches* RALPH's *attention. He turns gravely
to the TV set, for the moment forgetting* GEORGE *outside.
Gunfire subsides and the dialogue is brought up loud:*)

DIALOGUE

—Save your ammunition, they'll come back.
—How LONG HAVE WE GOT?
—Till sundown. They'll hit us again after dark.
—Let's make a run for it now!
—We'll have to abandon the wagons if we make a run for it.
The Rio Grande is at least five miles south of here.
—Mount the women, one woman behind each man on the
hawses, unhitch the hawses! Then stampede the cattle. That'll
give us a cover while we make our break.
—What is our chances, you think?
—You want a *honest* answer or a *comforting* answer?
—Give me the honest answer.
—The comforting answer would have been fifty-fifty: I'll
leave you to imagine the honest answer.
—Rosemary? Come here a minute. Take this pistol. There's
five shots in it. Save the fifth shot for yourself. Now git on
this hawss behind me.
—Oh, Buck! I'm so scared!
—*Git up!* O.K., sweetheart?
—Yes!
—Hold onto me tight. Dusty, when I count ten, start the
cattle stampede.

(*He starts counting, slowly.*)

GEORGE (*to himself as he paces the terrace*): Now I don't
even want her. If she asked me for it, I wouldn't give it to
her, the way I feel now.

(*Sneezes.*)

Catchin' a cold out here! What's he doing in there, the motherless bastard? BATES! REMEMBER ME?

RALPH (*opening the door*): I thought you'd gone faw your wife.

(RALPH *chuckles and holds the front door open as* GEORGE *withdraws his head from the window and reappears a moment later on the terrace.*

(RALPH *lets him in.*)

GEORGE: Will you look at that? A Western on Christmas eve, even! It's a goddam NATIONAL OBSESSIONAL.

RALPH: Yep, a national homesickness in the American heart for the old wild frontiers with the yelping redskins and the covered wagons on fire and—

GEORGE: Will you look at those miserable shorthorn cattle! Those cows, in this corny Western?

(*They both face the TV. There is a pause.*)

RALPH: Yep—an undignified beast. Man? Buddy? I don't have too much confidence in the project of the Dignified West Texas Longhorn Ranch, even now, but I will go along with you. Don't ask me why. I couldn't tell you why, but I will go along with you. Want to shake on it, Buddy?

GEORGE: That champagne ought to be cold now, let's break out that champagne now.

RALPH: It'll be still colder when you've picked up your wife.

GEORGE: I told you my policy, don't interfere with it, huh?

RALPH: Women are vulnerable creatures.

GEORGE: So's a man.

RALPH (*crosses to the kitchenette door*): I'll open up the champagne while you pick up your wife.

GEORGE: Ralpho? Man?

RALPH: Huh?

GEORGE: Now I know why I come here. You're a *decent! square!*

(*The kitchen door swings closed on them;* CAROLERS *are singing out front. After a moment* ISABEL *appears before the house with the dog.*

(*A* LADY CAROLER *appears on the terrace with a collection plate.*)

ISABEL: Oh—I'm afraid I don't have any money to give you, but—

(*She knocks at the door.*)

Wait!—till they answer the door, I—

(*Raucous voices are heard within.*)

—Some people regard the celebration of the birthday of Jesus as a, as a—sort of a—occasion, excuse for!—just getting drunk and—*disgusting!* I'll probably have to go round the back to get in. . . .

(*Great howls of hilarity have been coming from the back of the cottage, drowning out* ISABEL's *efforts to draw attention to the front door.*)

I'm very sorry, I just don't have any money.

(*The* CAROLER *accepts this in good grace and leaves.*

(ISABEL *goes around through the carport. A few seconds later* GEORGE, *in a state of Wild West exuberance, comes charging out of the kitchen with the champagne bottle, shouting:*)

GEORGE: POWDER RIVER, Powwwww-der RIv-errrr!—a mile wide and—

RALPH: TWO INCHES DEEP!

(*He follows him out as* ISABEL's *head appears through the open window in the dim bedroom: she lifts the dog through and hoists herself over the sill.*)

GEORGE: Git me a pitcher with ice and two cans of that Ballantine's ale and I will make us BLACK VELVET!

RALPH: Huh?

GEORGE: Man, you know Black Velvet!

(*He is back in the kitchen.*)

I made it that time in Hong Kong when we had those girls from the—

(RALPH *has gone in behind him. The door swings shut as* ISABEL *picks up the bedside phone in the bedroom.*)

ISABEL: Operator? I want a cab right away, it's an *emergency, yaiss!*

(*Slight pause.*)

Yellow Cab? Checkered! Well, please send a cab right away to— Oh, my goodness, I can't tell you the address, oh, I'll—I'll find out the address and I'll call you right back, right away. . . .

(*She hangs up with a little stricken cry, followed by convulsive sobs that she stifles forcibly. On the bed, in the pink-shaded lamplight, she looks like a little girl making a first discovery of life's sorrow. Instinctively she reaches out for the Infant of Prague; at the same time, the* CAROLERS *start singing below the terrace: "I Wonder as I Wander." This is a sentimental moment, but not "sticky."*)

Little Boy Jesus, so lonesome on your birthday. I know how you feel, *exactly!*—

(*She clasps the infant to her breast, tenderly.*)

—just exactly, because I feel the same way. . . .

DIM OUT

INTERMISSION

ACT THREE

No time lapse.

The men return with an open, foaming bottle of champagne, and pass it back and forth between them before the fireplace, not noticing that the dog has returned or suspecting ISABEL's *presence in the bedroom.*

GEORGE: I put them in five categories. Those that worship it, those that love it, those that just like it, those that don't like it, those that just tolerate it, those that *don't* tolerate it, those that can't stand it, and, finally, those that not only can't stand it but want to cut it off you.

RALPH (*following him with glasses, chuckling*): That's more than five categories.

GEORGE: How many did I name?

RALPH: I don't know. I lost count.

GEORGE: Well, you know what I mean. And I have married into that last category. What scares me is that she has had hospital training and is probably able to do a pretty good cutting job. You know what I mean?

RALPH: Ha ha, yeah. Wel-l-l. . . .

(*He sets the glasses down and takes the bottle from* GEORGE. *The little parlor is flickering with firelight.*)

GEORGE: Which class did you marry into? Into the same category?

RALPH: No. She got to like it. More than I did even.

GEORGE: Now you're braggin'.

RALPH: Love is a very difficult—occupation. You got to work at it, man. It ain't a thing every Tom, Dick and Harry has got a true aptitude for. Y'know what I mean? Not every Tom, Dick or Harry understands how to use it. It's not a— offensive weapon. It shouldn't be used like one. Too many guys, they use it like a offensive weapon to beat down a woman with. All right. That rouses resistance. Because a woman has pride, even a woman has pride and resents being raped, and most love-making is rape with these self-regarded—experts! That come downstairs yelling, "Oh, man, Oh, brother," and hitching their belts up like they'd accomplished something.

GEORGE (*getting the allusion and resentful*): You mean me?

RALPH: Naw, naw, will yuh listen a minute? I've got ideas on this subject.

GEORGE: A self-regarded expert!

RALPH: You know Goddam right I'm an expert. I know I never had your good looks but made out better.

GEORGE: One man's opinion!

RALPH: Look! Lissen! You got to use—TENDERNESS!— with it, not roughness like raping, snatch-and-grab roughness but true tenderness with it or—

GEORGE: O.K., build yourself up! If that's what you need to!

RALPH: Naw, now, lissen! You know I know what I'm sayin'!

GEORGE: Sure, self-regarded expert!

(*They are both pretty high now.*)

RALPH: I know what went wrong last night at that Cape Girardeau motel as well as if I had seen it all on TV!

GEORGE: What went wrong is that I found myself hitched up with a woman in the "cut-it-off" category!

(ISABEL *is listening to all this in the bedroom. She stands up and sits down, stands up and sits down, barely able to keep from shouting something.*)

RALPH: Aw, naw, aw, naw. I will tell you what happened. Drink your champagne. What happened, man, is this! You didn't appreciate the natural need for using some tenderness with it. Lacking confidence with it, you wanted to hit her, smash her, clobber her with it. You've got violence in you! That's what made you such a good fighter pilot, the best there was! Sexual violence, that's what gives you the shakes, that's what makes you unstable. That's what made you just sit on the straw mats with the Tokyo dolls, drinking sake with them, teaching them English till it was time to come downstairs and holler, "Oh, man, oh, brother" like you had laid them to waste!

(*There is a slight pause.* GEORGE *is sweating, flushed.*)

GEORGE: Who in hell ever told you I—

RALPH: I heard it directly from them. You just sat up there drinkin' sake with 'em an' teachin' 'em English, and then you'd come down shouting, "Oh, man, oh, brother!" like you had laid 'em to waste.

GEORGE: Which of them told you this story?

RALPH: *Which* of them? ALL! EV'RY ONE!

(*They pause.* ISABEL *sits down on the bed again, raises her hands to either side of her face, slowly shaking her head with a gradual comprehension.*)

GEORGE: Man, at this moment I'd like to bust your face in!

RALPH: I'm tryin' to help you. Don't you know that I am tryin' t' help you?

(*A pause. They look away from each other in solemn*

reverie for some moments. ISABEL *rises again from the bed but still doesn't move. After some moments she sits back down. She is crying now.*)

RALPH (*continuing gently*): You have got this problem.

GEORGE: In Tokyo I never told you—

RALPH: What?

GEORGE: I was choosey. I had a girl on the side. I mean a nice one. One that I wanted to keep to myself, strictly. I didn't want to expose her to a bunch of—

RALPH: Aw, now, man, you don't have to start fabricating some kind of a *Sayonara* fantasy like this!

GEORGE: How about Big Springs, Texas?

RALPH: What about Big Springs, Texas, besides being boring, I mean, what *else* about it?

GEORGE: Plenty. I fixed you up there. You never got nowhere in Big Springs, Texas, till I opened it up for you.

RALPH: Baby, don't be sore.

GEORGE: Sore, I'm not sore. You've done your damndest to make me feel like a phony, but I'm not sore. *You're* sore. Not *me. I'm* not sore.

RALPH: You sure are shaking.

GEORGE: Yeah, well, I got this tremor. . . . Jesus, my goddam voice is got the shakes too! But you know it's the truth, in Big Springs, Texas, we had the best damn time you ever had in your life, and I broke the ice there, for you.

RALPH: I don't deny that women naturally like you. Everybody likes you! Don't you know that? People never lowrate you! Don't you know that? I like you. That's for sure. But I hate to see you shaking because of—

GEORGE (*cutting in*): Look! We're both free now. Like two birds. You're gonna cut out of this High Point over a Cavern. And we'll buy us a piece of ranchland near San Antone and both of us—

RALPH: Yeah, yeah, let's go back to what we wuh tawkin' about. *Tenderness.* With a *woman.*

GEORGE (*getting the allusion and resentful*): *You mean* about such a thing as that when here you are, night before Christmas, with just a cocker spaniel and presents under a tree, with no one to *take* them from you!

RALPH (*abruptly*): *Hey!*

GEORGE: *Huh?*

RALPH: Th' *dawg* is back. How *come?*

GEORGE: The dog come *back,* tha's all. . . .

(ISABEL *comes out of the bedroom in coat and hat.*)

ISABEL: Yes, I brought the dog back.

(*A pause, rather long.*)

RALPH: We, uh, we—saw you going up to the wrong— Spanish-type cottage. . . .

ISABEL: I haven't discovered the *right* one, Mr. Bates.

RALPH: I ain't discovered it either.

GEORGE: What kept you so long in the wrong one?

ISABEL: They invited me in and made me sit down to a lovely buffet supper while they looked up the High Point Bates in the phone book.

(*She pauses.*)

I heard your very enlightening conversation from the bedroom. You're a pair of small boys. Boasting, bragging, showing off to each other. . . . I want to call a cab. I'm going downtown, George.

(He crosses unsteadily to the phone, lifts it and hands it to her with an effort at stateliness.)

Thank you.

(To RALPH)

Do you know the cab number?

GEORGE: Whacha want, yellow, checkered or what? I'll git it for yuh!

RALPH: Put down th' phone.

ISABEL: I'll get one.

(He dials the operator.)

GEORGE: Leave her alone. Let her go downtown. She's free to.

(RALPH takes the phone from her and puts it back in the cradle.)

ISABEL: Do I have to walk?

(She goes to the door, opens it and starts out.)

There's a car in front of your house, Mr. Bates.

RALPH *(rising with sudden energy and rushing to the door)*. YEP! IT'S HER OLD MAN'S CAR! Dorothea's papa, my ex-boss!

ISABEL: Perhaps he'll be kind enough to—

RALPH: Go back in, little lady! Stay in the bedroom till I git through this! Then I'll drive you downtown if you're still determined to go.

(He has drawn her back in the house.)

SET DOWN, GEORGE! For Chrissakes. Little lady, will you please wait in the bedroom till I get through this hassle with her old man?

ISABEL: It's all so ridiculous. Yes, all right, I will, but please don't forget your promise to take me downtown right afterwards, Mr. Bates!

(*She returns to the bedroom with dignity.* MR. *and* MRS. MCGILLICUDDY *appear before the house.*)

(*They are a pair of old bulls.*)

MRS. MCGILLICUDDY: The first thing to discuss is their joint savings account.

(MR. MCGILLICUDDY *hammers the knocker on the door.*)

I wish you'd listened to me an' brought your lawyer.

MR. MCGILLICUDDY: I can handle that boy. You keep your mouth out of it. Just collect the silver and china and let me handle the talk.

(*He knocks again, violently, dislodging the Christmas wreath attached to the knocker.* MRS. MCGILLICUDDY *picks it up.*)

Now what are you gonna do with that Christmas wreath? You gonna crown him with it?

(RALPH *opens the door.*)

RALPH: Well, Mr. and Mrs. *Mac!*

MR. MCGILLICUDDY (*handing him the wreath*): This come off your knocker.

RALPH: Ha, ha, what a surprise!

MRS. MCGILLICUDDY: We've come to pick up some things of Dorothea's.

RALPH: That's O.K. Take out anything that's hers, but don't touch nothing that belongs to us both.

MRS. MCGILLICUDDY: We've come with a list of things that belong exclusively to Dorothea!

MR. MCGILLICUDDY: Is it true that you called up Emory Sparks at the place you quit your job at and asked him to come over here tonight and make you a cash-on-the-barrel offer for everything in this house?

RALPH: Nope.

MR. MCGILLICUDDY: Then how come Emory's fiancée called up Dorothea to give her that information?

MRS. MCGILLICUDDY (*impatiently*): Come on in here, Susie.

(SUSIE *is the colored maid. She enters with a large laundry basket.*)

Is that the biggest basket you could find?

SUSIE: Yes, ma'am, it's the laundry basket.

MRS. MCGILLICUDDY: It isn't the large one. You'll have to make several trips up and down those slippery front steps with that little basket.

MR. MCGILLICUDDY: Haven't you got any ice-cream salt?

RALPH: You want to make some ice cream?

MR. MCGILLICUDDY: Susie, before you go down those steps with my daughter's china, you'd better collect some clinkers out of the furnace in the basement.

RALPH: How is she going to get clinkers out of an oil-burning furnace?

MR. MCGILLICUDDY: Oh, that's right. You burn oil. I forgot about that. Well, Susie, you better tote the basket of china down the terrace. Don't try to make the steps with it.

RALPH: She's not takin' no china out of this house.

MR. MCGILLICUDDY: You're not going to sell a goddam thing of my daughter's in this house!

RALPH: All I done was call up Emory Sparks because he's about to get married and invited him over to take a look at this place because I've got to unload it and I can't wait a couple of months to—

MR. MCGILLICUDDY: Now, hold on a minute, war hero!

RALPH: I don't like the way you always call me war hero!

MR. MCGILLICUDDY: *Why?* Ain't that what you *were?*

GEORGE: You're goddam right he was! I flown over seventy bombing missions with this boy in Korea and before that in the—

MR. MCGILLICUDDY: Yes, yes, yes, I know it backwards and forwards, and I know who you are. You are Haverstick, ain't you?

GEORGE: Yeah, you got my name right.

MR. MCGILLICUDDY: Well, Haverstick, the war's over and you two bombers are grounded. Now, Susie, go in the kitchen and get that Mixmaster and that new Rotisserie out in the basket while I collect the silver in that sideboard in there.

RALPH: Susie, don't go in my kitchen. You want to be arrested for trespassing, Susie?

MRS. MCGILLICUDDY: Stuart, you'd better call that policeman in here.

RALPH: NO KIDDING!

MRS. MCGILLICUDDY: We anticipated that you'd make trouble.

RALPH: How does Dorothea feel about you all doing this?

MR. MCGILLICUDDY (*at the door*): OFFICER!—He's coming.

RALPH: How does Dotty feel? What is her attitude toward this kind of—

(*He is trembling. His voice chokes.* GEORGE *rises and puts a hand on* RALPH's *shoulder as a young* POLICE OFFICER *enters looking embarrassed.*)

MR. MCGILLICUDDY: You know the situation, Lieutenant. We have to remove my daughter's valuables from the house because we've been tipped off this man here, Ralph Bates, is intending to make a quick cash sale of everything in the house and skip out of Dixon tomorrow.

RALPH: THAT'S A GODDAM LIE! WHO TOLD YOU THAT?

MRS. MCGILLICUDDY: Emory Sparks' fiancée is Dorothea's good friend! That's how we got the warning. She called to enquire if Dorothea was serious about this matter. How did Dotty feel, how did she FEEL? I'll tell you! SICK AT HER STOMACH! VIOLENTLY SICK AT HER STOMACH.

RALPH: I should think so, goddam it. I should THINK so! She's got many a fault she got from you two, but, hell, she'd never agree to a piece of cheapness like this any more'n she'd believe that story about me callin'—

MR. MCGILLICUDDY: How could there be any possible doubt about it when Emory Sparks' fiancée—

RALPH: Will you allow me to speak? I did call Emory Sparks and told him my wife had quit me because I had quit my job, and I merely suggested that he come over and kind of look over the stuff here and see if any of all this goddam electric equipment and so forth would be of any use to him since it isn't to me and since I got to have some financial—

(*He becomes suddenly speechless and breathless.* GEORGE *embraces his shoulder.*)

GEORGE: Now, now, son, this is going to work out. Don't blow a gasket over it.

RALPH: I think you folks had better consider some legal angles of what you're up to here.

MR. MCGILLICUDDY (*puffing, red in the face*): Aw, there's no legal angle about it that I don't know, and if there was, I could cope with that, too. I'm prepared to cope with that trouble. You got no goddam position in this town but what I give you!

RALPH: *Oh!* Uh-huh—

(MRS. MCGILLICUDDY *has gone to the bedroom and discovered* ISABEL *in it.*)

MRS. MCGILLICUDDY: *Stuart, they have a woman in Dotty's bedroom!*

RALPH: George's wife is in there.

MRS. MCGILLICUDDY: How long have you been planning this?

(*She knocks on the bedroom door.*)

Can I come in?

ISABEL: Yes, please.

(MRS. MCGILLICUDDY *enters the bedroom.*)

MRS. MCGILLICUDDY (*coldly*): I've come to pick up some things that belong to my daughter.

ISABEL: I told my husband we'd dropped in at the wrong time.

MRS. MCGILLICUDDY: May I ask who you are?

ISABEL: I'm Mrs. George Haverstick. You probably saw my husband in the front room.

MRS. MCGILLICUDDY: Your husband's an old friend of Ralph's, one of his wartime buddies?

ISABEL: Yes, he is, Mrs.— I didn't get your name.

MRS. MCGILLICUDDY: All I can say is "Watch out," if he's an old friend of Ralph's!

ISABEL: Why?

MRS. MCGILLICUDDY: Birds of a feather, that's all.

(MRS. MCGILLICUDDY *opens the closet and starts piling clothes on the bed. In the living room,* MR. MCGILLICUDDY *takes a seat in silence.*)

ISABEL: Are you sure you're doing the right thing?

MRS. MCGILLICUDDY (*calling out the door*): Susie!

SUSIE (*entering*): Yes, ma'am?

MRS. MCGILLICUDDY: Take these clothes of Miss Dotty's out to the car.

(SUSIE *carries out the clothes.*)

ISABEL: I think young people should be given a chance to work things out by themselves.

MRS. MCGILLICUDDY: You have no idea at all of the situation. And I'm sure you have your own problems if you have married a friend of my daughter's husband. Is he living on his war record like Ralph Bates is?

ISABEL: He has a distinguished war record and a nervous disability that was a result of seventy-two flying missions in Korea and, and—more than twice that many in—

MRS. MCGILLICUDDY: *I'm sick of hearing about past glories! Susie!*

(SUSIE *comes in again.*)

Now pick up all Dotty's shoes on the floor of that closet, put 'em in the bottom of the basket, put some paper over them, and then pile her little undies on top of the paper.— Then! If you still have room in the basket, collect some of the china out of the sideboard and cupboards. Be very careful with that. Don't try to carry too much at one time, Susie. That walk and those steps are a hazard.

(*There has been a prolonged silence in the front room during the scene above, which they have been listening to.*)

MR. MCGILLICUDDY (*at last*): Well, you seem to be living the life of Riley. French champagne. Who was the little girl I saw come out and go back in?

RALPH: Mrs. George Haverstick.

MR. MCGILLICUDDY: That means as much to me as if you said she was a lady from Mars.

RALPH: There's no reason why it should mean anything to you. I just answered your question.

MR. MCGILLICUDDY: Why do you feel so superior to me?

RALPH: Aw. Did you notice that?

MR. MCGILLICUDDY: From the first time I met you. You have always acted very superior to me for some unknown reason. I'd like to know what it is. You were employed by me till you quit your job today.

RALPH: Does that mean I had to feel inferior to you, Mac?

MR. MCGILLICUDDY: You've started calling me "Mac"?

RALPH: I'm not employed by you, now.

MR. MCGILLICUDDY: If there was a war you could be a war hero again, but in a cold war I don't see how you're going to be such a hero. A cold-war hero, ha, ha, is not such a hero, at least not in the newspapers.

(*Gathering confidence*)

Huh? Why don't you answer my question?

RALPH: Which, Mac?

MR. MCGILLICUDDY: Why you feel so rutten superior to me.

RALPH: Can I consider that question? For a minute?

MR. MCGILLICUDDY: Yeah, consider it, will you? I fail to see anything *special* about you, war hero!

(*He lights a cigar with jerky motions. The two younger men stare at his red, puffy face with intolerant smiles.*)

GEORGE: Let me answer for him. He feels superior to you because you're a big male cow, a spiritual male cow.

RALPH: Shut up, George. Well, Mr. Mac? Let me ask you a question. Why did you ask me to marry your daughter?

MR. MCGILLICUDDY: DID WHAT? I NEVER! Done any such thing and—

(MRS. MCGILLICUDDY *snorts indignantly from the open bedroom door.*)

RALPH: You mean to say you've forgotten that you suggested to me that I marry Dotty?

(MRS. MCGILLICUDDY *advances from the bedroom door, bearing a French porcelain clock.*)

MR. MCGILLICUDDY: I never forgotten a thing in my adult life, but I never had any such recollections as that. I do remember a conversation I held with you soon after you started to work at Regal Dairy Products an' come to my office to quit because you said you weren't gittin' paid well enough an' th' work was monotonous to you.

RALPH: That's right. Five years ago this winter.

MR. MCGILLICUDDY: I gave you a fatherly talk. I told you monotony was a part of life. And I said I had an eye on you, which I did at that time.

RALPH: How about the rest of the conversation? In which you said that Dotty was your only child, that you had no son, and Dotty was int'rested in me and if Dotty got married her husband would be the heir to your throne as owner of Regal Dairy an' its subsidiaries such as Royal Ice Cream and Monarch Cheese, huh?

MRS. MCGILLICUDDY: HANH!

RALPH: An' you hadn't long for this world because of acute diabetes and so forth and—

MRS. MCGILLICUDDY: HANH!

RALPH: And I would be shot right into your shoes when you departed this world? Well, you sure in hell lingered!

MRS. MCGILLICUDDY: ARE YOU GOING TO STAND THERE LISTENING TO THIS, STUART? I'm not!

MR. MCGILLICUDDY: Be still, Mama. I can talk for myself. I did discuss these things with you but how did you arrive at the idea I asked you to marry my daughter?

MRS. MCGILLICUDDY: HANH!

(GEORGE *goes to look out the window as if the scene had ceased to amuse him.*)

RALPH: What other way could it be interpreted, Mac?

(*He is no longer angry.*)

MR. MCGILLICUDDY: I offered you a splendid chance in the world which you spit on by your disrespect, your superior—!

RALPH: I respect Dorothea. Always did and still do.

MR. MCGILLICUDDY: I'm talkin' about your attitude to me.

RALPH: I know you are. That's all that you care about, not about Dorothea. You don't love Dotty. She let you down by having psychological problems that you brought on her, that you an' Mrs. Mac gave her by pushing her socially past her social endowments.

MRS. MCGILLICUDDY: WHAT DO YOU MEAN BY THAT?

RALPH: Dotty was never cut out to boost your social position in this city. Which you expected her to. You made her feel inferior all her life.

MRS. MCGILLICUDDY: *Me? Me?*

RALPH: Both of yuh. I respected her, though, and sincerely liked her and I married Dotty. Give me credit for that, and provided her with an—offspring. Maybe not much of an off-spring, but an offspring, a male one, at least it started a male one. I can't help it if she's turnin' him into a sissy, I—

MRS. MCGILLICUDDY: MY GOD, STUART, HOW LONG ARE YOU GONNA STAND THERE AND LISTEN TO THIS WITHOUT—

MR. MCGILLICUDDY: *Mama, I told you to keep your mouth outa this!*

RALPH: Yeah, but I MARRIED your baby. Give me credit for that. And provided her with an—offspring!

MRS. MCGILLICUDDY: What does he mean by that? That *he* had the baby, not Dotty?

MR. MCGILLICUDDY: Mama, I told you to keep your mouth out of this.

MRS. MCGILLICUDDY: He talks like he thought he did Dotty a FAVOR!

RALPH: Now, listen. I don't want to be forced into saying unkind things about Dotty. But you all know damn well that Dotty was half a year older than me when I married that girl and if I hadn't you would have been stuck with a lonely, unmarried daughter for the rest of your lives!

MRS. MCGILLICUDDY: *Oh*, my—GOD!

MR. MCGILLICUDDY: Let him talk. I want to hear all, all, all! he has to say about Dotty.

RALPH: You're *going* to hear it, if you stay in my house! I put up a five-year battle between our marriage and your goddam hold on her! You just wouldn't release her!—although I doubt that you wanted her always unmarried.

MRS. MCGILLICUDDY: WHAT MAKES YOU THINK SHE WOULD HAVE STAYED UNMARRIED?

RALPH: The indications, past history, when I met her—

MRS. MCGILLICUDDY: This is too sickening. I can't stand it, Stuart.

MR. MCGILLICUDDY: A bum like you?

RALPH: Don't call *me* a bum!

MR. MCGILLICUDDY: What in hell else *are* you? I give you your job which you quit today without warning! Carried you in it despite your indifference to it for—for—for—five—

RALPH: Wait! Like I said. I still respect your daughter, don't want to say anything not kind about her, but let's face facts. Who else but a sucker like me, Ralph Bates, would have married a girl with no looks, a plain, homely girl that probably no one but me had ever felt anything but just— SORRY FOR!

MRS. MCGILLICUDDY: OH GOD! STUART, ARE YOU GOING TO STAND THERE AND LET HIM GO ON WITH THAT TALK?

RALPH: HOW IN HELL DO YOU FIGURE HE'S GOING TO STOP ME?

MRS. MCGILLICUDDY: OFFICER! CAN'T YOU GET THIS MAN OUT OF HERE?

OFFICER: No, ma'am. I can't arrest him.

RALPH: ARREST ME FOR WHAT, MRS. MAC?

GEORGE: That's right, arrest him for what?

MRS. MCGILLICUDDY: Stuart? Take out the silver. I don't know where Susie is. We should have come here with your lawyer as well as this—*remarkably—incompetent—police-man!*

MR. MCGILLICUDDY: Susie took out the silver.

GEORGE: Naw, she didn't. I got the goddam silver. I'm sitting on it!

(*He sits on silver, then rises and stuffs it under sofa pillow, having been discomfited by the forks.*)

MR. MCGILLICUDDY: I guess I'll have to call the Chief of Police, who's a lodge brother of mine, and get a little more police co-operation than we have gotten so far.

OFFICER: O.K., you do that, Mister.

MR. MCGILLICUDDY: He'll call you to the phone and give you exact instructions.

OFFICER: That's all right. If he gives 'em, I'll take 'em.

(MRS. MCGILLICUDDY *has charged back into the bedroom to collect more things.*)

RALPH: Mr. McGillicuddy, you are the worst thing any person can be: mean-minded, small-hearted, and CHEAP! Outstandingly and notoriously cheap! It was almost two months before I could *kiss* Dorothea, sincerely, after meeting her father! That's no crap. It wasn't the homeliness that threw me, it was the association she had in my mind with *you!* It wasn't till I found out she despised you as much as I did that I was able to make real love to Dotty.

MR. MCGILLICUDDY: My daughter is *crazy* about me!

RALPH: You're crazy if you *think* so!

(MRS. MCGILLICUDDY *comes out of the bedroom.*)

MRS. MCGILLICUDDY: All right. All of Dotty's clothes have been taken out. I think we may as well leave now.

MR. MCGILLICUDDY: How about the TV? Which I gave DOTTY *last* Christmas?

RALPH: You want the TV? O.K.! Here's the TV!

(*He shoves it to the door and pulls the door open.*)

Take the TV out of here—an' git out with it!

MRS. MCGILLICUDDY: What is that under the tree? It looks like a new fur coat!

RALPH: That's right. A seven-hundred-and-forty-five-dollar sheared-beaver coat that I'd bought for Dotty for Christmas! —but which I have just now presented to Mrs. George Haverstick as her weddin' present.

MR. MCGILLICUDDY: The hell you have! How did you git hold of seven hundred and—

RALPH: From my savings account.

MR. MCGILLICUDDY: That was a *joint* account!

MRS. MCGILLICUDDY: STUART! TAKE THAT COAT! GO ON, PICK UP THAT COAT!

RALPH: By God, if he touches that coat, I'll smash him into next week, and I never hit an old man before in my life.

MRS. MCGILLICUDDY: OFFICER! PICK UP THAT COAT!

RALPH: I'll hit any man that tries to pick up that coat!

OFFICER (*putting down the phone, which he has been talking into quietly*): I talked to my chief. He gave me my instructions. He says not to take any action that might result in publicity, because of Mr. Bates having been a very well-known war hero.

MR. MCGILLICUDDY: Come on, Mama. I'll just have to refer this whole disgusting business to my lawyer tomorrow, put it all in his hands and get the necessary papers to protect our baby.

MRS. MCGILLICUDDY: I just want to say one thing more! Ralph Bates, don't you think for a moment that you are going to escape financial responsibility for the support of your child! Now come on, Stuart!—Isn't it pitiful? All that little boy's Christmas under the tree?

RALPH: Send him over tomorrow to pick it all up. That can go out of the house, the little boy's Christmas can go. . . .

(*They all leave.* ISABEL *enters from bedroom.*)

ISABEL: Mr. Bates! I don't believe that this is what your wife wanted. I'll also bet you that she is outside in that car and if you would just stick your head out the window and call her, she would come running in here.

(DOROTHEA *comes onto the paved terrace and knocks at the door.* RALPH *does not move. She knocks again, harder and longer. He starts to rise, sits down again.*)

George, let his wife in the house.

GEORGE: Let's just keep out of this. I reckon he knows what he's doing.

(*A car honks. A* WOMAN'S VOICE *is heard.*)

WOMAN (*off*): Dorothea! Come back. We'll get the police!

DOROTHEA (*calling at the door*): Ralph? Ralph? It's Dotty! I want the child's Christmas things!

RALPH: HE'LL GET THEM HERE OR NOWHERE!

DOROTHEA: *I'm not going to leave here without the child's Christmas things!*—Ralph.

RALPH: *Let him come here alone tomorrow morning.*

DOROTHEA: *You can't do that to a child.*—Ralph!

(*The car honks again, long and loud.*)

RALPH (*shouting back*): Put the kid in a taxi in the morning and I'll let him in to collect his Christmas presents!

MRS. MCGILLICUDDY (*appearing behind* DOROTHEA): Dorothea! I will not let you humiliate yourself like this! Come away from that door!

DOROTHEA: Mama, stay in the car!

WOMAN: Your father won't wait any longer. He's started the car. He's determined to get the police.

DOROTHEA: RALPH! (*She has removed the door key from her bag.*) I'M COMING IN!

WOMAN: *Dotty, where is your pride!*

(DOROTHEA *enters and slams the door. The* WOMAN *rushes off, crying "Stuart!"*

(DOROTHEA *stares at* RALPH *from the door. He gazes stubbornly at the opposite wall.*)

DOROTHEA: I could tell you'd been drinkin' by your voice. Who are these people you've got staying in the house?

RALPH: Talk about the police! I could get you all arrested for illegal entry!

DOROTHEA: This is your liquor speaking, not you, Ralph.

RALPH: You have abandoned me. You got no right by law to come back into this house and make insulting remarks about my friends.

DOROTHEA: Ralph? Ralph? I know I acted—impetuously this mawnin'. . . .

RALPH: Naw, I think you made the correct decision. You realized that you had tied yourself down to a square peg in a round hole that had now popped out of the hole and consequently would be of no further use to you. You were perfectly satisfied for me to remain at that rutten little desk job, tyrannized over by inferior men, for as long as my— heart kept beating.

DOROTHEA: No, Ralph. I wasn't. My aim for you was your aim. Independence! A business of your own!

RALPH: Not when you were *faced* with it.

DOROTHEA: You sprung it on me at the wrong moment, Ralph. Our savings account is at a very low ebb.

RALPH: Our savings account is all gone, little woman. It went on Christmas, all of it.

(*He pokes at the fire. There is a pause. The fire crackles and flickers.*)

DOROTHEA: *Mama* says you—bought me a *fur coat* for Christmas.

RALPH: Yeah, she took a look at it. Enquired the price. Wanted to take it off with her.

DOROTHEA: You wouldn't have bought me such a beautiful coat if you didn't still care for me, Ralph. You know that, don't you?

RALPH: I made a decision affecting my whole future life. I know it was a big step, but I had the courage to make it.

DOROTHEA: I've always admired your courage.

RALPH: Hah!—I break the news. You walked right out on me, Dotty, takin' my son that you've turned into a sissy.

He won't want these boys' toys under that tree. What he'll want is a doll and a—*tea* set.

DOROTHEA: All of these things are a little too old for Ralph Junior but he'll be delighted with them just the same, Ralph.

(*She takes off her cloth coat.*)

I'm going to try on that wonderful-looking beaver.

RALPH: It's not going out of the house, off you or on you, Dotty.

(*She puts on the beaver-skin coat.*)

DOROTHEA: Oh, how lovely, how lovely! Ralph, it *does* prove you love me!

RALPH: It cleaned out our savings account.

DOROTHEA: Both of us have been guilty of impetuous actions. You must've been awfully lonely, inviting a pair of strangers to occupy our bedroom on Christmas Eve.

RALPH: George Haverstick is not any stranger to me. We both of us died in two wars, repeatedly died in two wars and were buried in suburbs named High Point, but his was hyphenated. H-i-hyphen-Point. Mine was spelled out but was built on a cavern for the daughter and grandchild of Mr. and Mrs. Stuart McGillicuddy. Oh, I told him something which I should have told you five years ago, Dorothea. I married you without love. I married you for—

DOROTHEA: Ralph? Please don't!

RALPH: I married you for your stingy-fisted old papa's promise to—

DOROTHEA: *Ralphie! Don't! I know!*

RALPH: —to make me his Heir Apparent! Assurances, lies! Even broad hints that he would soon kick off!

DOROTHEA: Ralph?

(*She puts her hand over his mouth, beseechingly.*)

Don't you know I know that?

RALPH: Why' you accept it? If you—

DOROTHEA: I was so—

(*She covers her face.*)

RALPH: Cut it out, have some pride!

DOROTHEA: I *do!*

RALPH: In *what?*

DOROTHEA: In *you!*

RALPH: Oh, for the love of— In me? Why, I'm telling you I'm nothin' better'n a goddam—

DOROTHEA: I know, don't tell me again. I always knew it. —I had my nose done over and my front teeth extracted to look better for you, Ralphie!

RALPH: "Ralphie!" *Shoot* . . .

(ISABEL *raps discreetly at the bedroom door.*)

Huh? What is it?

ISABEL: I've made some coffee.

DOROTHEA: I *did* improve my appearance, didn't I, Ralph? It was extremely painful.

RALPH: Don't claim you done it for me! Every woman wants to improve on nature any way that she can. Yes! Of course you look better! You think you've won a *argument?*

DOROTHEA: *Me? What* argument? *No!* I've come back *crawling!*—not even embarrassed to do so!

(ISABEL *comes in from the kitchenette with coffee.*)

Oh! Hello. I didn't know you were—

ISABEL: Mrs. Bates, I'm Isabel Haverstick. I took the liberty of making some coffee in your sweet little kitchen. Mrs. Bates, can I give you some coffee?

DOROTHEA: Thanks, that's awfully sweet of you, Mrs. Haverstick. It's nice of you and your husband to drop in on Ralph, but the situation between Ralph and me has changed. I guess I don't have to explain it. You see I've come home. We only have one bedroom and Ralph and I have an awful lot to talk over.

ISABEL: I understand perfectly. George and I are going to go right downtown.

DOROTHEA (*softening*): You don't have to do that. This sofa lets out to a bed and it's actually more comfortable than the beds in the bedroom. I know, because other times when we've had a falling out, less serious than this time, I have—occupied it.

(*With a little, soft, sad, embarrassed laugh.*)

Of course, I usually called Ralph in before mawnin'. . . .

ISABEL: Oh, but this is no time for strangers to be here with you!

DOROTHEA (*now really warming*): You all stay here! I insist! It's really not easy to get a hotel room downtown with so many folks coming into town for Christmas.

ISABEL: Well, if you're sure, if you're absolutely certain our presence wouldn't be inconvenient at all?—I do love this room. The fire is still burning bright!—and the Christmas tree is so—pretty.

DOROTHEA: I'll tell my mother and father, they're still outside in the car, to drive home and then we'll all have coffee together!

(*She rushes out in her beaver coat.*)

ISABEL: I like her! She's really nice!

RALPH: She came back for the fur coat.

ISABEL: I think she came back for you.

RALPH: She walked out on me this morning because I had liberated myself from a slave's situation!—and she took the kid with her.

ISABEL: You're just going through a—period of adjustment.

RALPH: We've been married six years.

ISABEL: But all that time you've been under terrible strain, hating what you were doing, and maybe taking it out on your wife, Ralph Bates.

(DOROTHEA *returns.*)

DOROTHEA: All right. I sent them home, much against their objections. I just slammed the car door on them.

RALPH: They comin' back with the police?

DOROTHEA: No. You know they were bluffing.

ISABEL: I think you two should have your coffee alone in your own little bedroom. We'll all get acquainted tomorrow.

DOROTHEA: Ralph?

RALPH (*sadly*): I don't know. We're living over a cavern. . . .

(*He follows* DOROTHEA *into the bedroom. It remains dimly lighted.*)

DOROTHEA: But Mama's took all my things! I forgot to ask them back from her. I'll just have to sleep jay-bird since she took even my nighties.

RALPH: Yes, she was fast and thorough, but didn't get out with that seven-hundred-buck beaver coat.

DOROTHEA: I like your friends. But the girl looks terribly nervous. Well-bred, however, and the boy is certainly very good-looking!

RALPH: Thanks.

(*The bedroom dims out as* DOROTHEA *enters the bathroom. A silence has fallen between the pair in the living room.*)

ISABEL: Coffee, George?

GEORGE: No, thanks.

ISABEL: Moods change quickly, don't they?

GEORGE: Basic attitudes don't.

ISABEL: Yes, but it takes a long time to form basic attitudes and to know what they are, and meantime you just have to act according to moods.

GEORGE: Is that what you are acting according to, now?

ISABEL: I'm not acting according to anything at all now, I—

(*She sits on a hassock before the fireplace.*)

I don't think she came back just for the coat. Do you?

GEORGE: It's not my business. I don't have any opinion. If that was her reason, Ralph Bates will soon find it out.

ISABEL: Yes . . .

DOROTHEA (*at the door*): Excuse me, may I come in?

ISABEL: Oh, please.

DOROTHEA: Mama took all my *things!* Have you got an extra nightie that I could borrow?

ISABEL: Of course I have.

DOROTHEA: I forgot to take anything back. . . .

(ISABEL *opens her overnight bag and extends a gossamer nightgown to* DOROTHEA.)

Oh! How exquisite! No!—that's your honeymoon nightie. Just give me any old plain one!

ISABEL: Really, I have two of them, exactly alike. Please take it!

DOROTHEA: Are you sure?

ISABEL: I'm positive. You take it!

(*She holds up another.*)

See? The same thing exactly, just a different color. I gave you the blue one and kept the pink one for me.

DOROTHEA: Oh. Well, thank you so much.

ISABEL: If you'd prefer the pink one—?

DOROTHEA: I'm delighted with the blue one! Well, g'night, you folks. Sweet dreams.

(*She returns to the dark bedroom.* RALPH *is prone and motionless on the bed. A tiny light spills from the bathroom door.* DOROTHEA *enters the bathroom and closes the door so the bedroom turns pitch-black.*)

GEORGE (*grimly*): D'ya want me to go outside while you undress?

ISABEL: No, I, I—I'm—just going to take off my *suit. I* —I, I have a *slip* on, I—

(*She gives him a quick, scared look. The removal of her suit is almost panickily self-conscious and awkward.*)

GEORGE: Well. Ralph and I have decided to—

ISABEL (*fearfully*): *What?*

GEORGE (*finishes his drink, then goes on*): Ralph and I have decided to go in the cattle business, near San Antone.

ISABEL: Who is going to finance it?

(*She has turned out the lamp.*)

GEORGE: We think we can work it out. We have to be smart, and lucky. Just smart and lucky.

(ISABEL *drops her skirt to her feet and stands before the flickering fireplace in a slip that the light makes transparent.*)

ISABEL: We all have to be smart and lucky. Or unlucky and silly.

(DOROTHEA *comes out of the bathroom. Light from the bathroom brightens the bedroom, where* RALPH *is slowly undressing.*)

RALPH: All right, you're back. But a lot has been discussed and decided on since you cut out of here, Dotty.

DOROTHEA (*picks up something on the dresser*): Good! What?

RALPH: Please don't rub that Vick's Vap-O-Rub on your chest.

DOROTHEA: I'm *not!* This is Hind's honey-almond cream for my *hands!*

RALPH: Aw.

(*She starts taking off her shoes.*

(*In the living room:*)

GEORGE: What're you up to?

ISABEL: Up to?

GEORGE: Standin' in front of that fire with that transparent thing on you. You must know it's transparent.

ISABEL: I honestly didn't even think about that.

(ISABEL *crouches by the fire, holding her delicate hands out to its faint, flickering glow.*

(*In the bedroom:*)

RALPH: All right. Here it is. George and me are going to cash in every bit of collateral we possess, including the beaver-skin coat and his fifty-two Caddy to buy a piece of ranchland near San Antone.

DOROTHEA: Oh. What are you planning to do on this—

RALPH: —ranch? Breed cattle. Texas Longhorns.

(*A pause.*)

DOROTHEA: I like animals, Ralph.

RALPH: Cocker spaniels.

DOROTHEA: No, I like horses, too. I took equitation at Sophie Newcomb's. I even learned how to post.

RALPH: Uh-huh.

DOROTHEA: For a little ole Texas girl she sure does have some mighty French taste in nighties!

RALPH: I don't imagine she suffers from psychological frigidity.

DOROTHEA: Honey, I never suffered from that. Did you believe I really suffered from that?

RALPH: When your father proposed to me—

DOROTHEA: Ralph, don't say things like that! Don't, don't humiliate me!

RALPH: Honey, I—

DOROTHEA: PLEASE don't humiliate me by—

RALPH: HONEY!

(*He goes up to her at the dressing table. Sobbing, she presses her head against him.*)

You KNOW I respect you, honey.

ISABEL (*in the other room*): What an awful, frightening thing it is!

GEORGE: What?

ISABEL: Two people living together, two, two—different worlds!—attempting—existence—together!

(*In the bedroom:*)

RALPH: Honey, will you stop?

DOROTHEA: Respect me, respect me, is that all you can give me when I've loved you so much that sometimes I shake all over at the sight or touch of you? Still? Now? Always?

RALPH: The human heart would never pass the drunk test.

DOROTHEA: Huh?

RALPH: If you took the human heart out of the human body and put a pair of legs on it and told it to walk a straight line, it couldn't do it. It never could pass the drunk test.

DOROTHEA: I love you, baby. And I love animals, too. Hawses, spaniels, longhorns!

RALPH: The Texas longhorn is a—dignified beast.

DOROTHEA: You say that like you thought it was TOO GOOD FOR ME!

RALPH: How do I know that you didn't just come back here for that sheared-beaver coat?

(*Living room:*)

ISABEL: I hope they're getting things ironed out between them.

GEORGE: Why?

ISABEL: They need each other. That's why.

GEORGE: Let's mind our own business, huh?

(*Bedroom:*)

DOROTHEA: You'll just have to WONDER! And WONDER!

(*Living room:*)

GEORGE: It's a parallel situation. They're going through a period of adjustment just like us.

(*Bedroom:*)

RALPH: All my life, huh?

DOROTHEA: And I'll have to wonder, too, if you love me, Ralph. There's an awful lot of wondering between people.

RALPH: Come on. Turn out the light. Let's go to bed-ville, baby.

DOROTHEA (*turning out the light*): His or hers?

RALPH: In West Texas we'll get a big one called OURS!

(*In the living room*, GEORGE *has turned on TV and a chorus is singing "White Christmas."*)

GEORGE: Aw. You hate "White Christmas."

(*He turns it down.*)

ISABEL: I don't hate it now, baby.

(*He turns it back up, but softly.*)

DOROTHEA: I'm lookin' *forward* to it. I always wanted a big one, OURS!

RALPH: There's more dignity in it.

DOROTHEA: *Yes!*

(*She giggles breathlessly in the dark.*)

ISABEL (*in the living room*): I think they've talked things over and are working things out.

(*Bedroom:*)

RALPH: Yes. It makes it easy to know if—I mean, you don't have to wonder if—

(DOROTHEA *giggles in the dark.*)

That long, long, dangerous walk between "His" and "Hers" can be accomplished, or not. . . .

(*Living room:*)

ISABEL: I didn't know until now that the shakes are catching! Why do you keep standing up and sitting back down like a big old jack-in-the-box?

(*A low rumble is heard. It builds. Something falls off a shelf in the kitchenette. Crockery rattles together.*)

WHAT'S THIS!?

GEORGE: Aw, nothin', nothin'.

RALPH (*entering the doorway*): Well, she jus' slipped again!

DOROTHEA (*appearing behind him*): Did you all feel that tremor?

ISABEL: Yes, it felt like an earthquake.

DOROTHEA: We get those little tremors all the time because it seems that this suburb is built over a huge underground cavern and is sinking into it, bit by bit. That's the secret of how we could afford to buy this nice little home of ours at such a knockdown price.

ISABEL: It isn't likely to fall in the cavern *tonight?*

DOROTHEA: No. They say it's going to be gradual, about half an inch every year. Do you all mind if I turn on the light a second to see if there's any new cracks?

ISABEL: No, I'll—put on my robe.

(*She does. The room is lighted.*)

DOROTHEA: Yais! Ralph? A *new* one! This one is a jim-dandy, all the way 'cross the ceiling! See it, honey? All the way 'cross the ceiling. Well—

(*A pause.*)

We will leave you alone now. I still feel badly about you having to sleep on that folding contraption.

RALPH: Anything I can do? Anything I can—

DOROTHEA: Ralph! Leave them alone. Merry Christmas!

(*She shuts the door.*)

(*Pause.* ISABEL *stands before fireplace in the fourth wall.*

(*Pause.*)

GEORGE: Isabel? Little Bit? Marriage is a big step for a man to take, especially when he's—nervous. I'm pretty—nervous.

ISABEL: I know.

GEORGE: For a man with the shakes, especially, it's a—big step to take, it's—

ISABEL: I know what you're trying to tell me.

GEORGE (*taking seat on high stool near fire*): Do you, honey?

(*He looks up at her quickly, then down.*)

ISABEL: Of course I do. I expect all men are a little bit nervous about the same thing.

GEORGE: What?

ISABEL: About how they'll be at love-making.

GEORGE: Yeah, well, they don't have the shakes. I mean, not all the others have got a nervous tremor like I've got.

ISABEL: Inside or outside, they've all got a nervous tremor of some kind, sweetheart. The world is a big hospital, and I am a nurse in it, George. The whole world's a big hospital, a big neurological ward, and I am a student nurse in it. I guess that's still my job!—I love this fire. It feels so good on my skin through this little pink slip. I'm glad she left me the *pink* nightie, tonight.

GEORGE (*huskily*): Yeah, I'm glad she did, too.

(ISABEL *retires to slip into her nightgown.*)

I wish I had that—little electric buzzer I—had at—Barnes. . . .

ISABEL: You don't need a buzzer. I'm not way down at the end of a corridor, baby. If you call me, I'll hear you.

(*She returns and hugs her knees, sitting before the fire-place. He rests his head on his cupped hands. She begins to sing softly:*)

> "Now the boat goes round the bend,
> Good-by, my lover, good-by,
> It's loaded down with boys and men,
> Good-by, my lover, good-by!"

RALPH (*in the dark other room*): She's singin'!

(*Pause.*)

DOROTHEA: Papa said you told him that I was—homely! Did you say that, Ralph? That I was homely?

RALPH: Dotty, you used to be homely but you improved in appearance.

DOROTHEA: You never told me you thought I was homely, Ralph.

RALPH: I just meant you had a off-beat kind of face, honey, but—the rest of you is attractive.

DOROTHEA (*giggles*): I always knew *I* was homely but you were good enough lookin' to make *up* for it! Baby—

(ISABEL *is singing again, a little forlornly, by the fire-place.*)

ISABEL:
   "Bye low, my baby! Bye low, my baby!

Bye low, my baby! Good-by, my lover, good-by!"

(GEORGE *whistles softly.*)

Was that for me?

GEORGE: Come here!

ISABEL: No, you come here. It's very nice by the fire.

(*In the other room, as the curtain begins to fall:*)

DOROTHEA: Careful, let me do it!—It isn't mine!

(*She means the borrowed nightgown.*)

(*In the front room,* GEORGE *has risen from the bed and is crossing to the fireplace as:*)

THE CURTAIN FALLS

About the Author

Tennessee Williams (Thomas Lanier Williams) was born in Columbus, Mississippi on March 26, 1914, and lived there until he was twelve, when his family moved to St. Louis. His education at the University of Missouri (1931-33) was inerrupted for financial reasons, but he later (1938) received his B.A. from the University of Iowa. Tennessee Williams started writing and publishing poetry when very young, while simultaneously holding a variety of jobs—starting with a clerical position in the shoe company that also employed his father. His first real recognition came in 1940 when he received a Rockefeller fellowship and his first play, *Battle of Angels*, was produced by the Theatre Guild in Boston. His first financial break, which enabled him to give full attention to his writing, came with an offer from MGM, which he accepted, abandoning his job as a movie usher. After six months of work in Hollywood, he devoted his time to writing *The Glass Menagerie*, the initial success which established him as one of the leading American playwrights.

Since that time, his plays have been made into movies, produced on TV, turned into operas and ballets—*A Streetcar Named Desire, Summer and Smoke, The Night of the Iguana, Cat on a Hot Tin Roof,* and *The Glass Menagerie,* to name just a few. In May of 1969 Tennessee Williams was awarded the Gold Medal for Literature by the American Academy of Arts and Letters and the National Institute of Arts and Letters. He died on February 25, 1983.

He is the author of the following works: *Baby Doll, Battle of Angels, Camino Real, Cat on a Hot Tin Roof* (winner of the Pulitzer Prize and Drama Critics' Award). *Dragon Country* (short plays, including *In the Bar of a Tokyo Hotel*), *The Eccentricities of a Nightingale, Eight Mortal Ladies Possessed* (stories), *The Glass Menagerie, Hard Candy* (stories), *In the Winter of Cities* (poems), *Kingdom of Earth (The Seven Descents of Myrtle), The Knightly Quest* (stories), *Memoirs* (autobiography), *The Milk Train Doesn't Stop Here Anymore*, *Moise and the World of Reason* (novel), *The Night of the Iguana* (winner of the Drama Critics' Award), *One Arm & Other Stories*, *Orpheus Descending*, *Out Cry*, *Period of Adjustment*, *The Roman Spring of Mrs. Stone* (novel), *The Rose Tattoo*, *Small Craft Warnings*, *A Streetcar Named Desire* (winner of the Pulitzer Prize and Drama Critics' Award), *Suddenly Last Summer*, *Summer and Smoke*, *Sweet Bird of Youth*, *27 Wagons Full of Cotton*, *The Two-Character Play*, *Vieux Carré*, and *Clothes for a Summer Hotel*.

⊘ SIGNET BOOKS   Ⓒ SIGNET CLASSIC

ALL THE WORLD'S A STAGE

(0451)

☐ **FOUR PLAYS BY TENNESSEE WILLIAMS: SUMMER AND SMOKE, ORPHEUS DESCENDING, SUDDENLY LAST SUMMER and PERIOD OF ADJUSTMENT.** Love, hate, comedy, tragedy, joy, sorrow, passion, violence—all come alive in these four magnificent plays. (520157—$4.95)*

☐ **THREE BY TENNESSEE WILLIAMS: SWEET BIRD OF YOUTH, THE ROSE TATTOO and THE NIGHT OF THE IGUANA,** three of the Pulitzer prize-winning author's most brilliant plays. (521498—$4.95)

☐ **CHEKHOV: THE MAJOR PLAYS by Anton Chekhov. New translation by Ann Dunnigan. Foreword by Robert Brustein.** (522702—$3.50)

☐ **IBSEN: FOUR MAJOR PLAYS, Volume I, by Henrik Ibsen.** *The Master Builder, A Doll's House, Hedda Gabler,* and *The Wild Duck.* New translation with Foreword by Rolf Fjelde. (524063—$3.50)

☐ **IBSEN: FOUR MAJOR PLAYS, Volume II, by Henrik Ibsen.** *Ghosts, An Enemy of the People, The Lady from the Sea,* and *John Gabriel Borkman.* New translation by Rolf Fjelde. (522117—$2.95)

*Prices slightly higher in Canada

Buy them at your local bookstore or use this convenient coupon for ordering.

NEW AMERICAN LIBRARY
P.O. Box 999, Bergenfield, New Jersey 07621

Please send me the books I have checked above. I am enclosing $_____
(please add $1.00 to this order to cover postage and handling). Send check or money order—no cash or C.O.D.'s. Prices and numbers are subject to change without notice.

Name_____

Address_____

City _____ State _____ Zip Code _____
Allow 4-6 weeks for delivery.
This offer, prices and numbers are subject to change without notice.